D0224646

Introducing Language and Society

This accessible and entertaining textbook introduces students to both traditional and more contemporary approaches to sociolinguistics in a real-world context, addressing current social problems that students are likely to care about, such as racism, inequality, political conflict, belonging, and issues around gender and sexuality. Each chapter includes exercises, case studies and ideas for small-scale research projects, encouraging students to think critically about the different theories and approaches to language and society, and to interrogate their own beliefs about language and communication. The book gives students a grounding in the traditional concepts and techniques upon which sociolinguistics is built, while also introducing new developments from the last decade, such as translanguaging, multimodality, superdiversity, linguistic landscapes, and language and digital media. Students will also have online access to more detailed examples, links to video and audio files, and more challenging exercises to strengthen their skills and confidence as sociolinguists.

RODNEY H. JONES is Professor of Sociolinguistics at the University of Reading, where he teaches sociolinguistics and language and digital media on both the undergraduate and postgraduate levels. He has published widely in the areas of sociolinguistics, discourse analysis, computer-mediated communication, and health communication. His other textbooks include *Discourse Analysis*, 2nd edition (Routledge, 2018), and *Understanding Digital Literacies*, 2nd edition, with Christoph Hafner (Routledge, 2021).

CHRISTIANA THEMISTOCLEOUS is an Associate Professor in Sociolinguistics at the University of Reading, where she teaches modules in sociolinguistics, language and gender, and research methods. Her research interests fall within the areas of societal multilingualism, linguistic landscapes, and digital media. She has published widely in major sociolinguistic journals and books, and her current work, which explores language in conflict zones, has been funded by the British Academy.

Introducing Language and Society

RODNEY H. JONES
University of Reading

CHRISTIANA THEMISTOCLEOUS
University of Reading

CAMBRIDGE
UNIVERSITY PRESS

University Printing House, Cambridge CB2 8BS, United Kingdom

One Liberty Plaza, 20th Floor, New York, NY 10006, USA

477 Williamstown Road, Port Melbourne, VIC 3207, Australia

314–321, 3rd Floor, Plot 3, Splendor Forum, Jasola District Centre, New Delhi – 110025, India

103 Penang Road, #05-06/07, Visioncrest Commercial, Singapore 238467

Cambridge University Press is part of the University of Cambridge.

It furthers the University's mission by disseminating knowledge in the pursuit of education, learning, and research at the highest international levels of excellence.

www.cambridge.org
Information on this title: www.cambridge.org/highereducation/isbn/9781108498920
DOI: 10.1017/9781108689922

First published 2022

Printed in the United Kingdom by TJ Books Limited, Padstow Cornwall

A catalogue record for this publication is available from the British Library.

Library of Congress Cataloging-in-Publication Data
Names: Jones, Rodney H., author. | Themistocleous, Christiana, 1979- author.
Title: Introducing language and society / Rodney H. Jones, University of Reading ; Christiana
    Themistocleous, University of Reading.
Description: Cambridge ; New York, NY : Cambridge University Press, 2022. | Includes bibliographical
    references and index.
Identifiers: LCCN 2021038899 | ISBN 9781108498920 (hardback) | ISBN 9781108712859 (paperback)
Subjects: LCSH: Sociolinguistics.
Classification: LCC P40 .J66 2022 | DDC 306.44–dc23
LC record available at https://lccn.loc.gov/2021038899

ISBN 978-1-108-49892-0 Hardback
ISBN 978-1-108-71285-9 Paperback

For Jan Blommaert 1961–2021

Contents

Figures

Tables

Preface

This book is intended as an introductory text in sociolinguistics for students living in a world in which many of our traditional assumptions about languages and their speakers, about social categories such as class, gender, race, and 'nation', and about communication and 'meaning' themselves are being questioned. It is a generation that is witnessing unprecedented disruptions to their lives brought on by pandemic diseases, environmental threats, increasing inequality, and a resurgence of nationalism and authoritarianism around the globe. And it is a generation faced with important questions about the relationship between language and 'truth', and the relationship between individuals and the societies in which they live.

The fields of sociolinguistics and discourse analysis have long aimed to demonstrate the relevance of language studies for tackling the important social, political, and economic problems facing us. Along the way, it has developed a host of useful tools to understand how the way people use language affects their status, their social identities, and their opportunities in life, and the way language often serves as a tool for some groups of people to exercise power over other groups. In the last decade, however, in response to increasing globalisation and the increasing integration of digital technologies into nearly every aspect of our lives, a range of new concepts have been developed by scholars, concepts such as multimodality, superdiversity, and translanguaging. The methods that sociolinguists use to study the relationship between language and society are also changing, with traditional sociolinguistic interviews now being supplemented with approaches such as digital ethnography and the study of linguistic and semiotic landscapes.

This book is intended to give students a grounding in the traditional concepts and techniques upon which sociolinguistics has been built since the 1970s while at the same time introducing them to some of the newer concepts and techniques that have been developed to address more contemporary issues. One of its goals is to get students to think more critically about the traditional ways we conceive of language and society – not necessarily to dismiss these traditional approaches, but to interrogate them. But its most important goal is to help students understand the relevance of the study of language and society to confronting real problems in the real world.

Who This Book Is For

This book is really for anyone who is interested in the relationship between language and society and how that relationship impacts on people's lives. It's written in a way that is intended to make the ideas in it accessible to people without a strong background in linguistics or sociology or other social sciences. For this reason, it would be an ideal choice for introductory courses in sociolinguistics or 'language in society' at universities. But it is also suitable for more advanced students and even scholars who desire an easy-to-understand introduction to more recent intellectual developments in the study of language and society. The book draws upon examples from a wide range of national contexts, making it relevant to students and scholars all over the world.

How This Book Is Structured

The book begins with a short introductory chapter, which is followed by nine full chapters, each focusing on a different topic in sociolinguistics. Each of these chapters will introduce a number of key ideas and demonstrate how those ideas can be applied to understanding various aspects of language in society. Discussions of these ideas are punctuated by short activities that give readers a chance to think about and apply the ideas themselves.

Each chapter also includes a *Focal Topic* section in which some kind of real-world problem or phenomenon related to language and communication is discussed. In each of these *Focal Topic* sections we provide two case studies of how sociolinguists have used the ideas introduced in the chapter to try to understand these problems and to try to contribute to solving them. These case studies take the form of summaries of research articles that can be used to scaffold students' readings of the articles themselves.

Finally, each chapter ends with a list of suggested projects that involve students in actually collecting and analysing data using the concepts they have mastered by working through the chapters. At the end of the book there is a short section called *A Sociolinguist's Toolkit* in which we briefly review some of the main methods for doing sociolinguistic research that have been encountered in the book and offer advice about the practical issues students might encounter in carrying out their projects.

Teaching and Learning with This Book

Each of the chapters in this book builds upon the previous chapters, so it's strongly suggested that students work through the material in the order that it's presented. At the beginning of each chapter there is a list of the key terms covered in the chapter along with a short summary of what the chapter is about. When readers encounter these key terms (marked in **bold**) in the chapter itself, they can always consult the glossary at the end of the book if they

need to, for a concise definition of the terms. The activities in each of the chapters can be done individually, but they are particularly useful when done in a classroom setting in which students can discuss and compare their answers with other students. The projects suggested at the end of each chapter can be done either individually or in groups. Some teachers might want to turn some of these project ideas into assessed assignments for their courses.

What's Special about This Book?

The main thing that makes this book different from other coursebooks on sociolinguistics is that it attempts to engage students in critically evaluating some of the basic assumptions about language and society that have driven much of the work in sociolinguistics over the years and to make accessible to them more contemporary perspectives in the field. For this reason, it foregrounds concepts such as mobility, multimodality, and mediation, which may be less salient in other coursebooks.

Another important feature of the book is that it focuses on making students aware of the role of sociolinguistics in their everyday lives and of the relevance of sociolinguistic concepts to important social issues like racism, migration, political polarisation, and conflict.

The book includes plenty of material designed to support students and teachers, including activities in every chapter, a glossary of key terms, and guidelines for conducting research projects. There is also a companion website for this book (www.cambridge.org/jones-themistocleous), where students and teachers can go to find supplementary activities, explore the topics covered in the book more deeply, and get help carrying out their projects.

Introduction

Sociolinguistics and 'Wicked Problems'

PREVIEW

KEY TERMS

African American Vernacular English (AAVE)
communicative competence
sociolinguistics
speech community
wicked problems

In this introduction we will explain how sociolinguistics is relevant to helping us to solve real-world problems. We will also explore some of the challenges we face when we talk about concepts such as 'language' and 'society', and introduce some of the more recent concepts, theories, and practical tools that sociolinguists have developed to talk about and analyse the relationship between language and social life.

0.1 Introduction

This book is about the relationship between language and social life. By 'social life' we mean both the way we interact with other people in our daily lives and broader aspects of social life related to economics, politics, justice, technology, and the environment. The main goal of the book is to convince you that there *is* a relationship between language and social life and that *it matters*, that understanding more about language can actually help us solve our day-to-day problems of getting along with others as well as bigger problems related to economics, politics, justice, technology, and the environment.

In 2017, the World Economic Forum asked over 30,000 young people about the issues that they cared about most as part of its Global Shapers Survey (World Economic Forum 2017), and, not surprisingly, 'language' was not one of them. Instead, respondents said they were worried most about climate change, war, inequality, corruption, discrimination, and the access people have to economic and educational opportunities. At the same time, it can't be denied that language has some role in all of these problems: the way people use language to communicate ideas and manipulate people can influence the policies governments make about problems such as racism or whether or not citizens are willing to fight in wars. Language can be used as a weapon to maintain unequal power relationships or to make people feel like they are less important or that they don't belong. And whether or not individuals have access to particular languages or the languages they speak are respected and valued can have a dramatic impact on their economic and educational opportunities. In this book, we will not just explore the relationship between language and social life on a theoretical level; we will try to focus on the practical consequences of this relationship. In particular, we will explore how language contributes to the social problems that people are most worried about and how understanding how language functions in social life can help people to address these problems.

The field of study that you will learn about in this book is known as **sociolinguistics**. Sociolinguists study lots of things from the different ways people in different groups use language, to the attitudes and prejudices people have about the ways different people talk. Of course, understanding the relationship between language and social life alone won't solve any of the problems we mentioned above. Solving these problems requires input from lots of different kinds of people: scientists and engineers, psychologists and sociologists, politicians and entrepreneurs. The point we want to make in this book is that sociolinguists should also have a seat at the table.

Problems like those the young people who responded to the Global Shapers Survey said they worried about have been referred to as **wicked problems**, not because they are 'evil', but because they are difficult to solve and solutions inevitably involve the difficult task of getting people who think differently and speak different 'languages' (such as the 'language of science' or the 'language of business') to work together. The term was first used by design professor Horst Rittel and planning professor Melvin Webber way back in 1973 to describe problems that are made up of many different interdependent components, which are often themselves symptoms of yet other problems. Because of this, often when we try to solve one aspect of a wicked problem, we can actually make other aspects of it worse.

A good example of a wicked problem is income inequality. Although the gap between the rich and the poor in some countries is growing smaller, in many countries, especially large countries like China, India, and the United States, while the rich are getting richer, the poor are getting poorer. Income inequality is not just a problem in itself; it is associated with other problems such as rising crime rates, poor health, political inequality, and increased corruption in the public and private sectors. Figuring out the causes of inequality and coming up with solutions requires input from many different stakeholders, including economists, businesspeople, politicians, social workers, engineers, and educators. That's because inequality is not just an economic problem; it's a political, social, technological, and educational problem. But it is also a sociolinguistic problem.

Inequality is a sociolinguistic problem because, as we will explore in this book, *linguistic resources* (different kinds of 'language' and different ways of speaking, reading, and writing) are *valued* differently in different contexts, and *access* to these resources (the chance to learn different 'languages' and different ways of speaking, reading, and writing) are unequally distributed. In sociolinguistics there is considerable research – some of which we will talk about in this book – on how racial and class disparities as well as unequal opportunities in education and employment are made worse by unequal access to linguistic resources as well as by policies based on incorrect or biased ideas about language.

Inequality is also a sociolinguistic problem because our ideas about different groups of people, as well as our ideas about fairness and justice, are influenced by the way we talk about these people and these ideas. The way people talk about inequality can sometimes help perpetuate it by reproducing racist, sexist, or classist ideas.

Finally, inequality is a sociolinguistic problem because, as with *all* wicked problems, the people who need to get together to find solutions to it – rich people, poor people, politicians and businesspeople, engineers and educators – often have difficulty cooperating, not just because they may have different 'interests' and different 'agendas', but, because, as we said above, they speak different 'languages' – that is, they have different ways of reading and writing, speaking, and listening to others, which are inevitably associated with different ways of *representing* the world and assigning *value* to different things.

The field of sociolinguistics has changed a lot since the 1970s when it was established. But one thing that hasn't changed is that most sociolinguists are interested in how their study of language can help us to better understand and solve social problems. One of the first linguists to be called a 'sociolinguist' was William Labov. Labov was interested in how different features in people's speech function as markers of power and prestige. Among his most important contributions was his work on **African American Vernacular English (AAVE)** (which we will refer to later in this book as simply African American English), in which he challenged widespread assumptions that this variety is 'ungrammatical' or 'deficient', assumptions that reinforced racist myths associating intelligence with race. Labov's analysis revealed that AAVE has its own internally consistent rules of grammar and discourse, that it is, if you will, just as 'standard' as so-called 'Standard English'. In explaining the relevance of sociolinguistics to solving real-world problems, Labov (1982: 165–6) put it this way:

> Linguistics is said to be basic research that will give us more knowledge about mankind – but has no immediate application to the problems that most people are worried about … A distinctly different view is that linguistics is the study of an instrument of communication that is used in everyday life, an instrument that has evolved as a part of our social and biological history. This is the point of view that lies behind my own research. This approach isn't totally opposed to the other view, but it leads to different answers to the second question – what is linguistics good for? I would argue that linguistic research applies to a good many of the questions facing contemporary society: how to reverse educational failure in the inner cities; how to resolve conflicts and paradoxes that centre around bilingual education; how to implement the responsibility of the law to communicate to the public.

Another important pioneer in 'socially engaged' sociolinguistics was the anthropologist Dell Hymes, who questioned dominant ideas about *competence* in language that linked it to the mastery of grammatical rules. Hymes pointed out that real linguistic competence has more to do with one's ability to get things done in the real world and to show that one is a competent member of one's community, which he called **communicative competence** (Hymes 1966). Language, in this tradition, is always situated in webs of social relationships. It is a tool that people use to exercise and resist power, to show that they belong to particular groups, and to do things with other members of these groups that are important for their lives and livelihoods.

Over the years, sociolinguists have concerned themselves with a range of different social problems. Some of these problems have been more obviously 'linguistic' in nature – such as the right of people to speak the language of their choice, the sometimes negative effects of certain language policies on the education of minority children, the relationship between poverty and language 'death', and the way high-stakes language tests can sometimes discriminate against certain populations. But some of these problems have been less obviously 'linguistic' in nature, such as the role of communication in the spread of diseases such as COVID-19 and AIDS, the language-related barriers migrants face when applying for refugee status in different countries, the communicative dimensions of poverty, crime, drug abuse, homelessness, climate change, religious con-flict, terrorism and surveillance, and the spread of 'fake news' and white supremist propaganda over the Internet. All of these applications of sociolinguistics to social problems begin with an acknowledgement of the enormous power of language to shape human relationships and social realities, and of the potential for language to function both as a weapon to oppress people and as a tool to advance social justice.

More recently, things like the increased movement of people across the globe (partly as the result of war, poverty, and the effects of climate change) and the increased flows of information and culture through digital technologies, have compelled sociolinguists to come up with new ways of talking about and analysing the relationship between language and social life, and the main purpose of this book is to introduce you to some of these new concepts, theories, and practical tools for solving social problems.

Many of the pressures on sociolinguists to change the way they talk about language and society have, in fact, come *as a result* of wicked problems such as increasing inequality, changing forms of racism and discrimination, and the blurring of borders and transformation of trad-itional communities that has accompanied mass migration, as well as the blurring of boundaries and breakdown of traditional forms of expertise and authority that has accompanied the widespread use of digital tech-nologies. This is not surprising; wicked problems, by their nature, have a way of highlighting the inadequacy of many of the assumptions we have about the way the world works and the traditional tools we have at our disposal to solve problems in it, whether we are economists, politicians, climate scientists, or sociolinguists.

0.2 'There's No Such Thing as Society'

This famous quote comes from an interview that Margaret Thatcher, who was the UK prime minister at the time, gave to *Women's Own* magazine in October 1987. What Thatcher was really trying to say was that what mattered to her and to the British Conservative Party of her day was the goals and opportunities of *individual* citizens rather than the collective goals of the citizenry, and that she believed that people should be responsible for their own well-being rather than depending on (or looking after) other people. What Thatcher actually said was:

I think we've been through a period where too many people have been given to understand that if they have a problem, it's the government's job to cope with it ... They're casting their problem on society. And, you know, there is no such thing as society. There are individual men and women, and there are families. And no government can do anything except through people, and people must look to themselves first.

(Thatcher 1987)

Thatcher's musing about the existence of society was not just a philosophical exercise. It had real consequences on people's lives, serving as the basis for policies such as the privatisation of public services, the rollback of regulations on corporations, and the weakening of trade unions, which resulted in substantial increases in economic and health inequalities in Britain. Thatcher's words highlight the fact that even an idea as apparently self-evident as 'society' is not as self-evident as it may seem, and the way people understand society – how it works, who belongs to it, how people are supposed to relate to it, or even whether it exists in the first place – is influenced by people's *ideological positions* and *political agendas* and can end up having real material consequences on other people's lives.

The way we define 'society' also has a profound impact on the way we approach the study of language. Back in the late nineteenth and early twentieth centuries, pioneers in the study of language and society mostly saw society in terms of countries and ethnic groups. In fact, as we will discuss in Chapter 1, many people during this time regarded a 'common language' as the defining feature of a nation. Among these pioneers was the American linguist Leonard Bloomfield, who in 1933 proposed that the best way to study the relationship between language and society was to divide up society into what he called **speech communities**, which he defined simply as groups of people who speak the same language.

Later, however, sociolinguists like Labov and anthropologists like Dell Hymes and John Gumperz challenged this way of dividing up society as overly simplistic. Labov, for example, became interested in how other social divisions around things like race and class affected the way people talk, and Dell Hymes and John Gumperz re-envisioned speech communities as groups based not so much on sharing the same language as on sharing the same norms and attitudes about how people should *use* language. As Hymes (1974: 50–1) put it: '[a] speech community is defined ... as a community sharing knowledge of rules of conduct and interpretation of speech. Such sharing comprises knowledge of at least one form of speech, and knowledge also of its patterns of use.' This modified understanding of speech community focused on *participation* rather than membership, and Gumperz and Hymes emphasised that people naturally participate in multiple speech communities throughout their lives. This understanding of speech community also focused on language not as a system of grammar or collection of vocabulary items but as a *social practice* through which people negotiate their places in the social world.

Near the end of the twentieth century, sociolinguists became more and more interested in the *dynamic* ways people negotiate the multiple and overlapping communities that they belong to, and so came up with new ways of describing social groupings to help them to understand this dynamism. The sociolinguist Lesley Milroy (1987), for example, started to think of language speakers as part of complex *social networks* (see Chapter 3) characterised by strong and weak ties through which different ways of speaking and communicative norms were maintained and circulated, and, in the 1990s, the sociolinguists Penny Eckert and Sally

McConnell-Ginet began using the term *community of practice* (see Chapter 3), borrowed from the field of educational psychology, to describe groups of people who came together around common social practices. Whereas the definition of speech community advanced by Gumperz and Hymes focused on language as a social practice, the 'communities of practice approach' attempts to link the way people speak to a vast range of other social practices, such as what they wear, what they do for a living, and what sorts of political activities they engage in.

While all of these different ways of defining society and dividing it up have some practical utility for understanding the relationship between language and social life, as the twenty-first century has progressed, dividing people into classes, cliques, or communities, or even tracing the social networks they are part of has become increasingly challenging. One reason for this is the increasing *deterritorisation* (see Chapter 9) of people (García et al. 2016). Globalisation has brought with it an explosion of relocation, mass migration, and transmigration that has upended traditional associations of people (and their ways of speaking) with fixed geographical locations.

Another force that disrupts our more traditional ways of dividing up society is the Internet and the ways it facilitates both the rapid circulation of cultural products, including different ways of speaking, and the formation of new forms of *light communities* (see Chapter 4) based on a variety of new social and political affiliations and new communicative practices (such as 'memeing').

Because of these trends, the sociolinguist Jan Blommaert (2013a: 193) argues that 'there is a dramatic need to unthink and rethink some of the most basic concepts in social science – notions such as community, identity, and indeed citizenship'. '[S]ince the early 1990s', he explains:

> some fundamental changes have taken place in the ways in which all of these notions take shape in real life ... People from more places now migrate to more places, causing unprecedented forms of social and cultural diversity especially in the large urban centres of the world ... Adding to this complexity, the emergence and global spread of the Internet and other forms of mobile communication technologies – synchronous with the new forms of migration – have created a 'network society' (Castells 1996) in which people live and act in relation to long-distance, 'virtual' peers in sometimes enormous online communities. Taken together, these two forces have re-shaped social life around the world.

Part of the challenge that we need to address, then, when setting out to understand the relationship between language and social life – and to understand how that relationship is *relevant* to helping to solve real-world problems – is coming up with a way to talk about social life and social groups that captures this complexity. The key puzzle for sociolinguists, says the scholar Asif Agha (2007: 230), is figuring out how 'language is connected to the study of socio-political frameworks that motivate projects of minoritization, dominance and exclusion'. Just as Thatcher's definition of society as 'non-existent' had important political implications and material consequences, the way sociolinguists define society also has political implications, affecting the ways they are able to contribute to addressing 'wicked problems'.

0.3 'There's No Such Thing as Languages'

If the claim that 'there's no such thing as society' is surprising in a book about language and society, the claim that 'there's no such thing as languages' is probably even more surprising. But this is actually the view of many, if not most, linguists, including perhaps the most famous living linguist, Noam Chomsky, who wrote that the whole idea of 'separate languages' is really a 'socio-political' idea rather than a linguistic idea (1986: 15):

> We speak of Chinese as 'a language,' although the various 'Chinese dialects' are as diverse as the several Romance languages. We speak of Dutch and German as two separate languages, although some dialects of German are very close to dialects that we call 'Dutch' and are not mutually intelligible with others that we call 'German.' A standard remark in introductory linguistics courses is that a language is a dialect with an army and a navy (attributed to Max Weinreich). That any coherent account can be given of 'language' in this sense is doubtful; surely, none has been offered or even seriously attempted. Rather, all scientific approaches have simply abandoned these elements of what is called 'language' in common usage.

What Chomsky meant by this was not just that it is sometimes difficult to draw clear lines between different 'languages' and between 'languages' and 'dialects', a problem that we will discuss further in Chapter 1, but that the whole idea of 'languages' is just not very useful for his brand of linguistics. Rather than 'languages', what linguists like Chomsky are interested in is 'language' as a kind of innate human *capacity* governed by a set of structural rules or 'universal grammar' lodged inside the brain. Chomsky and his followers are mostly interested in understanding these rules rather than in understanding how people actually talk or what they think about how they talk. For them, the relationship between language and society is really irrelevant, since language is seen as a matter of the cognitive/psychological individual who develops 'language' no matter what 'speech community' they live in. So, in some respects, Chomsky saying that 'there's no such thing as languages' has some similarities to Margaret Thatcher saying that 'there's no such thing as society', since what both of them are saying is that they are more interested in the individual than the group.

Sociolinguists are different. While they would mostly agree with the statement 'there's no such thing as languages', what this means to them has more to do with the fluid and dynamic way that people use linguistic resources that frequently defies neat attempts to label 'what they are speaking' as a concrete thing. In fact, some sociolinguists prefer to use the verb 'languaging' (or sometimes 'translanguaging' or 'polylanguaging') rather than the noun 'language' to describe how people communicate verbally (see Chapter 5). Sociolinguists, or at least many of the sociolinguists you'll learn about in this book, think of languages as loose collections of complex and evolving form–function patterns that arise out of the needs and the constraints of actual communication.

But this doesn't mean that what other people call 'languages' (German, Dutch, Chinese) are not important. In fact, the way people divide up, classify, and most importantly, *assign value* to the way they (and others) talk is of primary importance to sociolinguists, because people's ideas about language are constructed out of their actual practices of speech and writing and the ideologies attached to these practices, and because these practices and ideologies have real material effects on people's lives. As the sociolinguists Sinfree Makoni and Alastair Pennycook (2007: 3) put it, 'while the entities around which battles are fought, tests are constructed and language policies are written are inventions, the effects are very real'.

So, what sociolinguists focus on is not just the way people actually talk, but also on the ways they think they *ought* to talk, and the ways they judge others for the ways they talk.

As Woolard (2004: 58) notes, ideas about the way people talk 'are never just about language, but rather also concern such fundamental social notions as community, nation, and humanity itself'. Sociolinguists are fond of saying that they are not so much interested in 'languages' as they are in the 'total linguistic fact' of a given situation (Silverstein 1985: 220), by which they mean all of the different, often unstable, ways people use linguistic resources in different situations and the way these resources take their meaning and their *value* from the situations in which they are used and the cultures in which these situations are embedded.

Makoni and Pennycook (2007), along with many other contemporary sociolinguists, believe that the main job of the sociolinguist should be, first of all, to *dis*-invent languages, that is, to challenge the ways that people divide up, label, and *value* the different ways people talk (which usually result in some people having economic, social, and political advantages over others), and, second of all, to *re-constitute* languages, that is, to figure out ways of describing what people are doing when they talk that don't just more accurately describe what's really going on but are also more useful for people in their fight for social recognition, equality, and justice. For Blommaert (2009: 268), this means reconstructing languages *not* as 'stable, closed, and internally homogeneous units characterizing parts of mankind, but as ordered complexes of genres, styles, registers, and forms of use: languages as *repertoires*' (see Chapter 2).

Just as it is important to carefully consider how we define and divide up society if we are going to figure out how sociolinguists can contribute to addressing the pressing social problems of our time, it is equally important that we consider how we define and divide up languages, and that we do so in a way that acknowledges and honours the diverse ways that people talk and the importance of these ways of talking for their individual and social identities.

0.4 What Now?

In the rest of this book we will guide you through a range of concepts, theories, and real-world examples that hopefully will help you to develop an appreciation for how sociolinguistics can enhance your understanding of the world around you and help you to contribute to making it better. Among other things, we will talk about how people 'imagine' languages and the effects these acts of imagining have on their lives and the lives of those around them, how people regularly mix together different linguistic resources from different sources in order to perform different kinds of identities and do different kinds of things, how digital technologies affect the way we use language and the consequences of this for our private and political lives, and how the ways we use language can perpetuate or challenge racism.

In each chapter we will also try to illustrate how what you have learnt relates to some important social issue such as citizenship, inequality, online harassment, gender and sexuality, migration, racism, and conflict. For each of these 'focal topics' we will introduce two articles written by contemporary sociolinguists working closely on these issues. While we will try to give a complete summary of what these scholars have said, you are also encouraged to seek out and read the original articles and perhaps other articles by these authors.

Finally, we also include a range of different activities in each chapter to give you a chance to test out the concepts that you are learning about, combine these concepts with things that you already know or think about language from your own experiences, and compare your ideas with those of other people you are learning alongside. At the end of each chapter, we provide a list of ideas for larger projects where you can apply the ideas that we have introduced to analysing data that you have collected yourselves.

CHAPTER

1 Imagining Languages and Their Speakers

PREVIEW

KEY TERMS

accent
codification
dialect
language
language ideologies
monolingual ideology
multilingual ideology
standard language ideology
verbal hygiene

In this chapter we will examine language ideologies – what people imagine languages to be and how they expect languages should be used. In particular, we will look at two powerful language ideologies: the monolingual ideology that says that monolingualism is better than multilingualism, and the standard language ideology, which says that there is one correct way of speaking a language and that other ways of speaking it are somehow inferior. At the end of the chapter, in the focal topic, we will explore the consequences that these ideologies have on people's lives.

1.1 Introduction

In November of 2018 graffiti began appearing around the district of Walthamstow in north-east London with the words SPEAK ENGLISH scrawled in white paint. Stella Creasy, the Member of Parliament for the district, was disturbed by this trend and posted the picture in Figure 1.1 online. The caption on her Instagram feed read, 'To whoever the sad sack is who is targeting Walthamstow with this hate crime graffiti- know that not only will we find you and make sure you are prosecuted, but you are not welcome in our area...'

Upon seeing the post, a local resident and artist named Chris Walker decided to Photoshop the image to reflect the actual linguistic diversity of the area, adding a WE to the sign, and listing after the verb SPEAK the words PANJABI, POLISH, BULGARIAN, BENGALI, FRENCH, LITHUANIAN, URDU, ROMANIAN, TURKISH, TAMIL and COCKNEY (Figure 1.2).

Taken together, this piece of graffiti and Walker's reworking of it reveal a couple of important things about the role of languages in social life. First is that people believe that languages exist as discrete, identifiable things. They often care very deeply about them, deeply enough to concern themselves with what language is spoken in a particular place. Second is the idea that particular languages *belong* to particular places, and, by extension, particular places *belong* to the speakers of particular languages. It's likely that the person who originally painted the graffiti was motivated by this idea. What is implied by the graffiti is that the language that *should* be spoken in England is English, and that the existence of other languages (and their speakers) in England is somehow unacceptable.

It is equally important to note the discomfort of Creasy and her Instagram followers, for whom the statement 'Speak English' scrawled in public places is seen as equally unacceptable, characterised, in fact, as a

FIGURE 1.1
Graffiti in Walthamstow

FIGURE 1.2
Photoshopped graffiti by artist Chris Walker

'hate crime'. So, while for some, the existence of more than one language spoken in a particular place is seen as a threat to the integrity of the nation, to others, the attempt to enforce the speaking of only one language is regarded as an act of violence. To the first group, the idea that English should be spoken in England is seen as a matter of common sense. To the second group, the idea that telling people that they should speak English in England is fundamentally racist is equally a matter of common sense.

However, these emotionally charged associations between languages and nations, languages and races, and languages and hate crimes become slightly muddled when we look at the list of 'languages' that the artist Chris Walker represents as being spoken in Walthamstow. Of course, some of these languages, such as French, are actually associated with a number of different nations (France, Canada, The Democratic Republic of Congo, etc.). Other languages on the list, Bengali, Panjabi, and Tamil, are associated with a single country (India), but are usually associated with particular regions of that country. One of the languages listed – Urdu – is (in its spoken form at least) sometimes labelled as a different language (Hindi). The strangest item on the list, though, is the last one – Cockney – which most people (at least most people in Walthamstow) would not consider in the same class as 'languages' like Polish, French, and Urdu. Most would consider it a *kind* of English, and, by representing it as something separate from English, the artist might have been making a joke. However, he also might have been trying to make a very interesting point about the degree of linguistic diversity that already exists *within* what people refer to as the English language.

In this chapter we will examine how people imagine languages, how they expect them to be used, and what they think about their users. Taken together, these things add up to what sociolinguists refer to as **language**

ideologies. Linguistic anthropologist Judith Irvine (1989: 255) defines a language ideology as 'the cultural system of ideas about social and linguistic relationships, together with their loading of moral and political interests'. The language ideology represented by the graffiti in Figure 1.1, for example, might be called the **monolingual ideology**. This is the set of social, political, and moral ideas that lead people to think that only one language should be used in a particular place. Another prevalent ideology which we will discuss is the **standard language ideology**, which leads people to believe that there is one 'standard' or correct way of speaking a language and that other ways of speaking it are somehow inferior or incorrect. At the end of this chapter we will explore the *consequences* that these ideologies have on people's actual lives when it comes to, for example, applying for citizenship in a particular country or making a case for asylum.

Activity: What Do You Think About Language?

We asked five people the question *'What do you think about language?'* We wanted to know people's views about language and why a particular 'language' is important to them. What kind of 'languages' did they like and want to learn, and why? What things confused them? How many 'languages' do they think are out there?

Read the responses that we got. Notice how our respondents use the labels 'language', 'dialect', and 'accent' and how they talk about the different ways that they and others speak. Discuss the following questions.

- What labels are used to name different ways of speaking?
- What are some linguistic features that they associate with these different ways of speaking?
- What are some attitudes they express towards these ways of speaking?
- What kinds of social groups or geographical entities are these different ways of speaking associated with? For instance, are they associated with nations, regions, areas, neighbourhoods, groups of people, etc.?

Respondent 1: I live and grew up in Wales, so the Welsh language is really important for me. Unfortunately, a lot of people stopped speaking Welsh because of the dominance of English. In the past, when the English took over Wales, it was forbidden to speak the language and there were strict rules in schools which saw children being punished for speaking Welsh. This meant that the language started to die out. It's so good though that the government in Wales made a lot of effort to revive the language. It's now taught in schools and universities, it is used in shops and traffic signs, on the radio and TV. I don't know if all these efforts will work because still not many people speak the language. For example, me, I'm fluentish in Welsh, but I mainly use English. I would like to learn more, but I wish I had the time to learn. There are a lot of older people speaking the language but mostly in more remote communities rather than urban centres.

Respondent 2: I live in a big urban city where more than 30 languages are spoken. The city has different areas that are somehow 'dedicated' to specific ethnic groups. Chinatown is located in the city centre. The 'Curry mile' is near the university area. The Jewish quarter lies between Chinatown and the Curry mile. At the edge of the city is my neighbourhood which is a Caribbean mish-mash, lots of people from Cuba, Jamaica and the Dominican Republic etc. Often when I walk in the city centre, I can hear other languages. I'm not 100% sure what they are but I think they sound Polish or Romanian. I guess you could say that I live in an ethnically diverse, multilingual place. I like listening to all these languages and I try to learn a few words when I go to those shops. I'm not always very successful . . .

Respondent 3: I come from the South of Italy and I speak a Neapolitan dialect. I went to study in the UK and my friends there were really surprised to find out that so many different dialects are spoken in Italy. Actually, almost each region has its own dialect and some of them are very different from one another to the extent that people cannot understand each other. It's quite funny but I am very used to it.

Respondent 4: I am originally from France and came to study in New York when I was 19. I fell in love with this place! You walk down the road and listen not just to all sorts of different languages from all over the world, but also different accents of English. I never realised that when I first moved here but now I think I become more and more aware of these differences. People from California sound quite different from those from New York or those who speak African American English or from people who migrate here from South America and they speak English. I really wonder how *I* sound to all these people. I think I still retained quite a bit of my French pronunciation but I think it's becoming less and less strong after living here for 20 years. I do want to keep it though as I feel that this is what makes me French, right? It is a symbol of who I am and where I'm from.

Respondent 5: I always wanted to live in Spain. After finishing my studies I found this opportunity to work in Seville for a year as an English language teaching assistant in a school. I arrived in Seville without knowing a word of Spanish. Well. . . I knew words like 'hola' and 'gracias' but that was about it! I thought because I speak English I was going to be able to communicate with everyone in the world. But, then I realised that this was not the case in the south of Spain as not many people speak English. I opened a bank account using a dictionary and I bought a TV. Most American/English films were dubbed in Spanish. The programmes also had Spanish subtitles. It might sound funny but I learned a lot by watching films and programmes on TV. Also, because people didn't speak English I was forced to use Spanish to be able to communicate. Although I never went to Spanish classes, in 3 months I was able to have a basic conversation like order a meal, or go to a shop! By the end of the year, I could speak well and I still do when I visit Spain. But I only use three tenses and I still don't know how to write!

1.2 Languages and Nations

"The moral entity – the grammatical being called a nation, has been clothed in attributes that have no real existence except in the imagination of those who metamorphose a word into a thing [. . .]"

(Thomas Cooper 1826)

As we have seen above, the idea that a country is defined by the language that the people in it speak, and the idea that people in a particular country should speak only one language seem like common sense to many people. These ideas are actually not very old; in fact, they really only became popular in Europe with the rise of *nationalism* in the eighteenth and nineteenth centuries. Before that, in Europe, people were commonly divided based on religious beliefs and loyalty to feudal lords.

What was meant by language at that time was basically Latin, the pan-European language of the Church. The ways people spoke to one another in daily life were not regarded as having an abstract existence beyond practical communication.

During the Renaissance, people started to develop the idea that the everyday ways they communicated constituted 'languages' and that these languages, along with other things, set them apart from other people. This was in part because people started to question the authority of the Catholic Church and partly because of technological advancements like the invention of the printing press, which resulted in the dissemination of the Bible translated into different local languages.

The *ideology* of nationalism itself, however, wasn't clearly articulated in Europe until the beginning of the nineteenth century. The crux of that ideology is that human beings are naturally divided into nations, that different nations are easily distinguished from one another by the culture and 'traditions' of their people, and that all nations have the right to govern themselves.

A number of scholars have argued that the existence of a common language was one of the main things that made people in the late eighteenth and early nineteenth centuries start to think of themselves as belonging to nations. Perhaps the most famous proponent of this idea is the historian Benedict Anderson (1991), who famously described the nation as an 'imagined community'. It is imagined, he says 'because the members of even the smallest nation will never know most of their fellow-members, meet them, or even hear of them, yet in the minds of each lives the image of their communion' (p. 6). Anderson argues that, with the invention of the printing press, people came to think of themselves as affiliated with others based on their ability to read the same texts. This idea that people shared a common language, he says, was one of the most important ingredients for the formation of common national identities. But others, including some linguists, have argued that these 'common languages' were *also imagined*, created to assist the ideological work of nation-building. And so, as the idea of the nation as a distinct geographical entity separated from other nations by borders was more and more widely accepted, so was the idea that languages are also distinct entities separated from other languages by borders.

The British historian Eric Hobsbawm in his book *Nations and nationalism since 1780* (2012: 51) insists that national languages 'are the *opposite* of what nationalist mythology supposes them to be, namely the primordial foundations of national culture and the matrices of the national mind'. Instead, he says, 'They are usually attempts to devise a standardized idiom out of a multiplicity of actually spoken idioms.'

One of the main results of the spread of nationalism, then, was the idea of *monolingual nations*. Whereas the European empires that preceded the modern nation such as the Holy Roman Empire and the Habsburg Empire had been **multilingual**, modern nations were founded on the ideology of 'One Language, One Nation'.

Germany is a good example of the relationship between language and nationalism. Before the nineteenth century, what is today called Germany was separated into more than 300 separate political entities. During the period of the French Empire (1804–1814), romantic philosophers and politicians began to imagine a nation free from the domination of Napoleon, and one of the main foundations for this vision was the idea that people who spoke the same language should be united with one another. The most famous of these philosophers was Gottlieb Fichte, who, in his 1806 treatise *Address to a German nation* wrote:

> Those who speak the same language are joined to each other by a multitude of invisible bonds by nature herself, long before any human art begins; they understand each other and have the power of continuing to make themselves understood more and more clearly; they belong together and are by nature one and an inseparable whole ... Thus was the German nation placed – sufficiently united within itself by a common language and a common way of thinking, and sharply enough severed from the other peoples – in the middle of Europe, as a wall to divide races not akin [...].
>
> (Fichte 1968 [1808]: 190–1)

Along with this notion that people who speak the same 'language' should live together, however, was born the notion that people who do *not* speak the language of a nation should not be tolerated within its borders. Fichte (1968 [1808]: 91) also wrote:

If ... [a nation] wishes to absorb and mingle with itself any other people of different descent and language, [it] cannot do so without itself becoming confused ... and violently disturbing the even progress of its culture.

It was this way of thinking about language and nationalism and culture, as the linguist John Joseph (2006: 127) points out, that would later 'lead to the development of "scientific racism" from the mid-nineteenth to the mid-twentieth century, with unspeakably horrible consequences'.

The monolingual ideology that accompanied the formation of European nations also became an important part of the national imaginaries of newer so-called 'immigration nations', such as the United States and Australia, which came about as a result of European imperialism and colonialism. In fact, as these countries began to absorb more and more speakers of different 'languages', the enforcement of this monolingual ideology was seen not just as a way to socialise immigrants into their new national identity but also as a matter of national security. In his famous 1919 address to the American Defense Society, for example, US President Theodore Roosevelt declared:

We have room for but one language in this country, and that is the English language, for we intend to see that the crucible turns our people out as Americans, of American nationality, and not as dwellers in a polyglot boarding-house.

(cited in Brumberg 1986: 7)

This invention of languages as part of the equipment Europeans used for imagining their own nations also played a part in the way they imagined non-European nations and non-European languages. Among the main ways that Great Britain controlled and administered its colonies, for example, was by deploying linguists to analyse the different ways people spoke in the territories they had conquered and divide them into languages. Among the most famous of these efforts was Sir George Abraham Grierson's *Linguistic Survey of India*, published in eleven volumes from 1898 to 1928. When he first arrived on the sub-continent, Grierson (1903: 350) bewailed the fact that the native people lacked an understanding of the idea of 'languages'. He wrote:

Few natives at the present day are able to comprehend the idea connoted by the words of a language. Dialects they know and understand. They separate them and distinguish them with a meticulous, hair-splitting subtlety, which to us seems unnecessary and absurd, but their minds are not trained to grasp the conception so familiar to us, of a general term embracing a number of interconnected dialects.

According to Grierson (1903: 350), nearly all of the names of Indian languages had to be invented by Europeans:

Some of them, such as Bengali, Assamese, and the like, are founded on words which have received English citizenship, and are not real Indian words at all, while others, like 'Hindostani', 'Bihari', and so forth, are based on already existing Indian names of countries and nationalities.

These quotes provide a perfect portrayal not just of the 'imagined' nature of different Indian languages, but also of the arrogance of European colonisers. These colonisers naturally assumed that their way of understanding and classifying the different ways people spoke was somehow superior to the understandings of the actual speakers.

Of course, no nation is really monolingual. As we will explore throughout this book, people as a rule have access to all sorts of different ways of talking that they deploy in different ways in different situations that sometimes have very little to do with what country they come from or live in (see Chapter 2). And, even in Europe, not all nations are built on monolingual ideologies. Some countries, such as Switzerland and Belgium, have cultivated multilingual identities. Others, such as Austria and Germany, have cultivated different national identities despite the fact that they share a 'common language'. Outside of Europe, multilingualism is the rule rather than the exception. More than 520 languages, for example, are spoken in Nigeria, and, according to former Papua New Guinea's prime minister Sir Michael Somare, Papua New Guinea has 832 different languages, making it the most linguistically diverse country on earth. Nevertheless, the notion that nations are somehow defined by the language that people in them speak, along with the idea that the existence of lots of different languages might constitute a threat to national unity, remains pervasive, not just in everyday discourse (such as the graffiti painted on the streets of Walthamstow), but also in the official laws and policies of many governments and institutions, and these ideas can affect the way people who speak in different ways are treated and the kinds of opportunities that they have.

At the same time, even the **multilingual ideologies** of places like Switzerland and Singapore can have the effect of including and excluding people, since they are also built upon the idea of languages as discrete entities often associated with particular groups of people. So, for example, in Singapore, until recently, people were restricted from learning languages in school that were not associated with the ethnic group they were seen to belong to (Chinese, Malay, or Tamil), and the African linguist Sinfree Makoni (2003) points out that the way the South African Constitution labels different African languages as separate entities not only ignores the similarities between these different ways of speaking but also can interfere with the educational opportunities of those who speak in ways that don't conform to the standardised versions of these languages.

1.3 Standard Language Ideology

The idea that 'languages' are real things that somehow function to define nations or groups of people leads naturally to the need to define what exactly is the 'common language' of a nation and to separate that 'language' from all of the other ways of speaking people engage in that don't necessarily conform to the 'common language'. In other words, as

Hannele Dufva and her colleagues (2011: 111) observe, 'the ideology of nationalism does not make a difference only horizontally – by drawing a boundary between any two languages – but also vertically, by elevating one variant – the variant chosen to be the "standard" language – over other usages'.

The label 'standard language' is usually reserved for the way the most powerful people in the society speak or the way people in the region where most of those people live speak. Thus, 'Standard French' is based on the way people in Paris talk, 'Standard Spanish' on the speech of the people in Castile, 'Standard British English' on the speech of the people living in south-east of the country, 'Standard German' on varieties of the central eastern region around Erfurt and Leipzig, and 'Standard Chinese' (or *Putonghua*, meaning 'common language') on the way people in the region around the capital Beijing speak. As one way of speaking comes to be accepted as the 'standard', people start to believe that this way of speaking is the true or original form of the language, and all other related ways of speaking are seen to be *derivations* and usually *distortions* of this original form. This, of course, is a myth, which is often encouraged by speakers of the 'standard' form: usually these other ways of speaking are just as old as the way of speaking that has been elevated to be the 'standard'.

In the last section we talked about the ideology of monolingualism, the set of ideas that leads people to believe that speaking only one language in one place is natural. The idea that one way of speaking used in a particular place is superior to others and the standard against which others are judged is called the **standard language ideology**. The linguist James Milroy (2007: 133) defines it as a set of 'language attitudes [that] are dominated by powerful ideological positions that are largely based on the supposed exist-ence of [a] standard form'. According to Milroy, the myth of a standard language is based on the unrealistic expectation 'that every sound should be pronounced in the same way by every speaker, and that all speakers should use the same grammatical forms and vocabulary items in exactly the same way . . . [and] that the language should not undergo change' (133).

Standard languages do not arise naturally; rather they are the result of deliberate social and political processes. According to Haugen (1966), the first step in language standardisation is choosing, out of all the ways of speaking available to a particular group of people, one to be the 'stand-ard'. This choice has nothing to do with how elegant, logical, or efficient that way of speaking is (though speakers of that variety often think this is the case). Rather, as we said above, it has to do almost exclusively with political and social power. This choice is subsequently legitimated through a number of different processes, including **codification**, involv-ing the formulation of standard forms of grammar, spelling, and pronun-ciation and the writing of dictionaries to record vocabulary. Some people insist that grammars are merely descriptions of the way people actually speak a language, but in reality they are careful *selections* of the way *some* people speak which end up ignoring and eventually censoring the ways other people speak (Dufva et al. 2011). Finally, this variety is promoted as the 'standard' through various channels in the society. One of the most important of these channels is the educational system. At school, children learn that certain ways of talking are correct, while others are incorrect, and when they learn to read and write, the written language they learn is based on the 'standard language'. The media also play an important role in the promulgation of the 'standard language', and sometimes there are even government-sanctioned agencies responsible for this, such as *L'Académie française* in France.

As with the ideology of monolingualism, the maintenance of the ideology of the 'standard language' depends on people becoming *emotionally invested* in it. Therefore, the 'standard language' is often associated not just with correctness but also with uprightness, morality, and civilisation in the discourse of teachers, politicians, and the media. Ability to speak the 'standard language' comes to be seen as a sign of intelligence, industry, social worthiness, and prestige. At the same time, maintaining and promoting the 'standard language' necessarily depends upon *stigmatising* people who do not speak that variety, portraying them as ignorant, backward, lazy, morally dissolute, and not even able to speak 'their own language'. In other words, the standard language ideology ends up being an excuse to discriminate against people who speak differently (and often also look different). As Milroy (2007: 135) puts it:

It is believed to be open to everyone to learn what the correct forms are; therefore, it is thought to be quite proper to discriminate – in employment, for example – against people who use non-standard forms. Although it is now unacceptable to discriminate openly against someone for reasons of ethnic group, social class, religion or gender, it is still acceptable to discriminate openly on linguistic grounds. Unfortunately, people do not usually realize that language stands proxy for these other social categories. As a person who uses non-standard linguistic forms will often be from a minority ethnic group or a lower social class, the effect of language discrimination is to discriminate against ethnic minorities and lower social class groups.

A related characteristic one finds in what Milroy calls 'standard language cultures' is a 'complaint tradition' (Milroy & Milroy 2012) in which politicians, educators, and media personalities are constantly raging against the supposed decline of the standard language, often as a result of its purity being compromised by the influence of foreign or minority ways of speaking. Part of this tradition are attempts at what the sociolinguist Deborah Cameron calls **verbal hygiene**, which she defines as 'practices … born of an urge to improve or clean up language' (1995: 1), such as campaigns for schools to go back to teaching 'the basics' (meaning the grammar of the 'standard language').

Not surprisingly, the impulse to police the borders of language is often linked with the impulse to police the borders of the country, making it more difficult for people who speak different languages to enter and more difficult for those who have entered to get ahead if the version of the national language they have learnt is different from the 'standard', an issue we will look at more closely at the end of this chapter.

Language standardisation, of course, is not always a bad thing. Milroy likens it to other kinds of standardisation such as the standardisation of currency or weights and measures, and notes standard varieties are usually more widely comprehensible and functional in a wider range of settings and activities. The process of language standardisation, as we discussed in the last section, can also help to unify people, giving them a sense of belonging to a group or a country. But the price of this is that it also acts to exclude people and separate the community that speaks the standard language from other communities.

Activity: 'Learn to Speak With a Fluent British Accent'

Look at the advertisement in Figure 1.3 and discuss the questions that follow.

1. How does this advertisement define a 'fluent British accent'? How does this definition reinforce the ideology of a standard language in the UK?
2. What sorts of *values* are attributed to speaking with this accent?
3. Who do you think this advertisement is intended for? What sorts of social rewards might these people attain from adopting a 'fluent British accent', and how might these rewards differ from those available to other people who adopt this accent?
4. Do you think there might be any disadvantages for these people in adopting this accent?

Learn to Speak with a Fluent British Accent

A British Accent that is Easy to Understand

Learn to read and speak with a fluent British Accent and be clearly understood. Learn the London accent. (Thames Estuary accent.)

- SEE clearly how the British Accent is spoken.
- Read and speak English words with a flawless British accent.
- Practice your British accent until it is perfect.
- Learn how to speak with a British accent without extra help. (All you need is the PDF eBook and occasional internet access.)

Are you learning English? Learn how to speak with a fluent British accent in weeks rather than years. The Thames Estuary accent is easy to learn.

It is a little known fact that an English Phonics course is a highly effective way to learn to speak with a British accent. The training course called 'Practice Reading and Speaking' is usually used to teach reading to all ages. However, you can use the cut down version of the phonics course 'PRS STUDENT GUIDE' effectively to learn to pronounce

Learn a British Accent

words with a perfect British accent. As an adult, you will likely have no problem reading the words in the course, but can you read all of them with a British accent? Use the course to practice speaking.

FIGURE 1.3
'Learn to speak with a fluent British accent'
(source: http://teachreading.info)

1.4 Languages, Dialects, and Accents

As should be clear from the discussion so far, when most people talk about a *language*, what they are usually referring to is what they imagine to be the 'standard' variety of that 'language' (e.g., English, French, Greek, Danish, Norwegian, Japanese, Arabic, Russian). Ways of speaking that are different from the 'standard' variety are often called **dialects**. The word dialect is usually used to refer to varieties of a given language which are associated with a particular region of a country and/or a particular sub-group within a community. It might be used, for example, to describe Geordie in the UK, Cypriot Greek in Cyprus, Cantonese in China, and Andalusian in Spain, because these are ways of speaking associated with particular places, or it might be used to describe a variety like African American Vernacular English (see Introduction), which is used in various urban communities in the US mostly by people of African American descent. Usually, dialects of the same language are considered to be different because they exhibit differences in grammar, pronunciation, and vocabulary. When varieties are different from the 'standard' only in pronunciation, people usually use the word **accent** rather than dialect.

There are all sorts of problems with these distinctions, however, when you actually look at the way people use them in real life. For example, while people refer to Norwegian and Danish as different 'languages', they are actually so similar that most speakers of Norwegian can easily understand speakers of Danish and *vice versa*. At the same time, while Shanghainese and Cantonese are regarded as 'dialects' of the same language, speakers of one of these two varieties are mutually unintelligible to speakers of the other. Serbian and Croatian are, like Danish and Norwegian, mutually comprehensible, but are written differently. Serbian, whose speakers are mainly Orthodox Christians, is usually written in the Cyrillic alphabet (the same alphabet used in Russian). Croatian, whose speakers are mainly Roman Catholic, is usually written in the Latin alphabet. Linguists like to refer to these varieties as a single 'language': Serbo-Croatian, but speakers of these varieties violently resist this label.

The same sorts of problems arise with the word accent. Strictly speaking, all people speak with an accent, in that their speech has phonological features that may differ from those of people with similar ways of speaking. Speakers of 'standard' accents, such as Received Pronunciation (RP) in the UK and General American in the US are not 'accent-less' – rather they speak with the accents of people from a particular region and (in the case of the UK) a particular social class. In fact, only about 3 per cent of the people who live in England actually speak with an RP accent. But, as Matsuda (1991: 1321) puts it, 'People in power are perceived as speaking normal, unaccented English. Any speech that is different from that constructed norm is called an accent.'

As we noted above when we were discussing the standard language ideology, whether a variety is considered a language, a dialect, or an accent is chiefly a matter of politics – the relative power that the speakers of one variety have over speakers of other varieties. Sometimes, however, the processes through which 'languages' get to be 'languages', 'dialects' get to be 'dialects', and 'accents' get to be 'accents' can be rather complex.

One example of this is the case of South Africa, which currently has eleven official 'languages'. If we exclude English and Afrikaans, which are European-derived 'languages', we are left with nine indigenous African 'languages'. Interestingly, five of these are linguistically very similar and speakers of them are mutually intelligible, so in other circumstances they might be considered 'dialects' rather than 'languages'. The explanation for this can be traced to missionary linguists during the colonial period, when what is now South Africa was divided into French, British, and Dutch territories, with linguists working in each territory coming up with their own ways of naming, describing, and writing the 'languages' they encountered. When South Africa gained its independence in 1961, politicians and linguists made an attempt to harmonise these 'languages' into one, but this was resisted, in some cases by the speakers of the 'languages' themselves, since people in each territorial group had come to consider themselves as distinct from other groups who had very similar ways of speaking. At the same time, treating these different ways of speaking as different 'languages', each with its own 'standard', has, in some cases, exacerbated social divisions and created obstacles for children being schooled in these 'languages'. Makoni (2003) notes that the way most people talk does not conform to *any* of these supposed 'standard languages', but rather resembles a kind of linguistic continuum across the region in which these 'languages' are supposedly spoken. He gives the example of the same sentences spoken in three different 'standard languages':

1. Standard siSwati: Indvodza iye edolobheni ekuseni.
   'The man has gone to town.'
2. Standard Xhosa: Indoda iye edolobheni kusasa.
   'The man has gone to town.'
3. Standard Zulu: Indoda iye edolobheni ekuseni.
   'The man has gone to town.'

The insistence by teachers that these 'languages' are utterly separate, he argues, can actually create problems for children learning them in school. He writes:

A child ethnically classified as Swati who produces the utterance *Indoda iye edolobheni kusasa* will be regarded as speaking incorrect siSwati, i.e. not speaking *pure* siSwati. She is pronouncing *indoda* as in Standard Xhosa and Zulu instead of *indvodza*. Similarly, a Zulu child who says: *Indoda iye edolobheni kusasa* will be said to be speaking incorrect Zulu because she says *kusasa* instead of *ekuseni*. The child's Zulu would thus be classified as incorrect even though it is correct Standard Xhosa!

(Makoni 2003: 143–4)

Not surprisingly, along with standardisation has come increasing efforts of verbal hygiene in South Africa, in which standard African languages are equated with moral purity and speakers of non-standard varieties, especially urban varieties which mix together the ways of speaking of different groups, are seen as morally irresponsible (Makoni 2003: 148).

A rather different example is Thailand. Saowanee and McCargo (2014) report that before 1939, Thailand, then known as Siam, was a multicultural society consisting of various ethnic groups who spoke different 'languages'. When the name of the country was changed to Thailand the government wanted people to develop a common sense of nationhood, and one way this was achieved was by elevating Central Thai or *Phasa Thai* to the 'standard language' and referring to all other varieties as 'dialects' of Central Thai, making them subordinate to it. One example is *Phasa Isan*, a way of speaking associated with the north-east part of Thailand, near the border with Laos. *Phasa Isan* is linguistically very different from 'Standard Thai', having lexical and phonological properties more similar to Lao than to Thai. Despite this, *Phasa Isan* is considered to be a 'dialect' of 'Standard Thai' instead of being recognised as a different 'language'. It is also important to mention that the subordination of *Phasa Isan* has led to its speakers being frequently characterised as 'unsophisticated', 'stupid', 'inferior', and 'socio-economically backward'.

Although labelling a certain way of talking as a dialect almost always has the effect of marginalising the people who speak that way, dialects can also help to reinforce a feeling of solidarity and social belonging among the people who speak them. This feeling can lead people to try to valorise and preserve their dialect as a way of resisting power or of emphasising their uniqueness or independence.

Of course, neither languages nor dialects are static, and new ways of speaking are developing all the time, especially under the influence of globalisation and urbanisation. New urban varieties, such as what has come to be known as Multicultural London English (see Chapter 9) are often influenced by the ways of speaking of many different immigrant groups as well as by popular culture and music, and in some cases, these varieties come to function as emblems of urban sophistication and youth culture. At the same time, there are inevitably people, self-proclaimed champions of the 'standard language', who go out of their way to criticise these new ways of speaking, and their criticisms (while often exhibiting no small degree of racism and xenophobia) are invariably based in the two ideologies that we have discussed in this chapter, the monolingual ideology that says that everybody in a particular place should talk the same, and the standard language ideology that says that there is only one true, correct, or 'moral' way of speaking a 'language'. This can be seen, for example, in the assessment that British historian David Starkey gave of Multicultural London English on the BBC TV show *Newsnight*, an assessment that exhibits the same kind of attitudes about language and society that likely led to the words 'SPEAK ENGLISH' being graffitied throughout the streets of Walthamstow.

The whites have become black. A particular sort of violent, destructive, nihilistic, gangster culture has become the fashion, and black and white, boy and girl, operate in this language together, this language which is wholly false, which is this Jamaican patois that has been intruded in England, and that is why so many of us have this sense of, literally, a foreign country.

(Mirror Online 2011)

Activity: Languages in South Africa

Take a look at the excerpt from the Constitution of the Republic of South Africa reprinted below and discuss the questions that follow it.

1. *The official languages of the Republic are:*
   Sepedi, Sesotho, Setswana, siSwati, Tshivenḍa, Xitsonga, Afrikaans, English, isiNdebele, isiXhosa and isiZulu.
2. *Recognising the historically diminished use and status of the indigenous languages of our people, the state must take practical and positive measures to elevate the status and advance the use of these languages.*
3. *(a) The national government and provincial governments may use any particular official languages for the purposes of government, taking into account usage, practicality, expense, regional circumstances and the balance of the needs and preferences of the population as a whole or in the province concerned; but the national government and each provincial government must use at least two official languages.*
   (b) Municipalities must take into account the language usage and preferences of their residents.
4. *The national government and provincial governments, by legislative and other measures, must regulate and monitor their use of official languages. Without detracting from the provisions of subsection (2), all official languages must enjoy parity of esteem and must be treated equitably.*
5. *A Pan South African Language Board established by national legislation must*
   (a) promote, and create conditions for, the development and use of -
      (i) all official languages;
      (ii) the Khoi, Nama and San languages; and
      (iii) sign language; and
   (b) promote and ensure respect for -
      (i) all languages commonly used by communities in South Africa, including German, Greek, Gujarati, Hindi, Portuguese, Telugu, Tamil and Urdu; and
      (ii) Arabic, Hebrew, Sanskrit and other languages used for religious purposes in South Africa.

— Constitution of the Republic of South Africa

1. How does the 'multilingual ideology' enshrined in the South African Constitution compare with the monolingual ideology evident in the laws and policies of other countries that you might be familiar with (for example Germany, Thailand, the United Kingdom)?
2. From what you know about the history of South Africa, what are some of the possible reasons for the adoption of this language policy?

3. What are some of the possible consequences of this policy?
4. The African linguist Sinfree Makoni (2003) argues that, by recognising nine African 'languages' as neatly divided bounded units, the South African Constitution ends up disadvantaging the very people it is meant to serve and reproducing the ways of dividing up 'languages' imposed on the local people by colonial invaders. What do you think of this critique? In what ways can a multilingual language policy like this continue to reproduce and reinforce a monolingual ideology and a standard language ideology?

1.5 Focal Topic: Language and Citizenship

The focal topic for this chapter is the relationship between language and citizenship. Not surprisingly, given the prevalence of the ideologies that we explored above, nations often turn to language as a means of controlling who they allow to live within their borders. They might, for example, require new immigrants to demonstrate a certain level of proficiency in the 'language' (or one of the official 'languages') of the country. This is the case in countries like the United Kingdom and France, but *not* the case in other countries such as Ireland, Israel, and Sweden. Another way governments might use language as a way to control immigration is by making sure that people who say they are seeking refuge from the dangerous political situation in certain countries really come from those countries by testing whether or not they speak the 'language' associated with that country. The two articles below are written by sociolinguists who are interested in these issues. The first is by Adrian Blackledge and discusses some of the ideological underpinnings of the British language policy for new immigrants. The second is by Mohammed Ateek and Simon Rasinger and discusses how a procedure known as 'Language Analysis for Determination of Origin' (LADO) is used to screen people applying for asylum in the UK.

As you will see, both of the articles demonstrate some of the real-world consequences of the language ideologies we have been discussing in this chapter: the monolingual ideology and the standard language ideology.

Blackledge, A. (2009) 'As a country we do expect': The further extension of language testing regimes in the United Kingdom, *Language Assessment Quarterly*, 6(1), 6–16   In this article Blackledge argues that the British government policy of making 'English proficiency' a precondition for both residency (known as 'indefinite leave to remain') and citizenship in the name of 'national unity' has the effect of discriminating against speakers of other languages and promoting inaccurate and harmful misconceptions about language.

Blackledge begins his article by talking about the power of language ideologies, especially the ideology of monolingualism, and how they have affected the ways people in Britain talk about language and immigration. He then reviews the history of government policies around language and citizenship since 2001, starting with *The Nationality, Immigration and Asylum Act*, 2002, which set out the requirements for applicants for British citizenship to take an English language test in order to demonstrate their proficiency in English (or Welsh or Scots Gaelic).

Discourses around language proficiency in the UK, Blackledge points out, are frequently and explicitly linked to ideas about 'British values'. In fact, one of the ways that English proficiency is tested is through a test of 'Life in the United Kingdom', which includes questions such as 'How often do most children in the UK receive their pocket money?', 'What is the distance from John O'Groats in the north of Scotland to Land's End in south-west England?', and 'Who is the monarch not allowed to marry?' Tests such as this, Blackledge argues, are not only poor measures of English proficiency, but also tie knowledge of the language to a collection of ideologically biased facts about (white) British culture.

Most of the article contains Blackledge's analysis of how the government justifies this requirement. One of the main justifications, he notes, is the claim that forcing people to speak English will increase social cohesion and give migrants equal opportunities in British society. He quotes the former prime minister Tony Blair, for example, announcing the extension of the language requirement to anyone who wishes to remain in the UK, whether or not they want to apply for citizenship, declaring:

We should share a common language. Equal opportunity for all groups requires that they be conversant in that common language. It is a matter both of cohesion and of justice that we should set the use of English as a condition of citizenship. In addition, for those who wish to take up residence permanently in the U.K., we will include a requirement to pass an English test before such permanent residency is granted.

In other documents published by the government, Blackledge points out the consistent claim that forcing people to demonstrate knowledge of English helps them to better integrate into British life. The consultation document, *Marriage visas: Pre-entry English requirement for spouses*, for example, states:

We want newcomers who come here with the intention to settle to make a meaningful contribution to our society and to our economy. It is therefore right that we should consider ways to assist a foreign spouse's integration into life here right from day one.

It goes on to argue:

A common language is fundamental to integration and cohesion for communities. We do believe there is a case for examining whether an English requirement for spouses before they arrive in the U.K., with the aim of long-term stay here, would help spouses integrate more quickly into the community, boost confidence in participating in employment, and make clear that, as a country, we do expect those intending to make the U.K. their long term home to recognise the importance of speaking English.

The ways such statements reflect and reinforce the ideology of monolingualism that we have discussed in this chapter are clear. In addition to this, however, Blackledge also suggests that the policy and the public discourse that accompanies it have the effect of demonising migrants by suggesting that speaking languages other than English is a *threat* to social cohesion. While most immigrants to the UK are likely to *want* to learn English, for many of them learning English will not really address the problems they face in the UK regarding integration and opportunities, many of which have their roots in systemic racism and economic disadvantages. Blackledge also points out that these economic challenges make it difficult for many migrants to access the kinds of educational opportunities they need to master English. As an alternative to the testing regime, he suggests that the government focus on providing resources to help migrants become more proficient in English.

Blackledge concludes by reminding us that, in any society, debates about language are often really debates about inclusion, multiculturalism, and the kind of society people wish to live in. In reality, he says, the UK is a multilingual, multicultural, and pluralistic society. English language testing for citizenship, rather than creating social cohesion, has the effect of marginalising minority languages and their speakers and of privileging not just 'English' but a particular variety of English which many 'natural born' citizens do not even speak.

Ateek, M., and Rasinger, S. M. (2018) Syrian or non-Syrian? Reflections on the use of LADO in the UK. In I. Nick (ed.) *Forensic linguistics: Asylum-seekers, refugees and immigrants.* Wilmington, DC: Vernon Press, pp. 75–93 Language Analysis for Determination of Origin (LADO) is a technique used by governments to determine the geographical origins of people who are applying for *asylum* (the right to live in a country based on claims that they would suffer persecution if sent back to the country they came from). LADO usually consists of an interview with an asylum seeker, which is recorded and subjected to linguistic analysis to compare the pronunciation, grammar, and vocabulary used by the claimant with the way others in the place they claim to be from speak. In many countries LADO is carried out by private companies and relies on so-called 'native speakers' of the language in question rather than trained linguists to do the analysis.

In many ways, this technique clearly reflects the ideologically charged myths about language that we have discussed in this chapter. The notion that all people from a particular place speak in a particular way is especially emphasised. In this article, Mohammed Ateek and Sebastian Rasinger report on a study they carried out of Syrian asylum seekers in the UK and their experiences with LADO. Due to an armed conflict between the Syrian government and opposition forces, as well as the rise of extremist groups in the country, over 40 per cent of the Syrian population had been displaced by the time this article was written. More than 8,000 of them had applied for refugee status or asylum in the UK.

Based on in-depth interviews with Syrian asylum seekers and lawyers who worked with them, Ateek and Rasinger point out four main problems with the use of LADO to test asylum seekers' claims of origin.

The first is the fact that often the process fails to take into account the sociolinguistic realities of the countries in question, instead depending on naive and inaccurate assumptions that everyone who claims to have come from a certain country should speak in a certain way. In reality, a wide variety of languages and dialects can exist in a given country. All sorts of factors can affect the way people speak: people often move around within their country of origin or spend time in other countries, and the ways of speaking in different regions of a country can change for various reasons, including contact with people from other regions. Syria is a good example of this, with the variety spoken in the eastern Syrian city of Deir Az-Zour, for example, being linguistically closer to the varieties found in Iraq than to those used in other Syrian cities. This can result in an asylum seeker from Eastern Syria being mistaken for an Iraqi. Most people, Ateek and Rasinger point out, possess complex linguistic repertoires (see Chapter 2). Their language may include lexical borrowing from neighbouring languages or dialects or influences from contact with speakers of different varieties due to travel. One of the asylum seekers Ateek and Rasinger interviewed, for example, had lived in Dubai from the age of 4 until the age of 18 and had been exposed to lots of different ways of speaking Arabic during that time. He said:

When I came back to Syria there were a lot of words that I did not know their meanings, but with time I learned and I used to ask people about their meanings. Even my friends in Hama used to tell me when I spoke that my accent was not the accent of Hama, it was more of Damascene accent although both of my parents are from Hama.

The second problem that Ateek and Rasinger uncover with LADO is the fact that the procedure for testing is often very predictable, leading many applicants to over-rehearse and even memorise their answers. In some cases, they argue that this might give the language analyst the impression that the applicant does not sound authentic or that they are 'trying too hard' to sound Syrian.

The third problem they reveal arises from the fact that sometimes people change the way they speak based on whom they are talking to, a phenomenon that we will discuss in more detail in Chapter 6. This is especially true in cases where one speaker has more power and the other speaker wishes to please them. One of Ateek and Rasinger's interviewees, for instance, was interviewed by a Lebanese person and found himself sometimes reproducing some the interviewer's Lebanese pronunciation.

Finally, Ateek and Rasinger point out that the way people talk in LADO interviews might be affected by their emotions or their attitudes towards the process. For example, their way of speaking might be coloured by the intimidating environment that is often created in the test-taking situation.

Ateek and Rasinger conclude that these issues, especially the lack of in-depth engagement with an applicant's sociolinguistic history, pose considerable questions regarding the validity of LADO as it is currently carried out. They suggest reforms to the process, the most important being the hiring of trained linguists rather than just interpreters or 'native speakers' with folk linguistic views to carry out the interviews and subsequent analysis.

Project Ideas

1. Interview a number of people about the different ways people in the neighbourhood, town, or region where they live speak. Pay attention to the different ways they describe these varieties (as 'languages', 'dialects', or 'accents') and the kinds of prestige or social values they assign to them.
2. Collect data from the media about how people talk about 'language standards'. Pay attention to complaints about 'falling standards' or 'bad language' and the kinds of evidence and reasons people give for these perceived phenomena. See if you can link these reasons to broader social issues such as immigration or generational conflict.
3. Research the policies that the country that you live in has regarding language and citizenship. Collect as many official documents and political speeches as you can about the issue and note the reasons that are given to justify the policy (for example arguments about 'integration' or 'diversity'). What sorts of language ideologies are reflected in these policies? What sorts of consequences do you think these policies might have on people living or wanting to live in the country?

CHAPTER

2 Resources and Repertoires

PREVIEW

KEY TERMS

codes
competency
genres
heteroglossia
icons, symbols,
and indexes
indexical
meaning
registers
repertoires
resources
semantic
meaning

In this chapter we will consider how people communicate not through 'languages' in the traditional sense, but through collections of *resources* – 'pieces' of language and other things like pictures, gestures, and clothing – which allow them to communicate not just what they mean but also who they are. Different people have access to different kinds of resources, which can create problems of inequality in society, an issue that we will take up in the focal topic section of this chapter.

2.1 Introduction

In the last chapter we talked about some of the different ways people think about language and some of the consequences these language ideologies can have on people's standing in the societies in which they live or their opportunities to become part of different societies. In this chapter we will introduce an alternative way of looking at language, one which focuses less on abstract 'languages' or 'dialects' and more on the different **resources** that people use to communicate with different kinds of people in different kinds of situations.

Figure 2.1 is a photograph of a section of what used to be the Berlin Wall. The picture of the two men kissing was painted in 1990 by Dmitri Vrubel and is called *My God, Help Me to Survive This Deadly Love*. There is a lot of background information you need to know to understand this painting. The first thing you need to know is that the two men are former General Secretary of the Central Committee of the Communist Party of the Soviet Union Leonid Brezhnev and former General Secretary of the Socialist Unity Party of the German Democratic Republic (GDR, what was known as 'East Germany') Erich Honecker. The painting is from an actual photograph taken on 4 October 1979, when Brezhnev, visiting East Berlin on the 30th anniversary of the GDR, gave Honecker what was known as a 'socialist fraternal kiss' in order to show his support. By the time this mural was painted, East and West Germany had been united and the part of the wall on which it was painted had been transformed into an open-air gallery. This background, and the placement of the mural in what was once East Berlin, helps us to understand the political meaning of the mural's title: *My God, Help Me to Survive This Deadly Love*, which is written in German below the painting and in Russian above and below it. What we are interested in here, however, is not just the mural but the graffiti which was subsequently written on top of it, the range of different 'voices' represented in this graffiti, and the range of different 'languages' used to express these voices.

Perhaps the most striking thing about this image is how many different kinds of **codes** we can find on it: we see words in what we would normally refer to as the 'languages' of German, Russian, and English, but we also see things like graffiti tags, most of which are almost impossible to interpret if we are not familiar with the local context. There are some words which, instead of just coming from a particular 'language', also come from a particular **register** or way of speaking associated with particular people with particular attitudes or social identities. The word 'faggots', for example, was originally a derogatory term for gay men used in American English, but it later spread both across the English-speaking world as well as into other 'languages'. But it may not be a word many readers of this book would use in a derogatory fashion, and if we were to hear someone use it in that way, we would probably associate it with certain kinds of opinions and political affiliations. But one thing

FIGURE 2.1
From the East-Side Gallery (Berlin)
(photo credit: young shanahan, licensed under CC BY 2.0)

that we can't really do is to assume that the person who wrote that word is a 'speaker of English' in the conventional sense, since this slur is known widely outside of the English-speaking world. At the same time, the way the word is written here – 'FAGGOT$' – with a dollar sign replacing the 's' makes interpreting the writer's message even more complicated.

Another piece of 'English' graffiti in the image is the phrase:

STOP HOMO-
PHOBIA
IN RU-
SSIA

This phrase seems to represent a very different 'voice', one which contrasts with the one represented by the word 'FAGGOT$'. Although these voices 'clash', it is difficult to know for sure how they are related to each other (partly because we don't know which piece of graffiti was written first). There does seem to be a relationship between this phrase and the picture of Brezhnev that it is written on top of, if one takes him to be an icon of the Russian government; although Brezhnev was long dead when the mural and the accompanying graffiti were painted, institutionalised homophobia has continued (if not increased) in Russia under Vladimir Putin.

What we see in this picture, however, is not just different codes and different registers, but also different **genres** – people using different forms of language to *do* different things. 'FAGGOT$' might be regarded as an *insult*, 'STOP HOMOPHOBIA IN RUSSIA' as a kind of political *slogan*, the English text below it, 'Love stories suck' as a kind of *commentary*, the English and Russian words 'My God, Help Me to Survive This Deadly Love' as *captions* (whose meaning is dependent on the picture they are associated with), and the graffiti tags as *signatures* which communicate that a particular person has been there.

This image, then, is a complex *conversation* among many different people carried out in many different languages, registers, and genres, reflecting the diverse and complex range of political and social opinions as well as the complex range of *communicative resources* present in contemporary Berlin.

But the main thing that we would like to point out here is that interpreting this text requires that we have some combination of **competencies** (which might include knowledge of German, Russian, American slang, global and local conventions regarding urban graffiti, Soviet history and the contemporary status of gay people in Russia), and that, depending on what configurations of competencies we bring to this image, we will experience it differently. We don't need to possess *all* of these competencies fully in order to 'get something' out of the image; it may, for example, be enough to know only that the German is German and the Russian is Russian and that the people kissing are two old dudes that had something to do with politics. We don't even need to have a complete command of all of these codes, registers, and genres in order to *contribute* to this conversation by adding our own graffiti. And this is not just true for this text. Many of the texts people encounter in the contemporary world are made from a mish-mash of different codes, registers, and genres, some of which they may not fully understand.

2.2 Heteroglossia

The Russian literary critic Mikhail Bakhtin (1981) argued that most texts and utterances are like this image, that whenever we use language we are always drawing on different resources and mixing together different 'voices', a phenomenon he called **heteroglossia**.

What we mean when we call this text 'heteroglossic' is not just that it was created by many authors, but also that it contains the 'voices' of lots of different *kinds of speakers*, representing different kinds of ideologies, and different kinds of opinions about things like politics, sexuality, nationality, love, and patriotism. Each of these bits of language 'points to' a particular world view and to the kinds of people who might have this world view.

Below is a text from a social media site which also contains different voices, but, rather than written by lots of different authors, as was the text above, this was written by a single author.

Dynamite Soul on 17 Dec 2008 19:04

Are you ready for some Super Dynamite Soul?

Plug und Mr. Edd droppen auf Krauty Schlager und German Freak Beats im wesentlichen Weird Stuff aus deutschen Landen. Musik zu der unsere Eltern gerne getanzt hätten, wenn sie ihnen so gekonnt servciert worden ware, wie es die Leipziger Funksoulbrothers auf diesem Mixtape tun.

Damenwahl!

Are you ready for some Super Dynamite Soul?

Plug and Mr. Edd drop on Krauty Schlager und German Freak Beats essential weird stuff from German soil. Music our parents would have danced to if only it was as well served as it is now by Leipzig's own Funksoulbrothers on this mixtape.

Ladies' choice!

(Androutsopoulos 2011: 291–2)

Here again we see a mixture of what we would conventionally call 'languages', in this case, German and English. But the English that begins the text is, again, a particular *register* of English, a kind of promotional discourse common to the music industry, and the German beneath it, peppered with English words – such as 'Freak Beats', 'Weird Stuff' and 'Mixtape' – as well as slang expressions like 'krauty'[1] – is hardly what is usually referred to as 'Standard German'. What is also interesting is that the music described in the post is also a 'weird' hybrid of soul/funk music and Schlager, which one online commentator describes as 'a form of pop so insipid and saccharine that it is possible the Communists built the Berlin Wall to keep it out' (Schuman 2017).

Again, this kind of text is not all that unusual. The kind of mixing of languages, registers, and styles that we see here, is, in fact, rather common, especially in parts of the world (or parts of the Internet) where people from different places and different backgrounds interact.

In the last chapter we discussed approaches to language that see 'languages' as predetermined, bounded, nameable 'things' which are 'spoken' by predetermined groups of people and are measured against some 'standard' of proper lexis and grammar. From the point of view of these approaches, the kinds of texts that we have been discussing here would be considered 'weird stuff'. But the closer we look at language *in use*, the more we see that this kind of diversity is the norm, even in what we might consider more conventional texts and verbal performances (see Chapter 5). Below, for example, is from a news story broadcast on a youth music radio station, reported by the sociolinguist Allan Bell (2014: 293).

Police in Napier are pretty stoked with the haul of pot they've grabbed. Over forty people arrested after a sting targeting cannabis growers seizing around twelve thousand plants worth around forty mill.

While most of us would describe this as 'English', the first sentence and the second sentence represent two very different registers or 'styles' (see Chapter 6) of English, the first, with its use of words like 'stoked', 'pot', and 'haul', representing a more informal, 'street' style of speaking, and the second, in which words like 'pot' and 'grab' are replaced with 'cannabis' and 'seize', representing a more formal journalistic register.

---

[1] A term originally associated with 'Krautrock' or Kosmische music, an experimental rock movement that arose in Germany in the late 1960s.

In this chapter we will look more at how language is *actually* used and understood. This involves coming to terms with the fact that communication is not accomplished through 'languages' in the sense that we talked about in the last chapter, but through people cobbling together 'pieces' of language (and other things like pictures, gestures, and graffiti tags) which they take from a range of different sources and which allow them to communicate not just 'meanings' but also attitudes, opinions, identities, and relationships. It also involves coming to terms with the fact that these pieces of language (and other things) are used and understood differently by different people in different circumstances. Finally, it involves coming to terms with the fact that different people have different degrees of *access* to these different resources, and the fact that any access (whether it be to resources like 'the English language', the history of East Germany, or knowledge of the finer distinctions between different kinds of 'krauty' music) is always *partial*. We always end up having to do our best with whatever resources are available to us.

Activity: Maya's Many 'Voices'

Maya was born in South Africa, where she lived with her family until the age of 7. Her family was originally from Cyprus, and her parents often spoke Greek at home. She learned English and Afrikaans at school. She also learned to recognise Xhosa, which is spoken widely in Cape Town where she was born, but she can't understand it. Maya's family moved to Cyprus when she was 7 and Maya went to a public school where the medium of instruction was 'Standard Greek'. She was also exposed to Cypriot Greek, the local variety, which she used with family members and friends. As she was growing up, she became interested in Japanese anime, and because of this she picked up a bit of Japanese. She also learned to draw anime figures, which she often shared with her other friends with the same interest that she had met online. These friends came from all over the world, and when they communicated, they often used a kind of English mixed with Japanese and other things like emojis. Later she went to London for university, where she studied art but also had to learn how to write 'academic English', which was a bit of a challenge. In her second year of study she took some Spanish classes and later went to Spain on an exchange programme for a semester. Now she is living back in Cyprus and her main way of communicating with her friends online is through Instagram. She also has her own YouTube channel which she uses to teach people about make-up, which is also one of her passions. In fact, she's a bit of a 'microcelebrity' on both YouTube and Instagram and knows how to use things like hashtags to attract more attention to herself.

Consider Figure 2.2 and discuss the kinds of *resources* (tools for speaking, writing, and expressing herself visually) that Maya has available to her and in what situations she would use each of these resources.

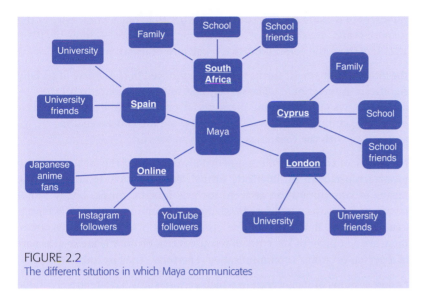

FIGURE 2.2
The different situations in which Maya communicates

2.3 Repertoires

If we think of real language use as a matter of the *resources* that people have available to them and the ways they deploy these resources in different situations, we can consider the collection of resources available to a particular person as that person's **communicative repertoire** (Rymes 2014). The word repertoire comes from the world of entertainment; it is used to refer to the stock of plays, songs, dances, and other things that a performing company or individual performer can perform. The idea of a communicative repertoire is not all that different: it's the stock of resources that a communicator is able to use in order to 'perform' communication. When we think about communicative resources in this way, we start to see how inadequate it is to talk about 'languages' in the conventional sense without also considering the different language varieties, registers/styles, and genres that we use to communicate.

The idea of communicative repertoires comes from work in linguistic ethnography conducted by John Gumperz and Dell Hymes. The whole point of linguistic ethnography is that linguists need to go out into the real world to discover how people *really* talk rather than basing their understanding of language on work done in laboratories or libraries. For Gumperz, most of this fieldwork was conducted in India and Norway, while Hymes worked primarily with Native American tribes. What they found out through this work was that, when people communicate, rather than simply encoding and decoding messages using discrete systems of 'language', they draw upon a rich collection of codes, registers, and genres that circulate within the communities to which they belong. In fact, as Hymes (1974) stressed, the status of 'belonging' to a particular community depends on one's ability to choose from and make use of these different resources in socially appropriate ways, rather than one's knowledge of the grammar and vocabulary of a particular 'language'. Gumperz (1964: 137–8) defined the communicative repertoire of a community as:

the totality of linguistic forms regularly employed in the course of socially significant interaction ... The verbal repertoire then contains all the accepted ways of formulating messages. It provides the weapons of everyday communication. Speakers choose among this arsenal in accordance with the meanings they wish to convey.

Nowadays, of course, sociolinguists usually don't limit the idea of communicative repertoires to 'linguistic forms', but also include non-linguistic means of communication as well, such as images, music, bodily movements, and resources associated with digital communication such as emojis (see Chapter 4). But if we confine ourselves for now to verbal resources, there are a number of key types of resources that ordinarily are seen as part of a person or group's communicative repertoire. They include:

Codes: systems of *signification* in which certain signs have relatively stable meanings. What are often called 'languages' or 'dialects' are types of codes. Communication requires shared codes, but using a shared code in itself does not necessarily enable successful communication.

Registers: ways of communicating associated with particular kinds of communicative activities or particular social identities (such as the ways of speaking we associate with people like scientists, professors, bikers, computer gamers, or even with particular genders or generations in particular places).

Genres: types of communicative activities or texts that are structured in predictable ways (such as stories, arguments, Instagram posts, political slogans, and graffiti tags).

Along with these resources, however, there is also a range of other resources that form part of an individual's or group's communicative repertoire, either as part of or separate from the resources listed above such as idioms (slang expressions), euphemisms, cultural references, forms of address, gestures, facial expressions, and even grammatical forms and ways of pronouncing certain words (see Chapter 3).

When Gumperz and Hymes talked in terms of communicative repertoires, they were mostly thinking of the resources available within *speech communities* (see Introduction). In fact, what they were most interested in was how people draw on community resources to signal membership in these communities. Having access to and being able to use the repertoire of a community in the way a member of that community 'should' was really what Hymes (1966) meant when he talked about *communicative competence* (see Introduction).

Recently, however, there has been more interest in how *individuals* form repertoires as they move across *different* communities and social networks. In other words, repertoires are seen as more a matter of the communicative resources people pick up through their temporary encounters with *multiple communities* as they move along their individual life trajectories, tools that they use not just to communicate but also to manage their social identities and their ever-changing affiliations with different social groups. The resources that are useful to us as teenagers become less important when we become young adults, and the resources that are important in our workplaces are less important when we are interacting with friends and family members. A person's communicative repertoire is always a 'work in progress'.

There are two things, then, that determine the contents of people's communicative repertoires: the degree to which different resources are made *available* to them in the different communities in which they participate, and the degree to which they are able to *master* these resources. We will return to these key issues of *access* and *mastery* below when we talk about language and inequality. For now it is important to stress that all of the resources in a person's communicative repertoire are to some degree *partial*, or, to use Jan Blommaert's (2010) word, *truncated*. Nobody, for example, can have total mastery of a particular code: nobody knows, for instance, all of the words in a 'language' like French or Swahili. So, what we mean when we talk about someone 'learning a language' is really a process of picking up 'pieces' of language that are useful for the kinds of social situations they might find themselves in.

The fact that we have not totally mastered these resources is not really a problem. No matter what degree of mastery we have over a code or a register or a genre, it still counts as part of our repertoire, and we are still able to use it to do things. A taxi driver in Hong Kong, for example, may know all of the names of the different hotels in the city in English, but may not be able to carry on an English conversation about what she had for lunch. Although her mastery of English is partial, it is still functional for the kind of job she needs to do.

Think back at how you interpreted the piece of the Berlin Wall that we talked about at the beginning of this chapter. The repertoire that you drew upon to understand it may have included a well-developed mastery of English, including a knowledge of homophobic slang words. Your mastery of German may be less well developed, and your knowledge of Russian may be limited to the ability just to recognise the Russian words as 'Russian'. Similarly, your knowledge of graffiti tags might have only been enough to allow you to recognise what you were seeing as graffiti tags, but not enough for you to recognise who they were written by or talk about the histories or reputations of the graffiti artists who placed them there. You may have been able to recognise the two kissing men in the picture as Leonid Brezhnev and Erich Honecker, but you may not be familiar with Brezhnev's 1979 visit to East Berlin when that kiss took place.

And so your ultimate understanding of the image was affected by the complex combinations of *unequal* competences that you brought to your reading of the image. Other people might bring different combinations of competencies to the image. A 'streetwise' Berlin graffiti artist looking at the image, for example, might be able to interpret the graffiti tags and tell you about the people who wrote them and the relationships they have with one another. This is not to say that one person's reading is necessarily better than another's. When it comes to interpreting texts, as well as producing them, everybody goes into the game with some set of partial and uneven resources. Sociolinguists Jan Blommaert and Ad Backus (2013) divide resources into those in which we have 'maximal competence', 'partial competence', 'minimal competence', and 'recognising competence'. But whatever our level of competence with a particular resource, they remind us, we are still able to use that competence to some effect when we are producing and interpreting texts and utterances.

Activity: Your Communicative Repertoire

Think of the different kinds of competences you have when it comes to the different resources in your communicative repertoire. In Table 2.1, give examples of different kinds of resources for which you have (1) maximal competence, (2) partial competence, (3) minimal competence, and (4) recognising competence. Discuss how you have used these resources in the past, focusing in particular on how even resources with which you have only minimal or recognising competence have still been useful to you in communication.

Table 2.1 Your communicative repertoire

Resources and competences	Name of resource	When and how you have used this resource
Codes (e.g., 'English', 'German')		
Maximal competence		
Partial competence		
Minimal competence		
Recognising competence		
Registers (e.g., 'the language of skateboarding')		
Maximal competence		
Partial competence		
Minimal competence		
Recognising competence		
Genres (e.g., academic essays, graffiti tags)		
Maximal competence		
Partial competence		
Minimal competence		
Recognising competence		

2.4 Indexicality

What does it mean when we appropriate different codes, registers, and genres, and why do people need so many different kinds of resources in their repertoires in order to participate in social life? To answer these questions, we need to consider the kinds of meanings that we convey with language. One kind of meaning that we convey is what is called **semantic meaning**, that is, the meaning of the words we are using. By using words like 'stoked' or 'enthusiastic', whose meanings are shared by the people who use them, we are able to communicate about a particular feeling we or others are experiencing. Even though both of these words have the same semantic meaning, however, it *does* matter which one we choose to use. By deciding to describe ourselves as 'stoked' rather than 'enthusiastic', we are creating a different kind of meaning, a kind of meaning that is less about the definition of the word and more about the kind of person we want others to think we are. This kind of meaning is called **indexical meaning**.

The idea of indexical meaning comes from the work of the semiotician Charles Peirce (1839–1914), who said that there are three kinds of relationships between a sign (for example a word, a gesture, or an image) and what it means (Peirce 1977). Some signs, which he called **icons**, get their meaning from the fact that they *resemble* what they are referring to. The simple picture of a man on the door of a male toilet communicates to us the gender of the people for whom the toilet is intended because it *looks like* a man.

Another kind of sign, which Peirce called a **symbol**, gets its meaning not from the fact that it resembles what it refers to, but rather because of some kind of *arbitrary* association that has been decided on by people in society and reinforced over a long period of time. The English word *man*, for example, does not look like a man, nor is there anything inherently 'manly' about the way it sounds. It's just a word/sound that has come to be associated with the meaning 'man' in the English language.

The third kind of sign Peirce talked about is called an **index**. Indexes are signs that take their meaning by 'pointing to' something in the external environment. An arrow on a road sign telling motorists to turn left is an index because it depends for its meaning on what it is pointing to. Similarly, when we see smoke, the smoke 'points to' the fact that there must be fire somewhere. But indexes don't just 'point to' things in the physical environment. They also 'point to' things in the social or cultural environment, such as social groups, identities, activities, or collective stories or memories. Wearing a white lab coat, for example, 'points to' the identity of a scientist. Similarly, having a tattoo or piercings, having a particular kind of hairstyle, and saying the word 'stoked' rather than 'enthusiastic' might also point to particular social identities.

The social or cultural meanings of indexes come from the fact that, in a given society, certain kinds of signs come to be associated with certain kinds of people or certain kinds of activities or certain kinds of attitudes or political or ideological stances. The word 'faggot' does not just mean 'gay man' – it points to a particular attitude towards gay men, and also to what we imagine to be the kind of person who might have that attitude. Since these kinds of meanings are dependent on the social context in which they are formed, they are different in different social contexts and can even change depending on the person who is making them. A gay man calling himself 'queer', for example, means something different than a homophobic skinhead calling him 'queer', both *semantically* and *indexically*.

Because language can be used to create both semantic and indexical meaning, we are able to use linguistic resources in ways in which the indexical meaning is more important than what the words we are using actually mean. Figure 2.3, for example, shows a tee-shirt with English writing sold in Japan. Here the semantic meaning of the words 'DISCERN DWARF BRAVERY COME OVER EXHILARATE KITTEN' might be difficult to understand, but in the context in which this tee-shirt might be worn, that doesn't really matter; what matters is that they are 'English' which, as Blommaert (2010) notes, in the local Japanese economy of signs, often indexes modernity or cosmopolitanism.

A similar point can be made about the tee-shirt in Figure 2.4, manufactured by the British clothing company Super Dry and sold in the UK. Here,

FIGURE 2.3
Japanese tee-shirt
(photo credit:
r/monstercake)

FIGURE 2.4
British tee-shirt

the semantic meaning of the Japanese writing (which can be translated as 'for business use') is really immaterial to what the person who wears this tee-shirt is trying to say with their fashion choice. The indexical meaning of this phrase is not as a linguistic phrase but as a little 'piece' of Japanese language that, in the context of the UK, 'points to' a kind of hip, young identity.

Of course, it is possible for someone to wear the shirt in Figure 2.3 in a context where English is widely spoken and people orient more towards the semantic meaning of the odd English sentence, but in this case it would still have an indexical meaning. If worn by a certain kind of person, say a hip young Londoner, it might signal a kind of playful irony, a delight in the 'randomness' of the words. If worn by a tourist or a recent immigrant, it might signal a kind of 'out of placeness' or linguistic 'deficiency'.

The point we are trying to make is that no matter what the words that are printed on our tee-shirts or come out of our mouths 'mean' semantically, they always *also* convey indexical meaning, and that indexical meaning is partly a matter of where we are (the linguistic environment we are inhabiting) and who we are (the kinds of competencies we have with the different resources we are using and whether or not others think we have the 'right' to use those resources). So indexical meanings depend on how the resources we use 'fit' into the linguistic environments in which we are using them. What we mean when we speak of a linguistic environment is not just the different 'languages' and other resources that are used in a particular space, but the kinds of *values* these resources are afforded in this space.

The French sociologist Pierre Bourdieu (1977) saw linguistic environments as 'marketplaces' in which different resources are a bit like currency. Not only are some resources 'worth' more than others, but they can also be used to 'purchase' particular 'social goods'. In many societies, for example, mastery of what is regarded as the 'standard language' can be used to 'purchase' educational and economic opportunities. In communities of rappers, the ability to creatively use language that is very different from the 'standard' variety can confer upon a person a certain social standing (see Chapter 9). The symbolic value of different resources has nothing to do with their *intrinsic* value but results from the kinds of values they have in different 'marketplaces'.

The sociolinguist Jan Blommaert refers to the ways resources are valued in different environments because of their indexical meanings as *orders of indexicality* (Blommaert 2005). When the same resource is used in different environments it does not just *mean* something different, but it is also valued differently because it is being measured against a different order of indexicality. One example Blommaert gives is of a proficient speaker of Nigerian English, a variety with distinct phonological and grammatical features, whose way of speaking might be highly valued on the streets of Nairobi, indexing educational attainment or a high social status, but might be less valued on the streets of London. He says (2010: 127):

As soon as linguistic semiotic products start travelling across the globe, they travel across different orders of indexicality, and what counts as 'good language' in one place can easily become 'bad language' in another; what counts as an expression of deference can become an expression of arrogance elsewhere; what counts as an index of intellectual middle-class identity in one place can become an index of immigrant underclass identity elsewhere.

One of the reasons we have such a variety of resources in our communicative repertoires, then, is that we move through a variety of different linguistic environments throughout our lives and participate in a variety of different social groups, enacting different *identities* along the way. Just as we have repertoires of different resources at our command, we also have repertoires of multiple identities that we enact in different environments, and our ability to 'pull off' these different identities depends on our access to particular resources and on the linguistic environments that we find ourselves in. Even within a single linguistic environment we might deploy different kinds of resources and enact different kinds of identities for strategic reasons, for example to show our attitude towards different people or different situations. We will talk in more detail about how we use communicative resources to perform identities in Chapter 6.

While we have lots of flexibility in terms of how we deploy and mix the different resources in our repertoires when we communicate with others, we do not have complete freedom. Some resources are considered more appropriate or are more highly valued in particular environments, and this is something that we don't have much control over. We are, to some degree, compelled to use resources that 'fit' with the environment we find ourselves in, in order to 'fit in' with the people we are communicating with. We also usually have limited control over the resources that we have access to or mastery of in the first place, since that depends on the kinds of exposure to resources and educational opportunities we have been afforded throughout our lives.

And so communicative resources ultimately have to do with power. Some people have more power than others because their communicative repertoires contain resources that are more highly valued in particular environments. And which resources are valued is also a matter of power, decided on and perpetuated by those who are able to influence things like educational standards and public policies. As Blommaert (2018: 35) puts it, 'repertoires are traces of social norms ... traces of the compelling and often even coercive and consequential evaluative responses of others in our lives: traces of power'. Here we can return to Bakhtin's idea of 'voices' that we talked about above. Not only do we speak in different 'voices' in different situations, but, depending on the situation, some voices are considered more authoritative than others, and so the kinds of voices we have access to ultimately determines whether or not people will listen to us, that is, whether or not we 'have a voice' in deciding what happens around us.

Again, we have to stress that what makes one resource more valued than another in a particular linguistic environment is not the inherent superiority of that resource but is more commonly a matter of that resource being associated with people who already have power. It is also possible for some people to resist the orders of indexicality of a particular environment, to introduce less valued resources in creative ways in order to increase their status or their access to social goods. Indeed, some devalued codes might even accumulate a certain kind of indexical value in social contexts where they are otherwise seen as inappropriate, as when middle-class white kids in the US use African American Vernacular English in order to index a kind of 'cool' identity (see, for example, Cutler (1999)). The point is that any discussion of communicative repertoires has to take into account the *unequal values* that different resources are given in different circumstances, the *unequal access* different people have to different resources, and the *unequal burden* this places on different people when it comes to successfully moving from one social context to another. Most importantly, this inequality when it comes to communicative resources is a factor in other kinds of inequality, especially social and economic inequality.

2.5 Focal Topic: Language and Inequality

In this chapter's focal topic, we will further explore the relationship between language and inequality, especially when it comes to the communicative resources that people have access to and the consequences of not being able to deploy resources that are valued by powerful people and powerful institutions. These issues are highlighted in the two articles we will summarise.

The first article, by Jan Blommaert, explores the difficulties migrants face in asylum interviews in Belgium when they are not able to produce 'stories' in ways that are recognised and valued by the bureaucracy tasked with deciding the legitimacy of their asylum claims. In Chapter 1 we explored the difficulties asylum seekers might face because of people's over-simplistic understandings of 'language' and their ideas about how people from particular places are 'supposed' to speak. In this chapter the focus is more on the *genre* of the accounts asylum seekers are meant to produce in asylum interviews, how they organise these stories, and how their command of other resources (such as French, Dutch, and English) can affect their ability to tell those stories in ways that are considered legitimate.

The second article, by Maria Sabaté-Dalmau, describes the communicative repertoires of three homeless migrants from Ghana in a town called Igualada, located about an hour away from Barcelona. In particular, Sabaté-Dalmau explores the kinds of values her informants and the people around them assign to their Ghanaian English, along with the other codes they have (varying amounts) of competence in, and how they use their English to position themselves in relation to other migrants and to the local population. Even though these migrants have a much higher competence in English than the local residents of the city where they live, because the variety they speak is not as highly valued as so-called 'standard' varieties (from places like the UK or US), they are unable to use their linguistic competence to gain economic or social capital.

Blommaert, J. (2001) Investigating narrative inequality: African asylum stories in Belgium. *Discourse & Society,* 12(4), 413–49   In this article, Blommaert explores the ways African asylum speakers in Belgium tell stories of their lives in the countries that they came from and why they fear going back to those countries, and, in doing so, draw upon repertoires of narrative structures and 'languages' with which they have varying levels of competence.

He begins with a discussion of the work in sociolinguistics on narrative and inequality, especially that of Dell Hymes and Courtney Cazden (1980), in which they examined the stories that people from different backgrounds told in university classrooms and how some kinds of stories were more highly valued than other kinds. What this research shows, says Blommaert, is that '[t]he rights to use particular narrative modes are unevenly distributed, and this pattern of distribution disenfranchise(s) those who have to rely on "disqualified" narrative modes for conducting their business in society' (414).

For his study, Blommaert interviewed more than forty African asylum seekers in Belgium whose cases were pending and analysed the ways they told their stories and how these narratives compared with the kinds of narratives expected by officials in asylum interviews. In Belgium, as in most countries, the asylum procedure depends heavily on investigating applicants' stories about their motives for fleeing their countries and seeking asylum, and a large number of applicants are turned down because their stories are deemed inconsistent or incoherent.

Blommaert begins his analysis of the stories he collected by looking at difficulties that some of the narrators had in producing the 'standard' variety of the language used in the interview (usually Dutch, French, or English). Many of the speakers, for example, exhibited considerable hesitation, self-correction, and mid-sentence changes in topic. Many had difficulties choosing the right words, as well as difficulties with verb tenses and pronoun usage, both of which can be especially important in high-stakes narratives about asylum. Many asylum seekers, Blommaert notes, acquired the European languages in informal circumstances outside of school and so sometimes their speech might be influenced by registers that don't 'fit' well in official proceedings. He also notes that, even when storytellers display competence in the lexis and grammar of a particular code, they may lack 'metapragmatic competence', by which he means the ability to interpret the communicative intentions of the interviewer when it comes to things like indirect speech acts.

In the next part of his analysis, Blommaert focuses on the overall coherence of the stories, that is, how the stories fit together as logical narratives. One problem with stories told in simplified or 'truncated' versions of a particular code, he argues, is that they may not, on the surface, seem coherent, because speakers are less able to use the linguistic devices that are usually associated with the telling of stories, especially in official settings. Nevertheless, he argues, a close analysis of the stories does reveal obvious patterns of coherence – he labels this 'ethnocoherence' because they are patterns of coherence associated with people from different narrative traditions trying to formulate stories in codes they are less familiar with and in a context they are less familiar with. Sometimes the patterns of the stories are influenced by what they think their listeners may or may not understand about the situation in their countries, and this can sometimes distract from the logical flow of the narrative. Sometimes the necessity to give sometimes rather complex contextual accounts of the local circumstances in their home countries can interrupt the sequential flow of the narrative and make it seem muddled or inconsistent.

In the final section of the paper, Blommaert discusses how applicants' stories are evaluated by officials in the course of the asylum procedure. The kind of 'narrative analysis' done by officials, he notes, tends to stress things like linearity, facticity, logic, and rationality. Such a focus, he says, is highly culture-specific, reflecting the ideologies of language use and communicative practices of the officials rather than the applicants. Blommaert also talks about how the asylum seekers' narratives are converted into written forms created by the interviewers, losing many of the important features of the original oral narratives, and then they are combined with a range of other documents (certificates, letters, regulations) in ways that asylum seekers are ultimately 'responsible' for but have very little control over.

Asylum interviews are situations characterised by obviously unequal power relationships. What Blommaert's study demonstrates is that an important aspect of this inequality has to do with the mismatch between the kinds of texts asylum seekers are expected to produce and the *resources* they bring to the situation. These aspects of inequality are often 'invisible' since the communicative practices governing these situations are considered 'normal' and 'natural' and easily accessible to all, not accounting for the fact they may be culture-specific. A fundamental aspect of inequality in this and many other 'official' encounters is 'access to the discursive resources that shape who can talk when, in what ways, and with what effects' (Briggs 1996: 13).

Sabaté-Dalmau, M. (2018) 'I speak small': Unequal Englishes and transnational identities among Ghanaian migrants. *International Journal of Multilingualism*, 15(4), 365–82   One of the biggest challenges for many migrants is that the communicative resources that they bring with them may not be valued in their new homes in the same way they were in the places they came from. The fact is, most migrants have at their disposal communicative repertoires that are sometimes considerably richer than those of the people in their new places of residence, but rather than being rewarded for this, Sabaté-Dalmau says, their 'multilingualisms are silenced and sanctioned' (p. 366), and they are regarded as incompetent 'language-less' people (Blommaert et al. 2005: 203).

For many migrants, the main resource that mediates their communication with others is English, but because the variety of English they speak may not be highly valued in their resident societies, no matter how competently they can communicate, they are unable to turn their linguistic skills into economic opportunities. One might, for example, imagine the different kinds of economic opportunities available in Spain to a monolingual speaker of British English from the UK and a multilingual migrant from Africa who is just as competent in English, but speaks a different, less 'elite' variety. Even when the African migrant struggles to learn Spanish in order to 'integrate', they might be penalised for their 'accent' or poor command of grammar or vocabulary, whereas the British migrant speaking Spanish might be praised for their efforts.

In this article Maria Sabaté-Dalmau provides a window into the lives of a group of economically disadvantaged migrants from Ghana living in the Spanish city of Igualada. The three men she studied, in fact, were homeless during the period of the study, despite their relatively high education levels (one had been an English teacher in Ghana, the other an accountant, and the third a schooled cocoa farmer). They had left Ghana between 2000 and 2001 to escape violence in their home regions and moved to southern Spain to work in agriculture. Later they moved to Igualada to work in the textile industry but lost their jobs when the textile industry collapsed due to an economic recession. Partly because the communicative resources in their repertoires were devalued in the society in which they lived, they found themselves socially and economically marginalised, unable to make a living doing the things they did back in Ghana.

For her study, Sabaté-Dalmau interviewed the three men about their communicative repertoires and also observed the ways they communicated with others in their daily lives. In her analysis she paid particular attention to the way they talked about and used English with different people in different situations, and how these uses of English reinforced relationships of difference and inequality.

Sabaté-Dalmau's three informants had rich multilingual communicative repertoires. They spoke Ashanti, and also had command of other Ghanaian languages. They also had some competence in Arabic, which they sometimes used with Muslim acquaintances. They spoke mostly Spanish and English with the local population and with migrants from other places. They were particularly conscious of their competence in Spanish, which they compared favourably with that of other migrants. In fact, their Spanish competence gave them a degree of prestige within the community of migrants that they were unable to achieve in the wider society.

All three of the informants were highly competent (and literate) in English, having been educated in English back in Ghana. The variety of English they spoke was Ghanaian English (GhE), which has a range of distinct phonological, lexical, and grammatical features. In Ghana, their competence in English was a marker of education and of relatively high social status.

Nevertheless, in their conversations with the researcher, they often made self-denigrating remarks regarding their English proficiency, describing their competence as 'small'. One of the men even insisted to her (in English) that he spoke *no* English. In their conversations with other African migrants, however, they often confidently displayed their English ability, using English as a pan-African *lingua franca* and as an emblem of 'cosmopolitan Ghanaianness', education, and modernity.

Sabaté-Dalmau argues that the way her informants used English and regarded their own use of English in different situations mirrored the different 'orders of indexicality' that they inhabited at different times and in different places. In their dealings with the local population, the variety of English they spoke was devalued (even though their command of English was much better than most of the local Spanish and Catalan speakers). When communicating with other African migrants, on the other hand, their English was highly valued. The situation of these three men, says Sabaté-Dalmau, provides a good example of how 'situated forms of social distinction, difference and inequality among migrants living under precarious life conditions are entrenched in language' (p. 387) and how powerful 'orders of indexicality' are in dictating what kinds of speakers of a particular 'language' (such as English) come to count as 'legitimate' speakers.

Project Ideas

1. Interview someone who has lived in more than one country over the course of their lives and produce a 'case study' of their communicative repertoire and how it has changed over time. Pay special attention not just to the different linguistic resources they have available to them but also how their access to and mastery of these resources has changed at different points in their lives.

2. Conduct 'ethnographic fieldwork' in a community or organisation that you belong to (it might be a club you belong to, a group of friends with the same interest, an online community you participate in, or even your family). Spend some time observing how people interact in the group and noticing all of the different communicative resources (including codes, registers, genres, as well as non-verbal resources) that are used, when people use these resources, and how they learn how to use them. Then interview other members of the group and find out what they think about these resources, what role they play in being a member of the group, and which of them are the most highly valued.

3. Interview the members of a family in which children have grown up bilingual or multilingual. Find out how different 'language policies' at home and at school affect how the children use the different codes that they have access to.

4. Compile a small collection of texts from a particular social context. It might, for example, be a workplace, an online community, or a 'fan community' (for example, people who like to listen to a certain kind of music). Analyse the texts and try to determine the codes, registers, genres, and other communicative resources people need in order to understand these texts. Think about whether people need to be fully competent in all of these resources, and how different combinations of competence might result in different people understanding these texts differently.

Language Variation

PREVIEW

KEY TERMS

community of practice
covert prestige
dialectology
enregisterment
ethnography
language variation
linguistic resistance
linguistic variable
metadiscourse
overt prestige
prestige variants
rapid and anonymous interviews
social networks
social variable
sociolinguistic interviews
variant

In this chapter we will delve deeper into the connection between language and social meaning by exploring the traditional concern of sociolinguists with what is known as language variation. Variation means difference, so people who are interested in language variation are interested in how language use differs among different groups of people and the social meanings those differences might index. We will take a critical look at the different ways scholars have studied language variation, exploring how even small alterations in the way people talk can signal belonging or not belonging to a particular group, and we will also examine the social processes through which certain ways of speaking come to be associated with certain kinds of people. In the focal topic section we will look more closely at the issue of 'belonging'.

3.1 Introduction

In the last two chapters we talked about how traditional views of language are dominated by certain ideologies about what languages are and how they should be used. In the real world, rather than speaking particular languages (like French, German, and Chinese), people draw upon a range of different linguistic resources to *do* different things in different kinds of social situations. We also talked about how certain ways of speaking or writing are often associated with particular places, particular activities, particular kinds of people, or even particular attitudes or political stances.

In this chapter we will explore in more detail certain kinds of resources that people use on a daily basis. In particular, we will focus on small things like whether people pronounce their r's or their g's or whether they say 'I'm not' or 'I ain't'. Choosing, for example, to say 'I can't find my keys nowhere' vs. 'I can't find my keys anywhere' can reveal something about a person's identity and their social affiliation. The difference between two, or three, or four or even more ways of saying something is called **language variation**.

The study of sociolinguistic variation has its roots in traditional studies of 'dialects', also known as **dialectology**, that were popular in the nineteenth and early twentieth centuries. So, a lot of the work in language variation studies has as its starting point the kinds of ideas about language that we started to question Chapter 1: ideas about languages being stable, identifiable things, and the idea that some (more 'standard') ways of using language can be distinguished from less 'standard' varieties (often called 'dialects'). More recent work on language variation, however, has focused less on measuring different ways of speaking against a 'standard language' and more on the idea of how *difference* itself comes to index social meanings and social identities. In this chapter we will look at how and why ideas of language variation have changed over the years.

In the field of language variation studies, the main focus of investigation has traditionally been the **linguistic variable**. A variable is basically some linguistic element such as a word or a sound that can be produced in different ways. We already know from the last two chapters that different people talk differently, even when they are speaking the same 'language'. The concept of the variable is useful because it helps us to isolate *specific* ways that people talk differently. For example, we might focus on a specific difference in pronunciation such as the phoneme $/\theta/$ in the word 'thing', which some people in London pronounce *thing*, and others pronounce *fing*. Or we might focus on a grammatical difference such as whether or not people say 'I didn't talk to anybody' or 'I didn't talk to nobody'. Or we might focus on the different words people use to talk about the same things, such as 'sofa', 'couch', 'chesterfield', 'davenport', or 'divan'.

One particular way of producing a variable is called a **variant**. Whether or not people use one variant or another can be a signal of where they are from, or how old they are, or what kind of group they belong to. So different variants are part of the *repertoires* which they draw on to

FIGURE 3.1
Language variation in Geordie – Viz comic (photo credit: Fulchester Industries/Dennis Publishing)

communicate in different situations and often to signal something about their social identities.

Figure 3.1 is a cartoon from *Viz* that shows people using variants of English vocabulary, pronunciation, and grammar that may be different from those that you have in your linguistic repertoire. For example, they say 'lads' rather than 'boys', 'fellows', or 'guys', they pronounce 'you' as 'yuz', 'no' as 'nae', and 'right' as 'reet', and they use the word 'neither' where others might use the word 'either'.

For people in England, these kinds of words and ways of pronouncing them might signal a way of speaking associated with people living in the city of Newcastle upon Tyne, informally known as 'Geordies'. But they might also signal a kind of working-class, masculine identity. This fits in with the story that the cartoonist is trying to tell; the conversation is between a character named Sid the Sexist and his friend Baz, who has seen the film *The Full Monty* (1997) and is trying to convince his friends to perform with him as male strippers at bachelorette parties in Shiremoor Men's Club, located in a traditional working-class community in North Tyneside, formerly a coal-mining village.

In the next section we will review some classic studies from the early days of variationist sociolinguistics, which tended to focus on factors like 'class' and 'gender'. Then we will talk about some of the problems associated with using these labels to divide up people and talk about the varieties they use and learn about how later sociolinguists have tried to overcome these problems.

3.2 Variation and Social Groups

In any society, people belong to different groups, but the way they are divided into groups and the importance given to different kinds of group membership might be different in different societies. For example, people can be seen to belong to different social classes, like working or middle class. Societies also distinguish between men and women, gay people and straight people, younger people and older people, people living in rural or urban areas, people who come from different ethnic backgrounds, and people who belong to groups associated with professions, pastimes, or political orientations (such as 'biologists', 'bikers', or 'Brexiters').

For people who study linguistic variation, the different groups that people are associated with is also a kind of *variable* – something that varies from person to person. We might call this a **social variable**. The main thing variationist sociolinguists are trying to understand is the relationship between social variables and linguistic variables. Often this relationship is not as simple as it first seems, partly because people always belong to multiple groups at one time. It might be difficult to figure out what social variable is most important when it comes to the way they are speaking.

Finding a way of studying how and why different people produce different variables differently has been a major focus of sociolinguistics since the 1960s. One of the first people to study linguistic variables was William Labov (1963). When he first started studying language in the 1960s, he became interested in the ways different people talked on a small fishing island off the coast of Massachusetts in the US called Martha's Vineyard. During the summer, this small island had a lot of tourists from the mainland US, who often exceeded the number of local residents. The islanders themselves were struggling financially and depended on these tourists for their incomes. Many of the younger residents, in fact, left the island for a better life on the mainland. Labov focused his investigation on a few variables, one being the different way people pronounced words like 'light', 'ice', and 'nice'. The way people on the mainland usually pronounced these words was with the sound [aɪ], but Labov noticed that some people on the island pronounced it differently. While some of them used [aɪ], others used [əɪ], pronouncing the word 'light' in a way that sounded more like 'late'. Even more interesting was that some people *changed* their pronunciation depending on whom they were talking to, sometimes saying 'light' and sometimes saying 'late'.

As it turns out, the 'late' pronunciation was one that had existed on the island for a long time, probably since the seventeenth century. But over the years, more and more people on the island started to use the mainland [aɪ] pronunciation. Labov studied the way the different pronunciations were distributed across different kinds of groups on the island. He found that in recent years, the traditional [əɪ] pronunciation was making a comeback, especially among middle-aged people, mostly fishermen, and others who had decided to stay on the island rather than move to the mainland for economic opportunities. Labov theorised that the variant [əɪ] had a kind of social meaning for the people who used it, indexing authenticity, solidarity, and loyalty to the rural values associated with traditional life on the island. So, using the pronunciation might be seen as a form of **linguistic resistance** by the locals towards the tourists who were seen to be disturbing the social equilibrium of the island.

Labov's study in Martha's Vineyard showed not just that people who belong to different groups in a society may speak differently from people in other groups, even when they are using the same 'language', but also that they use these differences to construct their social identities, signalling that they belong (or *don't* belong) to these groups. Labov's study of Martha's Vineyard was one of the first that looked at the distribution of different variables in a specific community. Since then, other scholars have explored different groups around the world using some of the techniques developed by Labov.

After investigating language variation in Martha's Vineyard, Labov set out to explore language variation in a very different kind of context: the borough of Manhattan in New York City. One of the things he was interested in was the different ways people pronounced the variable /r/. When /r/ appears after a vowel in words like 'floor', 'door', 'car', and 'guard', some speakers pronounce the [r], and others make no [r] sound. We can call these different variants an 'r-full' pronunciation and an 'r-less' pronunciation. In the UK, the r-less pronunciation is a feature of the so-called 'standard' variety (though lots of people in different parts of the UK do produce [r] after vowels), whereas in the US, an r-full pronunciation is considered more 'standard' (though there are plenty of people in the US who do not pronounce [r] after vowels). The important thing is that the *social meaning* of how /r/ is pronounced – the kind of social identities it *indexes* – is different in different places and within different social groups.

One thing that Labov was interested in was whether or not the way people in Manhattan pronounced the /r/ variable was associated with their social class. Of course, deciding what social class people belong to is a complicated issue – and something we will discuss further later in this chapter. The way Labov solved this problem was to visit three different department stores in New York, each of a different status, which he determined by the neighbourhoods the stores were located in, the newspapers they were advertised in, and the average price of different items sold in the stores. The three stores were Saks Fifth Avenue – the highest-ranking, Macy's – the middle-ranking, and Klein's – the lowest-ranking.

Pretending to be a customer, Labov went to each of the stores and asked the same question to the salespeople there, assuming that the speech of the salespeople would reflect the social status of the clientele that the stores served. In order to elicit speech that included the /r/ variable, he asked them where to find an item he knew was located on the *fourth floor*. He then pretended that he had not heard what they had said and asked the question again, prompting the salespeople to repeat their answers more 'clearly'. As a result, Labov was able to elicit four instances of the variable /r/ from each informant; two from the first, 'casual', answer and two from the second, more 'emphatic', response:

Casual response: fou<u>r</u>th (R1)   floo<u>r</u> (R2)
Emphatic response: *fou<u>r</u>th* (R3)   *floo<u>r</u>* (R4)

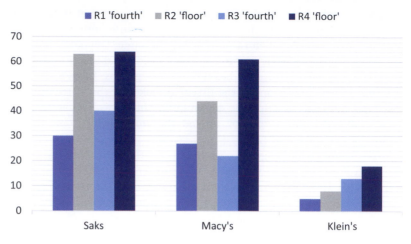

FIGURE 3.2
Percentage of r-full
pronunciation by
department store in
Labov's study
(adapted from Labov
1972)

This method of collecting data is known as a **rapid and anonymous interview** and its advantage in this case was that within just six and a half hours Labov was able to collect responses from 264 salespeople. Figure 3.2 shows the percentage of times the informants produced the [ɹ] (r-full) variant in each of the conditions.

Looking at the graph, you will notice a couple of patterns. First, and most importantly, the amount that informants pronounced [ɹ] increased based on the status of the department store. In other words, salespeople at Macy's pronounced [ɹ] more often in every condition than those at Klein's, and the salespeople at Saks, the store with the highest status, pronounced [ɹ] the most. Second, the salespeople in all of the stores usually pronounced [ɹ] more often the second time they said 'fourth floor', when they were trying to speak more clearly. Finally, Labov found that, at least in Macy's and Saks, people were much more likely to pronounce [ɹ] when it occurred at the end of the word ('floor') than when in occurred in the middle of the word ('fourth').

From this, Labov concluded that whether or not people pronounced [ɹ] was associated with social class, and that pronouncing [ɹ] more often after vowels was considered 'prestigious'. He also noted that the salespeople, no matter what store they worked in, were more likely to pronounce [ɹ] when they were paying more attention to their speech, suggesting that they believed that pronouncing [ɹ] after vowels made their speech clearer or more 'correct'.

One of the most interesting things that Labov's results showed was that the difference between the pronunciation in the middle-class department store was a lot closer to that of the upper-class store than it was to that of the lower-class one. In fact, the salespeople in Macy's used [ɹ] in the careful pronunciation of 'floor' almost as much as the salespeople in Saks. This is actually a consistent finding in studies of what might be called **prestige variants**, that middle-class people tend to aim towards producing them when they are paying attention to the way they speak, suggesting that they put a lot of stock in the prestige associated with them.

Activity: Replicating Labov's Study

Forty-six years after Labov's research, Mather (2012) carried out a replication of the study using the same method to collect the data. The only difference was that Mather had to replace Klein's department store because it closed down in the 1970s. Two other department stores were selected, Filene's Basement and Loehmann's, because like Klein's, they catered mainly to a working-class clientele. Because fewer salespeople were employed in these department stores compared to Macy's and Saks, both Filene's Basement and Loehmann's were surveyed to obtain a representative sample. The main findings from this study are presented in Figure 3.3. Look at the graph and answer the following questions:

1. What are the similarities between Mather's findings and Labov's?
2. What are the differences?
3. What can the studies tell us about how the social prestige of [r] changed between the times the two studies were done?
4. Why do you think people's pronunciation of [r] when it occurred in the middle of the word ('fourth') changed so much?
5. What do you think about the data collection method used by Labov and Mather? Is there anything about it you could criticise? What?
6. Do you pronounce your r's after vowels? Do you think there is a difference depending on where the /r/ appears in the word or whether or not you are speaking carefully? What about other people that you know (e.g., friends, neighbours, relatives, co-workers, teachers, and classmates)? What factors do you think may be associated with the use of [r] after vowels among the people that you know?

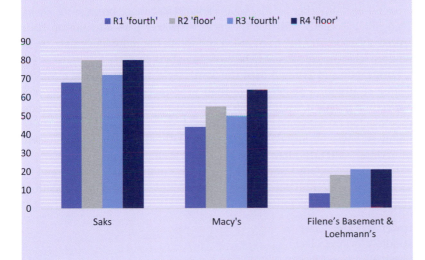

FIGURE 3.3
Percentage of r-full pronunciation by department store in Mather's study (adapted from Mather 2012)

In the 1970s the British sociolinguist Peter Trudgill was also keen to find out more about how language use differs among people who belong to different social groups. He focused his work in Norwich, his home city in the UK, and set out to explore twenty different phonological variables. One of these variables was the verb ending -ing, as in the words 'going', 'walking', and 'eating'. This variable is sometimes pronounced with the -ing sound [ŋ] (as in 'walking') and sometimes with an -in sound [n] (as in 'walkin'). The [n] variant, sometimes referred to as 'dropping your g's', can be found in lots of different varieties of English all around the world. Trudgill wanted to explore if the way people in the city he lived in pronounced -ing at the end of words was associated with their social class. He was also interested in finding out if it was associated with their gender.

In order to do this, he conducted **sociolinguistic interviews** with people. A sociolinguistic interview is an interview in which the investigator tries to get people to produce the variable or variables under investigation by engaging them in several different tasks, from reading aloud to engaging in casual conversation. Trudgill asked 122 informants from Norwich to do four tasks:

1. Have a casual conversation with the interviewer about life experiences;
2. Have a formal question–answer interview;
3. Read aloud a short passage;
4. Read a list of words.

The reason Trudgill chose these different tasks was that, like Labov, he wanted to alter the degree to which people were being 'careful' about the way they pronounced words. The idea was that when people were just chatting, without paying much attention to their words, they would reveal how they normally pronounced the variable. But, when they were doing things like reading word lists, where people are more likely to pay attention to their pronunciation, they would reveal something about how they thought certain sounds *should* be pronounced – in other words, what variants had more prestige for them. Trudgill's hypothesis was that the more a speaker pays attention to their speech style (i.e., moving from task 1 to task 4), the more likely they are to produce what are considered to be more 'standard' forms.

Both Labov and Trudgill used the word 'style' to describe the different degree of attention people pay to their pronunciation, labelling the pronunciation people use while reading 'formal style' and the pronunciation they use for casual conversation 'informal' or 'casual style'. Later sociolinguists, however, argued that style is actually much more complicated, something we'll talk more about later in this chapter and in Chapter 6.

Trudgill divided his informants by gender – males and females – and by social class, which he determined based on their occupation, education, and family income as follows:

Lower Working Class
Middle Working Class
Upper Working Class
Lower Middle Class
Middle Middle Class

Table 3.1 Percentage of [n] variant in Norwich by social class, gender, and style in Trudgill's study (adapted from Trudgill 1974)

Social class	Gender	Style			
		Word list	Reading passage	Formal speech	Casual speech
Lower Working Class	Male	66	100	100	100
	Female	17	54	97	100
Middle Working Class	Male	24	43	91	97
	Female	20	46	81	88
Upper Working Class	Male	0	18	81	95
	Female	11	13	68	77
Lower Middle Class	Male	0	20	27	17
	Female	0	0	3	67
Middle Middle Class	Male	0	0	4	31
	Female	0	0	0	0

Table 3.1 summarises Trudgill's findings. One thing that is clear from the table is that the more careful people were being about their pronunciation, the more they produced the [ŋ] variant, indicating that this is the pronunciation that they thought was more 'proper'. The table also shows that the men in Trudgill's study and those who belonged to the working classes were more likely to produce the [n] variant, and that women and people who belonged to the middle classes were more likely to produce the [ŋ] variant.

Trudgill theorised that one reason for this might be that, by producing the less 'prestigious', less 'proper', pronunciation, the men were indexing their affiliation with working-class culture, which is also often associated with masculinity. This is something that we saw in section 3.2., where the men in *Viz*'s cartoon used variants typical of Geordie speech to signal their working-class, masculine identities. In other words, although this variant might be considered less 'standard' by most people, for these working-class men, using it brought a different kind of prestige, making them sound more 'local', more 'manly', and more 'like their mates'. This kind of prestige is known as **covert prestige**.

While [n] in Trudgill's study was more popular with working-class men, the [ŋ] variant was more popular with women and with middle-class speakers. It is not surprising that, as in Labov's study, people of higher classes used the variant associated with more **overt prestige** – the prestige that is linked with variants which are thought to be more 'correct' (mostly because they are the ones that are normally used by more powerful people). The interesting question is why the women in the study seemed to prefer the 'prestige' variant. Some later studies have also found that women often prefer more 'standard' ways of speaking, but other studies have found that women are sometimes on the forefront of introducing *less* 'standard' ways of talking into a community. We will talk more about the complex relationship between gender and linguistic variation below.

The work of scholars like Labov and Trudgill was revolutionary, because it gave us a way to systematically study the different ways that people talk and to start to understand how even small differences, such as the way people pronounce /r/, can have important social meanings. They also helped to sensitise us to the relationship between social factors such as class and gender and linguistic variation. At the same time, there are limitations to this approach.

The first limitation is the privileging of categories like class and gender by researchers. Class and gender are no doubt important, but there are lots of other aspects of identity and group membership that might also be important that studies like those described above overlook. Furthermore, since this ground-breaking work was done in the late twentieth century, people have become more sensitive to how complicated things like gender and class can be: it's sometimes not so simple to divide people into binary gender categories or clearly delimited classes. The biggest problem, though, is the fact that these categories and the labels attached to them are imposed onto the participants by researchers based on the things they assume are important. Anthropologists call this kind of perspective an *etic* (or 'outsider's') perspective. Many sociolinguists nowadays promote a more *emic* (or 'insider's') perspective that tries to take into account the kinds of social categories and labels that are most relevant to the speakers themselves.

3.3 Social Networks

One way to avoid some of the problems described above is to focus less on social *categories* such as class and gender and more on social *relationships*. This is the approach taken by variationist sociolinguists like James and Lesley Milroy who, in the 1980s, started examining how people's **social networks** affect the way they talk. The main difference between this approach and the work that we have looked at so far is that research focusing on social networks does not aim to compare speakers based on the groups they belong to – groups that inevitably had been decided on by the sociolinguist prior to the research – but rather takes into consideration the webs of social relationships people are part of and the ways differing amounts of contact with different people in these webs affect the kinds of values they assign to different ways of speaking.

What do we mean by a 'social network'? In Chapter 2 we looked at the case of Maya, a young woman who was born in South Africa, moved to Cyprus as a child and then went on to study at university in the UK and Spain. As Maya moved from one location to another in her life trajectory, she established different kinds of connections, including close, long-standing connections with family members, connections of varying kinds with friends, connections with people who engaged with her in common activities, such as university classmates, connections with people with whom she had similar interests, such as fans of Japanese anime, and (often very loose) connections with people who were part of her online social networks, such as her Instagram and YouTube followers.

The first person Maya met when she arrived in the UK as a student was her flatmate Jodie, a girl from Scotland, who, similar to Maya, had come to London to study art. The two girls lived together, went shopping, joined a gym, and took the same art classes at university. Eventually they became very close friends. Maya and Jodie also worked part-time in a coffee shop owned by a Londoner couple, Anne and Adam. The coffee shop was located in Shoreditch, a famous area known as 'hipster paradise'. On Fridays after work, Maya, Anne, and Jodie often went shopping and then for a drink in Shoreditch's most famous street, Brick Lane. Maya was also learning Spanish at university and through these classes she established a friendship with Ricardo and his friends Juan and Ernesto from Venezuela. With them she shared interests in Latin music and dance. As we can see, during her university years, Maya established various kinds of relations and ties with different people. A partial representation of Maya's social network is illustrated in Figure 3.4.

As Maya was getting to know her new friends more and more, she started to adopt some of their speech features. This is quite natural. As we said in Chapter 2, as people move through their lives, they often acquire new resources, especially when they perceive that these resources have valuable social functions. From Jodie, Maya adopted the r-full

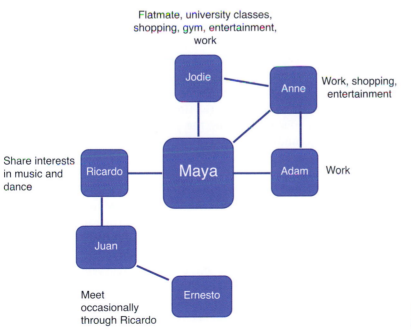

FIGURE 3.4
Maya's social network

pronunciation, a typical feature of Scottish speech. Maya also started to use some Spanish slang words that she learned from Ricardo. For instance, she would say 'He is chévere' meaning 'He is cool', 'She is my pana' meaning 'She is my good friend', 'This is so chimbo' for 'This is really bad' and 'That's fino' for 'That's cool.' She also learned some words from her Londoner friends, like 'This new place downtown is very sick' meaning 'This place downtown is very cool.'

Activity: Create Your Own Social Network

Write down the names of the people you interact with in a week. Now draw lines to create your own social network diagram. Indicate the kinds of relationships you have with each person. Think about how these different relations and ties you have with these different people might influence your linguistic practices.

1. How has your way of speaking been influenced by the different people in your network?
2. What sort of factors (e.g., how much you like someone or how much time you spend with them) determine how much influence someone has over how you talk?
3. Can you think of some specific features in your talk that you have picked up recently? Who did you get these features from? Why did you adopt them?
4. How does your media use affect the way you talk? In what ways are online social networks different from your physical social networks?

As we said above, **social network theory** was introduced into socio-linguistics in the 1980s by James and Lesley Milroy. Lesley Milroy (1987) was particularly interested in the way people talked in three working-class communities in Belfast, Northern Ireland, called the Clonard, the Hammer and Ballymacarrett. At the time of her study, social networks in Belfast were affected a lot by the political situation; people from Catholic backgrounds and Protestant backgrounds tended to have limited social contact with each other, but they did interact outside of their neighbourhoods at work and places of business. Each of these different neighbourhoods had different patterns of social and work-place connections. In Ballymacarrett, a long-established Protestant neighbourhood, most of the men worked in the local shipyard and rarely had contact with people outside of the neighbourhood, whereas the women were more likely to work outside the area. The Hammer was also a Protestant neighbourhood, but because of redevelopment, lots of people from this area had moved elsewhere, and so the social ties in this neighbourhood were less dense and varied than those in Ballymacarrett. The Clonard was a Catholic neighbourhood and a much poorer one. Many of the men were unemployed or forced to look for work outside the community in different places. The women also had to go out to work, but in their case, they tended to find work together.

In order to understand the kinds of social relationships people had in these communities and how they affected the way they talked, Milroy conducted an **ethnographic study**. Sociolinguists who conduct ethnographic studies spend a lot of time in the communities they investigate, not just conducting interviews like Labov and Trudgill, but also interacting with people on a more informal basis and getting to know something about their everyday lives.

Among the features of Belfast speech that Milroy was interested in were the variable /a/ in words like 'hat', 'grass', and 'man', and the deletion of /ð/ in words like 'mother' and 'together'. Some of her findings were similar to those of Trudgill and Labov, in that she found that the men in all three neighbourhoods tended to use variants that were generally considered less prestigious. But the difference between the speech of men and women was not the same in all of the neighbourhoods. In Ballymacarrett, for example, where most of the men worked together in the local shipyard and spent their spare time with their co-workers, who also happened to be their neighbours, the use of particular non-prestige, 'local' variants was more pronounced and consistent. The women in this neighbourhood, many of whom worked outside the area, used these variants less frequently. Milroy theorised that it was not masculinity that made the men talk the way they did, but their close-knit social network, which worked as a norm-enforcing mechanism. The men's close-knit network led them to use local variants as a symbol of solidarity and membership in the local community. This is something that we also saw in Labov's study of Martha's Vineyard, when the locals of a particular age and social class used variants which were associated with the local, traditional way of life on the island.

Interestingly, the situation in the Clonard was the reverse. It was the women who used the variants associated with the neighbourhood more than the men. Milroy also attributed this to the density of their social networks. Since the men in the neighbourhood were either unemployed or worked in different places, they were not able to maintain the kind of dense social networks the women, who worked outside the neighbourhood but tended to work together, were able to maintain.

Milroy's study highlights the importance of looking locally at specific communities and groups of people, instead of interpreting the social significance of variation on the basis of predetermined social categories like class and gender. Through **ethnography** Milroy was able to understand the complex relationship between the social dynamics in the three neighbourhoods and the use of different linguistic variables, and to dramatically demonstrate that linguistic differences that correlate with gender differences may have less to do with gender and more to do with other social factors.

3.4 Communities of Practice and Social Identity

In the introduction to this book we talked a bit about some of the difficulties associated with dividing people up into social groups when trying to study language and society. We talked, for example, about Gumperz and Hymes's notion of speech communities – communities of people who share the same communicative resources and ways of using them. But in Chapter 2 we argued that, over their lifetimes, people come to acquire lots of different kinds of resources as they move from community to community, and that what holds communities together is not just their shared sets of resources but also how useful these resources are in helping people to do things together. Doctors learn to talk like doctors partly because it helps them to do things with other doctors more efficiently, and the same can be said of skateboarders and sociolinguists. In such communities, ways of talking have both a practical value and an indexical meaning. Being able to talk like a skateboarder does not just make it easier for someone to 'do' skateboarding, but it also helps them to be accepted as a 'real' skater by other skaters.

This idea of communicative resources being connected with the common social practices people engage in is at the heart of the 'communities of practice' approach to language variation. The approach was pioneered by the sociolinguists Penny Eckert and Sally McConnell-Ginet (2003) in their work on language and gender. Like Milroy, Eckert and McConnell-Ginet questioned the use of gender as a stable social category in sociolinguistic studies, pointing out that people of the same gender in different communities might have very different linguistic practices, and that differences between men's talk and women's talk might have less to do with the fact that they are men and women and more to do with the different groups they belong to and the things they are using their linguistic resources to *do*.

This approach can be seen in Eckert's (1989) famous ethnographic study of students in a high school in suburban Detroit, which she called Belten High School. After spending a lot of time at the school, Eckert came to realise that the differences in the ways different students talked didn't have to do just with their membership in the social categories traditionally focused on in sociolinguistics, such as gender and social class, but also with categories that were unique to this particular environment. In other words, the students in the school had their *own* social categories, and these categories were associated not just with different ways of talking, but also with different ways of dressing, different musical tastes, and even different areas in the school where the students hung out.

Some kids in the school called themselves *Burnouts* while others called themselves *Jocks*. As Eckert got to know these two groups more and more, she noticed various differences between them. The Jocks engaged heavily in school activities, had dense friendship groups within the school, and were mostly university-bound. The Burnouts, on the other hand, rejected school and many of them had formed friendships with people in the urban area of Detroit by hanging around in parks and cruising strips. After finishing school, they were planning to get blue-collar jobs instead of going to university. According to Eckert, these two polarised social groups in Belten High constituted two distinct communities of practice.

As we said in the introductory chapter, a **community of practice** is a group of people who come together because they share a common cause, interest, or mission. People usually belong to different communities of practice at the same time, for example, in school, at home, in the workplace, at the gym, and so on. The idea of the community of practice enables us to observe how people make use of the different communicative resources in their repertoires strategically, to index membership in different communities at different times. It reminds us that identity is not something static, but something that can change from one context to another and through different stages in life.

In her study, Eckert observed that the Jocks and the Burnouts used certain linguistic variables differently. For example, the Burnouts used more 'negative concord' e.g., 'I didn't do nothing' than Jocks. Eckert theorised that negative concord had acquired some kind of social meaning in Belten High. By using negative concord, the Burnouts were constructing a style that was linked to rebelliousness, toughness, and an antiinstitutional and street-smart stance. But the Jocks, and especially the Jock girls, wanted to maintain a sophisticated, affluent, and squeaky-clean image, so they avoided linguistic variables that were associated with rebelliousness.

She also noticed that Burnouts were more likely to adopt pronunciations associated with urban Detroit, for example, pronouncing 'bus' like 'boss' and 'light' like 'loit'. Interestingly, she found that it was not just that Burnouts were more likely than Jocks to adopt these new 'hip' urban pronunciations, but it was the Burnout girls that were the most likely to adopt them. This finding stands in contrast to the findings by Trudgill (see above) and others that women are more likely to favour prestige variants. In fact, many other studies as well have shown instances where women (especially teenaged women) are at the vanguard of introducing new ways of talking into their communities (see, for example, Gal 1978; Otheguy & Zentella 2012)

Perhaps the most important lesson we can take from Eckert's study of Belten High is that when examining the relationship between linguistic variables and social variables, researchers need to take a more *emic* approach, focusing on the identities and group boundaries that are important *to the speakers themselves* rather than those that are important to the researcher.

A number of other scholars have also tried to gain 'insider' perspectives on the way people talk using ethnographic methods. Drummond (2018a, b), for example, studied the speech of adolescents at Pupil Referral Units in Manchester, UK, places where students are sent because their behaviour in mainstream schools is thought to be too disruptive. Drummond collected his data by observing and participating in activities in and out of class, recording spontaneous interactions and interviewing the students.

He reports that collecting data from this context was initially challenging as the young people viewed him with suspicion and some even refused to speak to him. But gradually he was able to gain the young people's trust.

A big part of this approach is respecting the lived experiences and native expertise of the people being studied, and some researchers have even handed over the data gathering process to participants themselves, making them, in effect, co-researchers. One example is Deborah Cameron's (1992) study in an Afro-Caribbean youth club in London in which she explored issues of racism, language variation, and ethnic identity by getting the young people to produce a video about their own thoughts and experiences about the way they used language and how others reacted to it. They aimed to share this video with wider audiences, like other youth clubs, who could use it as a tool to encourage discussion among young people on the importance of Afro-Caribbean linguistic heritage. Cameron called this approach 'empowering research' (see Appendix). Empowerment was also part of Drummond's (2018b) study. Based on his ethnographic study in the Pupil Referral Unit, he got participants to create scripted comic art scenarios of interactions that could be used by young people to talk through their experiences and also as resources for training teachers in how to serve such students better.

3.5 Enregisterment and Social Meaning

In Chapter 2 we talked about how using certain kinds of communicative resources in certain ways can come to *index* certain social identities, and in this chapter we have explored in great detail how even subtle differences in grammar or pronunciation can serve to 'mark' people as being from a particular region or belonging to a particular social group. But how does this come to be the case? How do certain ways of speaking acquire social meaning? For instance, how did the use of negative concord come to be associated with Burnouts at Belten High? How did r-less pronunciation come to be associated with working-class people in Manhattan? And why is the *-ing* pronunciation in Norwich gendered?

The sociolinguist Asif Agha (2003, 2007) argues that linguistic variables, styles, signs, or other communicative resources become linked with social identities, social groups, specific places, or specific activities through a process he calls **enregisterment**. Enregisterment comes about when people become aware of variations in the way different kinds of people communicate and that awareness gets mixed up with the values, prejudices, and preconceptions they have about these people. These associations between 'what these people are like' and 'how these people talk' become solidified over time through things like media representations and educational practices.

One example of enregisterment is the case of Pittsburghese which was studied by the sociolinguist Barbara Johnstone and her colleagues (2006, 2009, 2011, 2013, 2016). According to Johnstone, the speech of people in Pittsburgh, Pennsylvania, particularly working-class people who have lived there for a long time, has a number of distinct features. For example, they pronounce 'downtown' as *dahntahn* and 'wash' as *worsh*, and 'house' as *has*, refer to rubber bands as *gumbans*, use the word *yinz* as the plural form of 'you', and sometimes leave the auxiliary 'to be' off passive-voice constructions, i.e., 'it needs washed' rather than 'it needs to be washed'. But it wasn't until fairly recently that people thought of this way of speaking as 'Pittsburghese'.

Johnstone explains that in the past people in Pittsburgh who used these features lived in a close-knit community and were not geographically mobile. Therefore, they didn't perceive these features as being unique because everybody in their community spoke in the same way. As younger people in Pittsburgh started to be more mobile, however, they began to come into contact with people outside their community. Once they noticed the difference between the way they talked and the way others talked, these young people started to adopt ways of talking not associated with Pittsburgh. But they didn't totally abandon the features they had grown up with. Rather, they were able to select features strategically, to, for example, say [haʊs] for 'house' when they wanted to sound educated and cosmopolitan and [has] when they wanted to index their affiliation with the working-class culture of the neighbourhoods they grew up in. This is an example of how certain linguistic variants start to accumulate social meanings as people begin to notice them, to make distinctions between the people who use them and the people who don't, and then to attach their use with particular social identities or social practices.

These linkages between certain linguistic features and certain kinds of people are often reinforced through media artefacts such as films, television shows, and books. For example, Johnstone gives an example of a novelty book called *Sam McCool's New Pittsburghese: How to Speak Like a Pittsburgher* (McCool 1982; Figure 3.5), which is illustrated with sketches

FIGURE 3.5
Sam McCool's *How to Speak Like a Pittsburgher* (McCool 1982)

of working-class men doing things like "napping on the *cahch* ('couch')". The text and images in the book create an association between the local variety and specific kinds of people (mostly working-class people) doing specific kinds of activities.

A similar example of how media artefacts can reinforce enregisterment is the cartoon from *Viz* that we talked about in section 3.1. Beal (2000, 2009) studied this cartoon along with various other texts from the nineteenth century onwards to trace the enregisterment of urban varieties in two cities in the north of England: Newcastle upon Tyne and Sheffield. By studying these texts, Beal was able to determine how certain combinations of linguistic features used by people in these cities came to be recognised as 'Geordie' and 'Sheffield dialect' respectively.

Other kinds of artefacts as well can contribute to enregisterment. For instance, in Pittsburgh souvenir shops you can buy mugs, stickers, and tee-shirts with representations of 'Pittsburghese'. Figure 3.6, for example, shows a photo of a coffee mug with the word PITTSBURGHESE surrounded by various representations of local speech (*keller, jynt igle, the Mon, red up*). Through such artefacts, 'varieties' like 'Pittsburghese' become visible in the public arena and gain a certain social status. In this case, 'Pittsburghese' becomes associated not just with the city of Pittsburgh, but with ideas about authenticity and pride of place.

A lot of the early work in variationist sociolinguistics focused on identifying and describing different 'varieties' (such as 'Geordie' and 'Pittsburghese'). The idea of enregisterment reminds us that, like 'languages', none of these 'varieties' actually exist naturally. They are the result of processes of *imagining*, in which people start to notice features in the way particular people talk, assign values to these features and the people who use them, and then *talk about* these features. We use the word **metadiscourse** to refer to people *talking about the way people talk.*

FIGURE 3.6
Pittsburghese
(Johnstone 2016: 635)

Metadiscourse can be found in all aspects of our lives, from casual conversation to the exhortations of teachers to funny sayings printed on coffee mugs. Consider, for instance, the following examples:

1. In a story about her first visit to Pittsburgh, a woman described watching an interview with a working-class Pittsburgher on TV, claiming that she *'couldn't understand a word the man was saying'*.
2. On an online discussion forum about Pittsburghese, one participant wrote the following: *'If it's such an embarrassment to talk this way . . . if we sound stupid . . . how come I am a univ. prof and I still say gum bands [rubber bands], pop [soda], and drop the 'g' off any word ending in 'ing'?'*

(Johnstone 2016)

In these examples we can see that the two people make different kinds of associations with Pittsburghese. The first one reproduces standard language ideologies while the second one makes an attempt to challenge associations of Pittsburghese with lower education and the working class. These examples show some very important things: first of all, that enregisterment is always about people assigning *value* to different ways of speaking; second, that different kinds of values can be assigned to enregistered forms by different people; and finally, how people assign values, align themselves with or distance themselves from different ways of speaking, and engage in enregistering metadiscourse, have to do with their desire to show what groups they belong to and to assert their *belonging* within those groups.

3.6 Focal Topic: Youth Language and Belonging

The focal topic for this chapter is youth language and belonging. Adolescence has a particular significance in sociolinguistic studies because it is a stage in life when people are neither children nor adults. Adolescents have some autonomy and rights and sometimes even some economic independence, but of course not as much as adults. Adolescents are often required to stay in education and abide by specific rules of behaviour in terms of where they go and what activities they do. But at the same time, they have the freedom to develop their own identities, which might be in opposition to those their elders have in mind for them (Eckert 1997). This is often achieved through things like music, hairstyles, and dress as well as developing and using linguistic features that signal membership in specific groups.

The studies we present in this section combine traditional language variation approaches with ethnographic research to explore aspects of identity in two very different communities of practice. Mendoza-Denton's *Homegirls* study examines the everyday interactions and practices of female youth affiliated with the gangs of El Norte (the North) and El Sur (the South) in California. This is the first major ethnographic work looking at the dynamics of these gangs in relation to Latina identity. Bucholtz, on the other hand, focuses her study on a group of girl 'nerds'. In this study Bucholtz analyses the linguistic practices of 'nerd girls' and illustrates how the members who identify themselves this way negotiate aspects of their identities through their linguistic practices.

Both studies show that different kinds of semiotic and linguistic resources can project different kinds of social meanings. As young people apply these resources in their everyday lives, meanings emerge in local contexts, enabling them to project an array of identities and index their belonging to specific social groups. But belonging also inevitably involves exclusion, and sometimes entire groups (such as gang members or 'nerds') can find themselves marginalised in various ways (sometimes because of the way they talk). These studies can give us insights into how language use contributes to people's negotiations of 'who's in' and 'who's out', insights that we can apply to other social problems involving inclusion and exclusion.

Mendoza-Denton, N. (2008) *Homegirls: Language and cultural practice among Latina youth gangs.* **Malden: Blackwell** The Latin population is one of the fastest-growing ethnic groups in the US. In this study Mendoza-Denton examines the relationship among ethnic identity, linguistic practice, and gang affiliation in a community of practice that consists of young Latina females. What makes this study stand out is its combination of different approaches. Mendoza-Denton is inspired both by the variationist sociolinguistic tradition associated with scholars like Labov and the more ethnographic work of people like Penelope Eckert, and she also incorporates insights from discourse analysis and semiotics.

Mendoza-Denton begins her study by providing a very detailed account of her two-and-a-half years of fieldwork in a Southern California high school which she calls Sor Juana High. She introduces the readers to different aspects of the everyday lives of the girls who go to this school, and talks about how she met and managed to befriend members of the two opposing gangs in the school, the Norteñas (Northerners) and the Sureñas (Southerners). She then describes the differences between the two groups, highlighting the symbolic markers members use to distinguish themselves.

The Norteñas were mainly American-born and saw the US as their homeland. They adopted as part of their symbolic capital a specific type of American music they called 'Oldies', which included mostly African American artists from the late 1950s and early 1960s. The Sureñas were recent immigrants from Mexico who kept up with the latest youth culture developments in Mexico. They were great aficionadas of Banda music, a fast-paced polka popular in Mexican rural areas. The two gangs also used other kinds of symbolic practices to construct their identities. For example, the Norteñas wore red, had feathered hairdos and wore deep red lipstick. The Sureñas wore blue, had vertical ponytails and wore brown lipsticks. Different methods of applying eyeliner were also crucial for each gang's identification. All these symbolic markers were used to distinguish the girls and enable them to index their affiliation and belonging to either the Norteñas or the Sureñas gang.

Language was also used as a semiotic resource through which the two gangs set themselves apart. One of the variables Mendoza-Denton explored was the pronunciation of /θ/ in what she calls 'Th-Pro words' like 'thing', 'anything', 'something', and 'nothing'. When it comes to the pronunciation of these words, [notiŋ] rather than [nʌθiŋ] reflects a more Spanish-influenced phonology. Mendoza-Denton found that the Spanish-influenced pronunciation was disfavoured by other Latina and non-Latina girls in the school but used extensively by the girls in the gangs. This Spanish-influenced pronunciation had gained covert prestige among the Latina gang members. Similar patterns were identified for another variable, namely the raising of /ɪ/, which was also used more by the Latina gang girls compared to other girls in the school.

Through the examination of the relationship between sociolinguistic variables, everyday practices, and symbolic markers among the Norteñas and the Sureñas, Mendoza-Denton observed that despite their differences, both groups of Latina girls seemed to want to mark their Mexican ethnicity and, most importantly, to project a hardcore 'macha' gang identity. But as one gang girl explained, being macha is not about being masculine or unfeminine. It is about standing up for yourself and achieving egalitarian relationships with men.

Mendoza-Denton's study is important because it not only highlights how macha identity is constructed through the various resources (e.g., stylistic, symbolic, and linguistic choices) that the Latina girls had in their repertoire but also shows how gender categories are not simple, binary and fixed, but rather contingent and locally constructed through everyday practices of belonging.

Bucholtz, M. (1999) 'Why be normal?': Language and identity practices in a community of nerd girls. *Language in Society*, 28(2), 203–23 In this study Bucholtz uses the idea of communities of practice to investigate the linguistic practices associated with a less examined social identity in schools: the nerd. She starts by making reference to Eckert's study on the Jocks and Burnouts and the kinds of identities that these two groups projected through the different resources available in their repertoires. Both groups aimed to index some kind of 'cool' identity, which was achieved, as we have seen in section 3.4, using different linguistic variables and symbolic markers. The group that Bucholtz studied, on the other hand, seemed to aim at cultivating 'un-cool' identities.

Bucholtz conducted ethnographic fieldwork for one academic year at a high school in California. She identified a small cohesive group of friends, mainly European American girls, who formed a club which they called the 'Random Reigns Supreme Club'. This club consisted of four central members – Fred, Bob, Kate, and Loden – and two peripheral members, Carrie and Ada.

Bucholtz explains that not all high school students want to be considered 'cool'. In fact, members of the Random Reigns Supreme Club were quite proud of *not* being 'cool'. Bucholtz (1999: 213) writes:

Where cool girls aim for either cuteness or sophistication in their personal style, nerd girls aim for silliness. Cool girls play soccer or basketball; nerd girls play badminton. Cool girls read fashion magazines; nerd girls read novels. Cool girls wear tight T-shirts, and either very tight or very baggy jeans; nerd girls wear shirts and jeans that are neither tight nor extremely baggy. Cool girls wear pastels or dark tones; nerd girls wear bright primary colours.

Bucholtz's analysis of the specific features in the speech of the girls in this community of practice reveals how they used language to show how they *did not belong* to the group of 'cool kids'. Some of the ways they did this included avoiding the use of colloquial expressions, employing 'super-standard' and hyper-correct phonological and syntactic forms, and creating their own vocabulary using words from Greek and Latin.

What these girls were trying to do was to disassociate themselves from non-nerds and especially from 'cool' teenagers. Bucholtz argues that, contrary to popular perceptions, the nerd identity is not a stigma imposed by others but actually an alternative identity purposefully chosen by these girls. The nerd girls refused to engage in the pursuit of 'coolness' that preoccupied other students. Instead, through their language and other social practices, they were able to imbue nerd identity with a certain kind of social prestige.

Project Ideas

1. One place linguists sometimes look for signs of linguistic variation is in popular music. For example, Peter Trudgill studied linguistic variation in *Beatles* songs (1983) (see Chapter 6), Simpson (1999) compared the linguistic features of *Dire Straits*, *Meat Loaf*, and *Sade*, and Beal (2009) analysed the language of the indie band *Arctic Monkeys*. For this project, you should choose two singers or bands and identify linguistic variables that are produced *differently* by the singers or bands. Consider why these differences occur and think about the kinds of identities and social meanings the singers are trying to project with them.

2. Interview ten people from your local area to explore whether they 'hear' the social differences in the way others talk. Ask your informants if they noticed whether people in their community use different vocabulary, pronunciation, or grammar. Ask them to reflect why they think this is the case and what kind of social meanings and identities are projected through the use of different variants. What can you say from your research about how different varieties are *enregistered*?

3. Ask five friends to identify their key contacts and to draw a social network representing these contacts and indicating the kinds of relationships they have with each person. Ask your informants to reflect

how people in their social network may have affected the way they use language. Have they adopted any linguistic variants from other members in their social network?

4. Conduct ethnographic fieldwork in your classroom or a club you belong to. Identify the different kinds of social groups and the kinds of semiotic and linguistic resources they use in order to project different identities and group affiliations.

CHAPTER

4 Modes and Media of Communication

PREVIEW

KEY TERMS

algorithms

context

light communities

meaning potential

media

meme

modes

monomodal ideology

multiliteracies

multimodality

networked multilingualism

recombination

recontextualisation

resemiotisation

In this chapter we will consider different modes of communication other than language, such as images and emojis. We will also consider the different media that serve as carriers for communicative resources, and how they can affect the way these resources circulate, how they can be used, and by whom. We will also discuss how media, especially digital media, can affect the formation of different kinds of communities, and how different kinds of texts and other communicative resources circulate through these communities. Finally, in the focal topic we will discuss the role different modes and media play in the stigmatisation of the communicative practices of particular individuals or groups and the promotion of particular ideologies such as sexism and racism.

4.1 Introduction

In Chapter 2 we discussed Dmitri Vrubel's mural painted on part of the former Berlin Wall depicting Soviet leader Leonid Brezhnev and East German leader Erich Honecker engaging in a 'socialist fraternal kiss'. The painting, we said, was from a photograph taken in 1979, and at that time, the meaning the kiss conveyed was how much the Soviet Union supported East Germany. But the same kiss reproduced on a section of the dismantled Berlin Wall in 1990, a year after the collapse of East Germany and a year before the dissolution of the Soviet Union, had a rather different meaning, especially when combined with the caption *My God, Help Me to Survive This Deadly Love.* Finally, we saw how the kiss on the mural twenty-five years later, scrawled with homophobic and anti-homophobic graffiti, took on yet other meanings.

In 2011, more than a decade after Dmitri Vrubel's mural was painted, the French clothing manufacturer Benetton released an advertising and public service campaign with Photoshopped images of world leaders kissing in the same style as Brezhnev and Honecker. In most of these images, however, the leaders depicted kissing were adversaries. Figure 4.1, for example, of the exterior of a Benetton shop in Paris, shows then US President Barack Obama supposedly kissing then Chinese President Hu Jintao on the left, and Pope Benedict XVI kissing an imam on the right.

In these images, the kiss takes on a different meaning, especially when combined with the word UN*HATE* printed above the kissing figures. Here the kiss is asking us to imagine a world where even people who don't like each other are able to get along. Along with the slogan, UN*HATE*, however, the image also includes the company's logo: UNITED COLORS OF BENETTON, reminding people that the company that produced these messages is also in the business of selling clothes. For the Benetton company, producing these Photoshopped kisses with a message of world peace was a way of communicating to their customers that they are a

FIGURE 4.1
Benetton UN*HATE*
advertisement
(photo credit: Patrick
Kovarik)

FIGURE 4.2
Mural painted outside of the Keule Ruke restaurant in Vilnius, Lithuania (photo credit: Tim Snell licensed under CC BY-ND 2.0)

'certain kind of company' – a company that doesn't just care about selling clothes, but also about social issues. In Chapter 2 we talked about how talking in a certain way or wearing a tee-shirt with words written in a particular language can index particular kinds of social identities. They are ways of saying 'Look, I'm this kind of person.' In the same way, Benetton used these kisses to say, 'Look, we're this kind of company.'

In 2016, a similar kiss appeared on a mural painted on the side of the Keule Ruke hamburger restaurant in Vilnius, Lithuania, this one of then US presidential candidate Donald Trump kissing Russian President Vladimir Putin (Figure 4.2). When asked what kind of message he wanted to convey by commissioning artist Mindaugas Bonanu to paint this mural on the exterior of his restaurant, the owner, Dominykas Ceckauskas said simply, 'We see many similarities between these two "heroes" (Putin and Trump). They both have huge egos, and it's amusing to see they are getting along well' (Reilly 2016). Others, however, assigned more serious meanings to the image, taking it as evidence of 'misgivings in the Baltic States' following Trump's criticism of NATO (*Times of Israel* 2016). Later, gay rights activists in Europe argued about whether or not the picture of the two famously homophobic politicians was offensive or a clever queer political tactic (Hurley 2018), and even later, opponents of President Trump adopted the image as an icon of the President's alleged 'collusion' with Russia during the election that made him president. Meanwhile, in Vilnius the mural became somewhat of a tourist attraction, with couples, gay and straight, photographing themselves kissing in front of it and posting their images to Facebook and Instagram.

As time passed, however, other street artists altered the image, adding their own 'improvements'. In the version in Figure 4.2, for example, a joint has been added to Trump's hand and he is blowing smoke into Putin's mouth.

So far in this book we have been focusing on *verbal* resources for communication. But, as we said in Chapter 2, people have other kinds of resources available to them in their *repertoires* besides speech and writing.

They also make use of images, gestures, clothing, and other means to communicate, and just as with verbal language, people deploy these resources into different situations in order to do different kinds of things and to *index* different kinds of social identities.

As we can see from the examples above, a picture of two (male) politicians kissing can have very different meanings for different people depending on where and when they encounter it. Such an image can also be used to *do* lots of different things, including solidify a political alliance, advocate for world peace, question a politician's honesty, and market knitwear or hamburgers. Finally, by using such an image – painting it on the side of a business, using it in an advertisement, or sharing it with friends on social media – the people who do so are inevitably communicating to others that they are a certain kind of people, that they hold certain attitudes or beliefs or identify with particular groups. The social meaning of images like this is not random. Like linguistic resources, images build up meanings over time within the communities in which they are used, and people sometimes build on these conventional meanings to make new meanings.

But there is something else that is interesting about these images as well, and that is all of the different *material forms* in which they appeared – photographs, advertisements, paintings on walls, and photographs shared by people on Facebook and Instagram. All of these different material manifestations inevitably had an effect on how these images were circulated and who could see them. An image painted on a wall, for example, can only be seen by a limited number of people at once, but when it is transformed into a digital photograph and shared over the Internet it can be seen and commented on by millions. These different ways of circulating images also have an effect on how people might interpret the images. You might interpret an image differently if it's painted on a section of the former Berlin Wall than if it's on the side of a hamburger restaurant, if it appears in *Time* magazine, or if it appears in Donald Trump's Twitter feed.

In this chapter we will consider different **modes** of communication other than language, and how these modes are used, often in combination with language, to make meaning, perform social actions, and enact different kinds of identities. In particular, we will examine how the meanings and functions of different signs depend not just on who uses them but also on the **context** in which they are used. We will also consider the different material technologies or **media** that we use as carriers for our communicative resources, and the effect different media can have on how different resources circulate, how they can be used, and by whom.

4.2 Modes and Multimodality

Why should we worry about pictures of politicians kissing in a book about language and society? It is not just, as we said above, that linguistic resources form just part of our communicative repertoires. It is also that language use itself always involves and, in many cases, *depends* on these other resources. As Scollon and LeVine (2004: 1–2) put it:

[L]anguage in use, whether this is in the form of spoken language or text, is always and inevitably constructed across multiple modes of communication, including speech and gesture not just in spoken language but through such 'contextual' phenomena as the use of the physical spaces where we carry out our discursive actions or the design, paper and typography of the documents within which our texts are presented.

There is also an argument to be made that modes other than speech and writing are more central to our day-to-day communication than ever before. Of course, communication has always been **multimodal** – we have always gestured when talking, and written materials have always included images. Nowadays, however, technological advances, especially the rise of digital technologies, have made creating and sharing multimodal texts easier than ever before. Indeed, you can't really understand how people communicate over the Internet without taking into account forms of communication such as selfies, animated GIFs, TikTok videos, and emojis. At the same time, with the increased mobility of both people and information, people increasingly find themselves in situations in which they need to communicate with others who do not share the same verbal codes or whose competence with a shared verbal code is minimal. As Adami (2017: 2) puts it, 'When communication occurs in superdiverse contexts, with people sharing little or only partial background knowledge, we can predict that the multimodality of communication is enhanced, with non-verbal resources achieving a greater functional load.'

Modes are basically different systems for communicating. In face-to-face interaction, as Scollon and LeVine say, we don't just communicate through speech, but we use gestures and physical space. We also communicate through the clothes we wear, and through the way we handle objects. At a distance we communicate through writing that is printed in different fonts and sizes and colours, as well as with sound effects and music, images, and symbols such as emojis. All of these different ways of communicating can be considered modes. We call modes *systems* for communicating since they operate systematically. The discourse analysts Carey Jewitt and Gunther Kress (2003: 1) define a mode as any 'regularized, organized set of resources for meaning making'.

Just because modes are organised, though, doesn't mean that the meanings of particular words, gestures, colours, shapes, fonts, and images are fixed. As we have seen in the last three chapters, both the *semantic* meanings and the *indexical* meanings of the resources we use are to some degree fluid and contextual. This fluidity of meaning is particularly obvious when it comes to some of the most common signs that we exchange on an everyday basis. When we tap the ❤ on someone's Instagram post, for example, we may be expressing that we 'like' what was posted, but we may really be expressing that we like the person who posted it and would probably tap on the ❤ no matter what they posted, or we may be doing so because we expect them to tap on the ❤ on our posts.

Similarly, the emoji 😂 can have a range of different meanings, depending on how and when we use it and with whom. It might express happiness, embarrassment, or frustration. It might mean that we think something or someone is funny, ridiculous, absurd, or totally unacceptable, or it might be used to signal that something that we have just written is not really serious. We might even use it just because we can't think of any other way to reply to someone's message. So the meaning of 😂 depends on the context in which it is used, including the words or other emojis it's used with.

Like codes, genres, registers, and linguistic variables such as /r/, modes can also convey *indexical meaning*. That is, they can 'point to' particular social identities or attitudes in different communities. For example, if you use a lot of emojis, you might be communicating not just the semantic meaning of the emojis you are using, but also that you are 'the kind of person who uses a lot of emojis', which in different contexts might make people think you are expressive and energetic or emotional and childish. People might even take it as an expression of your 'masculinity' or 'femininity' (see, for example, Pérez-Sabater 2019). So the indexical meaning of using emojis, or of using a particular emoji such as 😂 also depends on context.

While the meaning of different words, symbols, icons, images, and sounds is not fixed, it is also not random. In other words, ❤️ probably cannot mean 'I hate your post' and 😂 probably cannot mean 'Let's go for pizza.' Rather, different communicative resources can be used to express a *range* of semantic and indexical meanings. The linguist M. A. K. Halliday (1978) talked about linguistic resources as having **meaning potential**, and the same can be said of graphic resources like emojis and pictures of politicians kissing. The meaning potential of a particular communicative resource refers to the kinds of meanings that a resource allows a person to express (including the kinds of social identities it allows them to enact) in a particular context. The other side of meaning potential is that particular resources also function to *limit* the kinds of meanings people can make (and thus the kinds of people they can show themselves to be). Meaning potential is *socially constructed*, that is, it builds up over time among different groups of people as they use particular communicative resources in particular ways, and so the meanings that are assigned to particular sounds, words, grammatical features, images, articles of clothing, and even smells (see Pennycook & Otsuji 2015) end up reflecting the 'reality' or world view of particular communities, societies, or cultures (Halliday 1978: 123).

Some scholars talk about the meaning potential of different modes in terms of *affordances* and *constraints*, an idea that comes from the evolutionary biologist J. J. Gibson (1979). For Gibson, affordances refer to what different things in an organism's environment are 'good for' – what they enable the organism to do. When we say modes have affordances we mean that they allow us to 'do' different things, specifically, to represent the world and interact with other people in different ways. As Kress (2000: 157) puts it: 'modes have different potentials, so that they afford different kinds of possibilities of human expression and engagement with the world'.

The mode of writing, for example, allows us to present our ideas in a linear, sequential logic that unfolds over time, whereas images allow us to 'show' meaning to an audience all at once. Images also allow us, in some cases, to show finer gradations of meaning – we can express not just 'red' but a particular shade of red. Emojis and animated GIFs allow us to communicate something about our attitude towards something or someone in ways that words may not. An affordance, when it comes to communication, however, is not necessarily something that allows you to communicate more 'clearly' or 'precisely'. In fact, sometimes the advantage of using one mode over another is that it allows us to be ambiguous, *not* to commit ourselves to saying something precisely. This is certainly one of the advantages of emojis like 😂 – they allow us to hint at a range of different meanings rather than saying something like 'that's ridiculous' or 'I'm so embarrassed!'

Activity: The Meaning Potential of Emojis

Look at the different emojis in Table 4.1. Write down what you think the *meaning potential* of these different emojis is – that is, the range of meanings that they can have based on your experience. Write down two or three example sentences illustrating how the emoji might be used to express different meanings.

Table 4.1 Emojis

Emoji	Range of possible meanings	Examples of how you might use it
a. 🔥		
b. 🙏		
c. 💁		
d. 😳		
e. 🤦		

Now, compare your answers with those of someone else. Do you have the same or different understandings of the meaning potential of these different emojis? How can you account for these similarities or differences?

Discuss the following questions:

- Do you use different emojis or use emojis differently when you communicate with different kinds of people? If so, why?
- Do you think people from different groups (different age groups, different genders, different cultural backgrounds) use emojis differently from you? If so, why do you think this is?
- What are the affordances of using emojis? How would the example sentences you wrote be different if you had left out the emoji or if you had tried to express the meaning conveyed by the emoji in words?

4.3 Resemiotisation, Recombination, and Recontextualisation

So, how do people make meanings and enact social identities using multiple modes?

In order to answer this question, we need to examine three processes that people engage in when they use multimodal resources: **resemiotisation**, **recombination**, and **recontextualisation**.

Resemiotisation refers to what happens when people try to express the same meanings using different modes. For example, I might tell you a story about my night out clubbing with my mates, explaining in vivid language what happened and how I felt about it. Or I might *resemiotise* this narrative into images, putting together the photos I took that night to create an Instagram 'story'. Although both of these stories are about the same night out, you would probably understand and experience them in very different ways. In my verbal story, for instance, I may be able to organise the events as a detailed narrative and include some evaluative commentary about what I thought about particular incidents or people. I could also try to arrange the pictures and videos in my Instagram story into a kind of sequential narrative, but I wouldn't be able to create links or fill in details about what happened in between the different pictures and videos. At the same time, I might not need to explain to you how I felt about the evening because you would be able to tell from the expression on my face and the faces of my friends. You might also feel like you were experiencing my night out more 'directly' rather than hearing about it as a narrated memory. In this regard, the Instagram story might also have certain advantages for me, allowing me to preserve in real time what happened to me since, especially after some nights out, I may not be able to remember everything that happened so clearly.

The important thing about resemiotisation is that it allows people to overcome the constraints of one mode by switching to another mode. At the same time, they also end up losing some of the affordances for meaning-making that the first mode provided. So, there's always a kind of trade-off. Resemiotisation changes the way I can represent reality, which means that the person I'm communicating with can understand or experience it differently. It also changes my opportunities for creating indexical meaning. Taking a selfie allows me to make use of all sorts of multimodal resources to communicate what kind of person I want you to think I am, such as my facial expression, my clothing, and the way I pose with my friends. Even the fact that I have an Instagram account and decided to share my night out with you via images already signals that I am a certain kind of person.

Finally, resemiotisation has an impact on the access different kinds of audiences can have to my story. If I'm telling you the story face-to-face, your understanding depends on us sharing a common code, in this case English. My Instagram story, on the other hand, depends much less on me sharing a verbal code with my audience, though they will still have to have some cultural knowledge of what a club is and what goes on during nights out. Of course, another big difference between these stories is that I can normally only share my spoken story with a few people at a time face-to-face, whereas I can broadcast my Instagram story to hundreds or even thousands of followers. But that difference has more to do with *media* than with modes (see below).

Recombination has to do with how people make meanings by combining and recombining different modes when they communicate. As we said above, all texts and interactions are to some degree multimodal, and their meaning depends not just on the meaning potentials of individual modes, but also on how they interact with one another. To continue with the example of the Instagram story of my night out, chances are that it won't just consist of images. I'm also likely to combine those images with funny captions, attach hashtags such as #partypeople or #instagood to them, superimpose icons or emojis on them, or apply filters or effects. The addition of any of these other modes might alter the meaning of the images. My captions, for example, might help explain what is depicted in an image, and my emojis might tell you something about my attitude towards what is depicted.

We are using the term *re*combination rather than just combination because it better captures the way we continually mix and match different resources in our repertoires. I might, for example, use the same emoji or the hashtag #instagood with different images, or I might reuse the images I used on my Instagram story for some other purpose. Communication is always a matter of recombining the finite supply of resources we have access to in new ways in order to make new meanings. And these new meanings that are made always in some way build upon the past meanings these resources were used to make in different combinations.

One particularly dramatic example of how recombination works in communication is in the ways people mix and match words and images in image macros. Image macros are a kind of internet **meme** normally consisting of a picture with some written text, usually placed above and below the picture. The reason people like image macros is that they allow them to be creative with the process of recombination, combining new words with old pictures or new pictures with old words. One of the most popular kinds of pictures people use in memes are pictures of cats, and one of the most popular pictures of cats is the image of 'grumpy cat', a photo of a grumpy-looking cat who was named Tardar Sauce.[1] The words accompanying the image are usually assumed to be attributed to 'grumpy cat' herself. For example, we might combine this picture with the words: 'I WENT CLUBBING ONCE/IT WAS AWFUL.' This, in fact, might be a funny meme for me to include in my Instagram story about my night out. This combination is actually a variation of an earlier combination of the 'grumpy cat' meme with the words 'I HAD FUN ONCE/IT WAS AWFUL', and one of the reasons the new combination 'makes sense' is because it reminds people of the earlier combination. It also fits into a general theme that governs 'grumpy cat' memes, that the words that are combined with the picture must be somehow 'grumpy'.

From this example, a few clear principles about how recombination works can be seen. The first is the fact that, when we combine one mode with another mode, we change the meaning potential of both of the modes. The meaning of the words 'I went clubbing once. It was awful' changes when these words are superimposed onto the face of 'grumpy cat' – specifically, a text that, in itself, is not particularly funny, becomes funny. The meaning of 'grumpy cat's' face also changes. Of course, her face will always be grumpy, but the words give a more specific meaning to her grumpiness and create a meme that I can share with my friends about my night out clubbing. Another important principle of recombination that we can see from this example is that often new combinations get part of their meaning from their relationship to old combinations.

Recontextualisation refers to the fact that the meaning of a particular modal resource can change dramatically depending on the context into which it is deployed. My Instagram story, for example, has one possible set of meanings when shared with my friends, but it would have a different possible set of meanings if it were taken out of the context of my friend group and introduced into a different context – if, for example, one of my friends showed it to my mother or my boss. Recontextualisation refers to the process of taking a 'text' (by which we mean any combination of semiotic resources) from one context and introducing it into a new context. The anthropologists Richard Bauman and Charles Briggs (1990: 72) say that recontextualisation has 'powerful implications for the conduct of social life'. What they mean is that it has a potentially big effect not just

---

1 See https://knowyourmeme.com/memes/grumpy-cat.

on the meaning of the text that has been recontextualised, but also on the status and relationships of the individuals involved in the process. Taking my clubbing pictures out of the context of my group of friends and introducing them into my workplace, for example, might have implications for my job or my relationship with my boss. For this reason, people are often careful about the contexts in which the texts they produce can be introduced. In fact, the philosopher Helen Nissenbaum (2009) argues that being able to control the *contexts* into which your words, images, and other kinds of communication are introduced is the essence of *privacy*.

But context itself is a rather complicated idea. By context we don't mean just the physical environment in which a text is deployed, but also the *social* environment (e.g., who is the audience for the text) as well as the *activity* in which the text is used (for example, dancing at the club or having a meeting at the office). Context is always something that we try to control, but it is also something that we can *create* using communicative resources. For example, adding the 😂 emoji to a message in an online chat can have the effect of changing the context of the chat, maybe turning a 'serious' conversation into a more light-hearted one.

Sometimes the words that we add to pictures in memes have the effect of creating a different context in which the picture can be interpreted. This is especially true when people use the 'when … and you're like' construction. For example, you might create a context for the picture of 'grumpy cat' by superimposing the words: 'WHEN YOUR FRIENDS SHOW YOUR INSTAGRAM STORY TO YOUR PARENTS/AND YOU'RE LIKE'.

In short, understanding the meaning potential of different kinds of multimodal resources is not a simple matter. Meanings are never stable but change as resources are recombined with other resources and as they circulate through the social world, travelling from context to context. This is true both for the semantic meaning potential of signs and for their *indexical* meaning, that is the way signs become associated with different kinds of people and the way they accumulate different kinds of *values*. To understand the opportunities people have for recombining resources and the ways different resources circulate through societies, gathering meaning along the way, we need to move on from talking about modes to talking about *media*.

4.4 Media

While modes are the semiotic systems that we use to create texts, media are the *material carriers* of these texts. For example, a picture of two politicians kissing can be conveyed by being painted on the side of a hamburger restaurant, by being printed in a newspaper or magazine, or by being shared on a social media platform. All of these conveyances – the brick wall, the print publication, and the digital platform – are examples of media. Media are extremely important when it comes to the social function of language and other semiotic resources because they help to determine how different kinds of texts and resources get circulated, who has access to them, and the kinds of meanings that different people are able to make with them.

Just like modes, media have different affordances and constraints, that is, they make some aspects of communication easier while limiting other aspects of communication. A microphone, for instance, has the affordance of allowing me to project my voice to a large number of people. This affordance, however, can constrain my ability to talk privately to the person standing next to me – so if I want to do that I will need to step away from the microphone or switch it off. A long article in a newspaper or magazine might afford me the opportunity to make a complex and nuanced argument about the relationship between Donald Trump and Vladimir Putin and its implications for geopolitics, but it may not be seen or read by as many people as a picture of the two men kissing that 'goes viral' on Facebook. So, messages are not just carried by media – they are to some extent also *shaped* by them.

The two main affordances and constraints of media when it comes to communication are that: (1) they enable and constrain the *resources* available to us to make meaning and how we are able to recombine these resources, and (2) they enable and constrain how we can control the *contexts* in which our messages appear (including who is able to access and reshare them). In other words, media affect *how we express ourselves* and *whom we can talk to*, and, for this reason, media help to determine the values that come to be associated with different kinds of resources, the kinds of social identities we are able to construct using these resources, and the way different groups of people in society who use these resources come to see themselves and be seen by others.

In Chapter 1 we talked about Benedict Anderson's argument that what sparked the growth of nationalism, enabling people to start thinking of themselves as 'French' or 'German' or 'British', was the printing press. Through the medium of print, people became exposed to common ideas, stories, and symbols of the nation. They also came to be exposed to a common written language, and once particular versions of 'languages' were written down and circulated widely, they eventually came to be regarded as 'standard' versions of the languages that people spoke.

In fact, the medium of print was largely responsible for making written language itself such a highly valued resource in many societies. Writing as a mode of communication did not just take on important communicative functions, but it also took on important symbolic functions, indexing 'civilisation', 'education', and 'intelligence'. In many societies, to be 'illiterate' was (and still is) synonymous with being uneducated or stupid. People came to associate writing with the development of science, history, philosophy, and, of course, literature, and to associate spoken communication with 'tribal', 'primitive' societies (see, for example, Ong 1982/2003).

This preoccupation with written language, however, began to change with the rise of electronic media such as the radio, film, and television, which allowed people to transmit modes other than writing (speech, sounds, images) over long distances. Walter Ong, in his 1971 essay entitled 'The literate orality of popular culture today' argues that these media have ushered in 'a new orality' (p. 21). Part of the reason these media have changed the status of modes like speech, gesture, and image was that they have introduced new affordances for how people can use these modes – now, for example, speech, like writing, can be easily *recontextualised* – lifted out of the context in which it was produced and conveyed into other contexts.

Digital media have further altered the range of modes that we can convey across contexts and how these modes can be combined. Now the modes of writing, speech, still and moving images, music, and other sound effects, as well as font, colour, and layout can be easily recombined and recontextualised, with even *embodied* modes (see Chapter 8) like gestures and facial expressions becoming prominent resources for communication across distances.

As a result, the whole idea of what it means to be 'literate' and the social values associated with literacy have changed. Rather than speaking of 'literacy' – the ability to produce and decipher written language, people now speak of **multiliteracies**, the ability to communicate effectively through multiple modes conveyed through multiple media. The multiliteracies perspective aligns with the 'sociolinguistics of resources' (Blommaert 2010) that we discussed in Chapter 2: modes, like 'languages' are not static systems for making meaning, but sets of 'dynamic representational resources, constantly being remade by their users as they work to achieve their various cultural purposes' (New London Group 1996: 64).

What this short history of media and modes tells us is that different media don't just make it more convenient for people to communicate with others in different ways. They also have the potential to change the *values* people assign to different communicative resources and so to alter their *ideologies* about language and communication. For example, because digital media enable people to mix different modes and codes together so easily, and also because they enable people themselves to mix so easily with people with communicative repertoires that are different from theirs, they have in many ways challenged both the *ideology of monolingualism*, which we discussed in Chapter 1, as well as challenging what we might call the **monomodal ideology** (the idea that one mode – usually written language – is superior to other modes of communication).

While media can have a dramatic effect on how we conceptualise and use language, it can also have an effect on how we conceive of 'society', manage our social relationships, and participate in different groups. That's because media help to create structures around communication, determining who can participate and how they can participate, and what sorts of resources they can use. These structures for interacting and sharing communicative resources are the scaffolding upon which different kinds of communities are formed.

One final but extremely important point about media has to do with power. Different kinds of media have an effect on who can control access to different kinds of resources and, to some extent, the ways these resources come to be valued by a society. When it comes to the medium of print, the powerful people are those who own the printing presses and so decide what gets printed and what doesn't. When it comes to broadcast media, the powerful people are those who have the resources to produce and broadcast content over the airways. The Internet, in many ways, has altered the relationships of power associated with older media, giving to ordinary people the power to create and broadcast content and to influence the ideas and behaviours of others. At the same time, digital platforms (such as Instagram, Google, Snapchat, and YouTube) are also controlled by powerful companies which design their products in ways that nudge people into creating certain kinds of content, having certain kinds of interactions with one another, and forming certain kinds of communities which optimise the profitability of these platforms.

Activity: Comparing Media

Think about your experiences with the different kinds of media listed in Table 4.2 and consider the affordances and constraints of the media in terms of the kinds of modes you can use and the ways you can control the contexts of your messages.

Table 4.2 Comparing modes

Medium	Modes (What modes are available to me and how can I mix them?)	Context/Recontextualisation (Who is 'part of' the conversation? Who has access to my message? Are they able to share it with other people? How can I control this?)
Telephone		
WhatsApp		
Snapchat		

How do these affordances and constraints affect whether or not you would use this medium to do certain kinds of things or to communicate certain kinds of messages?

4.5 How Digital Media Have Changed 'Language'

As we said above, digital media have changed the way people use language in two main ways. One has to do with the ease with which they allow people to *recombine* different communicative resources, including different codes, scripts, and modes. Part of this has to do with their technical affordances. The app Snapchat, for example, makes it easy for users to combine photographs, drawings, emojis, and written language using various scripts and fonts. Part of this, however, also has to do with the technological *constraints* of some digital media platforms, which compel

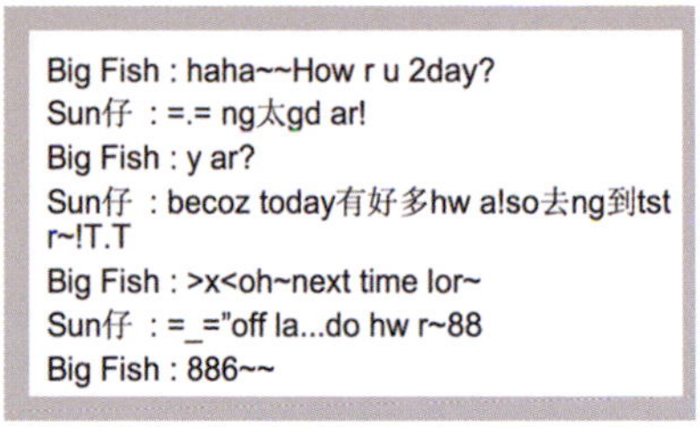

Big Fish : haha~~How r u 2day?
Sun仔 : =.= ng太gd ar!
Big Fish : y ar?
Sun仔 : becoz today有好多hw also去ng到tst r~!T.T
Big Fish : >x<oh~next time lor~
Sun仔 : =_="off la...do hw r~88
Big Fish : 886~~

FIGURE 4.3
ICQ chat in Hong Kong (adapted from Jones 2001)

people to come up with creative ways to communicate. Before it became easy to input Arabic into digital devices, for example, digital media users in Arabic-speaking countries developed a way of writing Arabic with Latin characters and numbers (sometimes also mixed with English words) called *Arabizi*. Similarly, one thing that helps to drive the development and adoption of resources like emojis, GIFs, and non-conventional spellings and punctuation are constraints the media place on using the nonverbal resources we normally use to manage face-to-face communication.

In her study of the way young people communicated on the chat programme ICQ in the early 2000s, sociolinguist Carmen Lee (2007) noted how internet users creatively made use of a range of different linguistic resources such as 'standard' written Chinese, Cantonese characters, Romanised Cantonese, English, English abbreviations, and emoticons and other typographical symbols, taking into account the affordances of these different resources for communicating their meanings as well as the technical constraints of the software they were using. Figure 4.3 is an example of such interaction.

One of the most striking things about such conversations is the way these young people recombined resources. The utterance ng 太gd (not too good) for example, is formed from the Romanised transcription of the Cantonese word for *not* (ng), the Chinese character for *too*, and an abbreviation of the English word *good*. Another notable thing about this text is how the interlocutors introduce features from spoken Cantonese into their written communication, such as the sentence-final particles ('ar', 'lor'), normally used the way intonation is used in English to convey a speaker's attitude towards what they are saying. Yet another interesting feature is the use of special slang terms and abbreviations specific to the digital communication of Hong Kong Cantonese speakers, such as 88 to mean *bye bye* (because the pronunciation of 88 in Cantonese is *bat bat*): in other words, *numbers* are used to indicate a particular sound pattern in *Cantonese* which is meant to express an *English* word. Such complex interactions between codes demonstrates how, in digitally mediated communication, it is sometimes difficult to identify what 'language' is being used.

These practices of mixing resources or, as we will refer to it in Chapter 5, *translanguaging*, seem natural in digitally mediated communication, not just because the technology makes it easy to mix languages and scripts and graphic elements in new ways, but also because the Internet, as Paolillo (2007: 424) puts it, 'represents a language contact situation of unprecedented scale'. Digital media have made interactions between people with access to very different sets of linguistic resources more common.

The media sociolinguist Jannis Androutsopoulos (2013: 185) refers to this phenomenon as **networked multilingualism**, which he defines as 'multilingual practices that are shaped by two interrelated processes: being networked, i.e. digitally connected to other individuals and groups, and being in the network, i.e. embedded in the global mediascape of the web'. What determines how people decide which resources to mix and how to mix them, he says, are the affordances and constraints of the technology itself (such as character sets and keyboards), users' access to networked resources (such as memes, GIFs, translation programs), and their understanding of the different audiences they are communicating with. The example Androutsopoulos gives is the way migrants in Germany with different language backgrounds communicate with their friends on Facebook, picking and choosing different elements from their communicative repertoires in order to accommodate the different linguistic competencies of their audiences.

Networked multilingualism has the effect of disrupting people's traditional understandings of the boundaries between different 'languages' and 'varieties', as different ways of writing become less tied to particular geographical places or bounded 'speech communities', and more linked to other factors such as the affordances of the medium, the complex configuration of audience members these media make possible, and the kinds of activities (such as 'Instagramming' or 'gaming') that people are engaged in.

It is for this reason that Philip Seargeant and Caroline Tagg (2011) advocate what they call a 'post varieties' approach to analysing language use on social media. What they mean by this is that rather than trying to identify and separate out the distinct language 'varieties' (such as 'Standard Written Chinese' or 'English'), and rather than trying to characterise the way people communicate online as a 'new' variety (such as 'chatspeak'), it is better to get away from the idea of varieties altogether and to recognise the ad hoc, creative, and situated ways people draw upon and recombine different resources in order to deal with the constraints of the media, the competencies and orientations of their audiences, and their own desires to index particular kinds of social identities.

Nevertheless, there have been attempts, both by linguists and by ordinary people, to *enregister* (see Chapter 3) the kind of language that people use online, treating it as a special 'variety' of language. The linguist David Crystal (2006), for example, back in the early 2000s, tried to describe the features of what he called 'Netspeak', including things like shortened forms and acronyms (such as BTW, LOL), unconventional spellings and punctuation, and emoticons. The most important question to ask in this regard, however, is not whether or not a variety called 'Netspeak' actually 'exists', but rather why people find it necessary to 'imagine' such a variety, and what social functions such processes of *enregisterment* might accomplish. These are the questions asked by sociolinguist Lauren Squires

(2010), who analysed the *metadiscourse* (see Chapter 3) about internet language in the media and in academic discourse. She found across the sources that she surveyed a relatively consistent set of features (such as acronyms, abbreviations, and respellings) that were thought to characterise internet language as well as a relatively consistent set of negative attitudes towards this 'variety'. Interestingly, when she analysed actual instant messaging conversations, she found that these features were actually relatively rare. She concludes that the enregisterment of internet language (or 'Netspeak') actually serves as a way of promoting the standard language ideology and anxieties about the effects of new technologies on communication. Others, such as Crispin Thurlow (2014), have similarly noted how metadiscourse about computer language often functions as a way of 'disciplining' young people and devaluing or marginalising their everyday social practices and social identities.

This last example points to an important trend that has developed online alongside the increased diversity of communicative resources and communicative practices – an increased tendency for people to want to *police* the linguistic performances of others, criticising and assigning value to the resources they use and how they use them. Of course, as we said in Chapter 1, people have always engaged in acts of what Cameron (1995) calls 'verbal hygiene'. The Internet only makes it easier for such evaluations to circulate and 'go viral', as we will see in our focal topic.

4.6 How Digital Media Have Changed 'Society'

Just as digital media have made us rethink some of our traditional ideas about the boundaries between different 'languages' and 'varieties', they have also forced us to rethink our old ideas about the boundaries between different kinds of groups in society. The media scholar Manuel Castells (2000) argues that digital technologies have brought about new configurations of social organisation and social identity. The reason for this is not just because they allow people to easily connect with others across long distances and across geographical and political borders, but also because they change the ways people manage the audiences they have for their communication and the *contexts* in which the texts and utterances they produce are experienced.

In the introduction to this book we talked about Gumperz and Hymes's (1972) notion of speech communities, groups of people who share communicative resources and ways of using them. Gumperz and Hymes, writing long before the invention of the Internet, focused on how membership in speech communities depends on people's participation in concrete 'speech events' in the physical world. Similarly, the concept of communities of practice used by sociolinguists like Eckert has traditionally been used to explore groups of people who engage in common social practices in physical spaces such as high schools. But how applicable are these ideas about social organisation to online environments in which people are not bounded by the constraints of the material world?

Early researchers of internet communication were very interested in the ways digital technologies facilitated the formation of 'virtual communities' (Rheingold 2000), groups of people with common interests, common goals, and (often) common communicative resources, who could gather together virtually for social and political purposes, and the early architecture of the Internet, dominated by 'newsgroups', 'bulletin boards', and 'online forums', seemed to encourage this kind of social organisation. With the development of social media platforms, however, the way people organised themselves and the way different communicative resources circulated online changed dramatically. The idea of 'communities' as stable and bounded groups of people became less relevant, and the idea of 'social networks' (see Chapter 3) seemed a much more appropriate way of describing how people interact online. After all, the Internet is itself a network, and social media sites gave people ways of organising themselves based not on shared interests or shared communicative resources, but on social relationships.

What this meant when it came to language and communication was that much more of the communication that people engaged in online involved *heterodox* audiences with different interests and access to different communicative resources. Although we can use technological methods (such as privacy settings) to filter and segregate our audiences, much of what we communicate online is available to a wide range of different kinds of people, which means we either have to adapt the way we use resources (such as different codes) in order to accommodate people with different configurations of competencies, or we need to adjust our communication so that it signals or 'hails' (Althusser 1971) the people that we want to pay attention to it. It also means that we tend to have much less control over the ways our messages circulate once we have posted them, that is, what kinds of contexts they might end up in. The internet scholars Alice Marwick and danah boyd (2010: 114) call this phenomenon 'context collapse'.

That is not to say that people don't organise themselves into 'communities' online. Online spaces are, in fact, full of activist groups, fandom communities, interest groups, video game 'clans', political 'tribes', and various clusters of 'trolls', 'hackers', and hate groups. The discourse analyst James Paul Gee (2004) calls these kinds of groupings 'affinity spaces', because they form around common 'affinities' towards different kinds of activities or ideas (such as playing an online game or supporting or opposing a particular political idea). Such spaces often have rather porous boundaries and sometimes have rather short lifespans, and people move easily in and out of them (often anonymously). Jan Blommaert (2017) contrasts these online communities with the more 'durable' kinds of communities we associate with physical spaces (for example, 'speech communities', 'communities of practice', the 'imagined communities' of nation states) by using the term **light communities**, which he defines as 'moments of tight but temporary ... groupness' which form around particular configurations of communicative resources and social practices, ranging from memes to conspiracy theories, to online 'challenges' issued via platforms like TikTok.

Of course, some of these communities are 'lighter' than others, and some of them seem to have a particularly 'heavy' quality to them because of the passion, enthusiasm, shared outrage or violence that those involved in them can display. A good example of this are social groupings associated with what has been called the 'Manosphere', which Blommaert (2017: 1) describes as an online zone of social activity in which 'men gather to exchange experiences and views on the oppressive role and position of women in their worlds, and often do so by means of ostensibly misogynist, sexist, (often) racist and (sometimes) violent discourse'.

The key thing to note about such groupings is the importance of specific configurations of communicative resources such as hashtags, memes, catchphrases, and other 'viral' signs in holding them together and attracting participants to them. But there are technological factors that contribute to the formation and maintenance of such communities as well, most important being the **algorithms** that govern how different kinds of texts get circulated online and how connections get formed between people based on the kinds of content that they create and share. These algorithms are often designed to circulate content to people based on what they have been engaged with in the past, and so can have the effect of reinforcing the opinions they already hold or their sense of belonging to groups that they already align to.

4.7 Focal Topic: Marginalisation and Harassment Online

At its inception, people thought that the Internet would bring all the different kinds of people in the world together into a 'global community' and expose them to ideas different from their own. To some extent this has happened. As we said above, the circulation of texts, the distribution of communicative resources, and the formation of online 'affinity spaces' is no longer limited by regional and national boundaries. At the same time, the opposite has also occurred: the Internet has in many respects brought about increased fragmentation of people into groups with different interests and different agendas, and an increased polarisation of opinions and antagonism among people with different views.

One reason for this is the manner in which digital networks facilitate the rapid dissemination of texts and communicative resources, sometimes of an extreme or incendiary nature. Another is the business model of the companies that own digital platforms, which compels them to maximise user engagement by channelling content to them that both reinforces the opinions they already have and inspires outrage against people who might hold different opinions. Social media sites also increase people's consciousness of social status, and the power of different communicative resources (such as hashtags, memes, and Instagram stories) for displaying status.

In this section we will consider how language and other semiotic resources that circulate on the Internet, undergoing processes of resemiotisation, recombination, and recontextualisation, can function to marginalise or belittle certain groups of people.

The first article, by sociolinguists Erhan Aslan and Camilla Vásquez, describes the case of a television interview with a teenaged girl speaking 'non-standard' English that 'went viral', sparking a heated online discussion about the propriety of the girl's linguistic performance as well as a barrage of image macro memes mocking her. The article shows how participatory online spaces like *YouTube* can function as sites where people assign value to particular ways of speaking and, in doing so, sometimes perpetuate racist and sexist stereotypes.

The second article, by media scholars Alice Marwick and Robyn Caplan, shows how common communicative resources (such as the term *misandry*) function to build a sense of community among a loose online network of bloggers, activists, and fringe groups known as the Manosphere, and how these resources are used to construct a unified vison of feminism as 'a man-hating movement which victimizes men and boys' (p. 543).

Both articles show how attention to the way communicative resources are commented upon and transformed as they circulate through digital networks can help us to understand how certain ideologies are negotiated and promoted within online affinity spaces.

Aslan, E., and Vásquez, C. (2018) 'Cash me ousside': A citizen sociolinguistic analysis of online metalinguistic commentary. *Journal of Sociolinguistics*, 22(4), 406–31   This article analyses the metadiscourse produced by commenters on YouTube and producers of internet memes around a viral video of a young white girl speaking in a way that resembles African American Vernacular English (AAVE). The analysis reveals how online collectives of internet users come together to police the linguistic performances of others in ways that often promote social inequality, the stigmatisation of minorities, and the perpetuation of the standard language ideology.

The video in question came from the US television talk show *Dr Phil* and depicts a 'troubled' teenager revealing examples of her delinquency (including lying, cheating, and stealing cars), eliciting the disapproval of the host, Dr Phil. At one point, in response to the audience laughing at her, the girl turns to them and says: 'Catch me outside, how about that', which she pronounces 'cash me ousside, howbow dah',[2] which causes Dr Phil to retort, 'What now, I didn't get that. Are you speaking English?'

The phrase quickly became the subject of online commentary and internet memes, many of which linked the girl's way of speaking to AAVE and various stereotypes sometimes associated with it, such as 'gangsta culture' (see Figures 4.4 and 4.5).

In order to examine the language ideologies circulating online around this 13-year-old girl's linguistic performance, Aslan and Vásquez collected

---

2 [kɛʃ mi ɑsːɑː hɑ bɑ dæʔ]

FIGURE 4.4
'Cash me ousside'
meme 1
(adapted from Aslan &
Vásquez 2018: 411)

FIGURE 4.5
'Cash me ousside'
meme 2
(adapted from Aslan &
Vásquez 2018: 412)

comments from *YouTube*, where the original video had been posted along with a host of remixes, dance performances, and meme reaction videos based on it. They collected the comments from the original and a meme reaction video with the most views, extracting those in which commenters were explicitly commenting on the girl's language. They coded the comments based on whether or not they were positive, negative, or neutral, and based on the social categories (for example race, region, education, and age) that were mentioned.

Perhaps not surprisingly, the vast majority of the comments contained negative evaluations of the girl's speech, many of them containing expletives, racial epithets, and insults (e.g., 'her speech and grammar are crap' and 'ENGLISH MOTHERFUCKER, DO YOU SPEAK IT?'). The most interesting thing, however, was the way these negative evaluations interacted with other social categories, especially race.

Some commenters associated the girl's speech with certain regions of the US (such as the South), but most of these were relatively neutral. Others commented on what they perceived to be the girl's educational background, making more negative comments, such as 'Go back to school and learn to speak proper English' and 'Get an English tutor.'

The most negative comments, however, were those that associated the way that the girl spoke with AAVE. Many of these promoted negative evaluations of this variety and the people who speak it and included offensive racial epithets, and some of them mixed misogyny with racism, linking the youth's use of this variety with alleged sexual behaviour with African American men.

Others, however, questioned the authenticity of the girl's performance (see Chapter 6) and accused her of appropriating a way of speaking that didn't rightfully belong to her in order to project a certain social image, attract attention, or gain notoriety (see Chapter 7). There were also commenters who, while they didn't mention race, class, or education, associated the girl's speech with particular kinds of places or identities that might index these categories, such as 'ghetto', 'street', 'trailer park', 'hoodrat', and 'gangsta'.

Aslan and Vásquez are careful to emphasise the *variety* of evaluations and associations attributed to the girl's linguistic performance. At the same time, their study shows how evaluations of other people's speech are often closely tied to the speaker's racial or ethnic identity as well as the racial or ethnic identities indexed by the communicative resources they deploy. Such evaluations often reproduce and make more visible racist attitudes, as well as attitudes about class and gender. It also shows how online spaces can function to amplify such judgements and the attitudes that underly them as metadiscourse about language in the form of memes and other kinds of digital texts that circulate through online networks and 'go viral'.

Marwick, A. E., and Caplan, R. (2018) Drinking male tears: Language, the Manosphere, and networked harassment. *Feminist Media Studies*, 18(4), 543–59   In this article, Alice Marwick and Robyn Caplan examine how misogynist speech circulates online and, in particular, how specific communicative resources and strategies come to function as emblems of internet users' affiliation to anti-feminist networked communities or affinity spaces.

They begin their argument by noting that, while often people think about online harassment as a matter of individual behaviour, such behaviour is increasingly promoted and supported by an online collective of bloggers, YouTubers, political activists, anti-feminist gamers, commenters, and trolls which make up the 'Manosphere'. The Manosphere may not be a coherent 'community' in the traditional sense, but its members are held together by a common set of communicative resource and harassment techniques which they use to signal their affiliation with like-minded others and to spread their ideology through digital networks.

Marwick and Caplan proceed to give a number of examples of 'networked harassment', including organised campaigns of abuse, cyberbullying, hacking, and other threatening behaviour against well-known women, especially queer women and women of colour. Among the most prominent cases they mention is a harassment campaign that began in 2014 against women game developers and media critics who sought to address sexist representations of women in video games conducted through the use of the hashtag #gamergate on platforms such as 4chan, Reddit, and Twitter. They quote Anita Sarkeesian, one of the women targeted in the campaign with death threats, slurs, and sexually violent language, talking about the collective nature of such harassment:

We don't usually think of online harassment as a social activity, but we do know from the strategies and tactics that they used that they were not working alone, that they were actually loosely coordinating with one another. The social component is a powerful motivating factor that works to provide incentives for perpetrators to participate and to actually escalate the attacks by earning the praise and approval of their peers.

(TEDx Talks 2012)

The main point that Marwick and Caplan make in their argument is that such collective harassment is made possible by the circulation of communicative resources such as hashtags, catchphrases, and memes that circulate quickly through subcultural online spaces where participants use them to frame feminists as 'villains' and themselves as 'victims'. In order to illustrate this, they trace the online circulation of the word *misandry* across three historical periods: 1990s Usenet newsgroups, early blog culture in the late 1990s and early 2000s, and social media and online press in the 2010s.

Misandry is defined as the 'dislike of, contempt for, or ingrained prejudice against men (i.e., the male sex)', but as it circulated over time through digital networks it came to be used as a synonym for feminism, creating a false equivalence between discrimination against men and discrimination against women.

Although the term *misandry* pre-dates the Internet, Marwick and Caplan show how the rise of digital networks from early Usenet groups to more recent social media spaces introduced affordances for the term to gain popularity and legitimacy, serving as a call-to-action for men who agreed with the characterisation of feminism as 'man-hating'. Most important is the way the term operated as a resource to link together disparate parts of the Internet where people with anti-feminist ideologies congregated and to facilitate the development of the kind of collective harassment strategies mentioned above.

At the same time, Marwick and Caplan show how digital networks can also facilitate *resistance* to such ideologies, noting how feminists appropriated the idea of *misandry* to create humorous memes such as the 'I drink male tears' campaign where women circulated pictures of themselves drinking from coffee cups with the words 'MALE TEARS' printed on them,[3] illustrating the processes of resemiotisation, recombination, and recontextualisation that we discussed above.

Project Ideas

1. Collect a sample of data from a social media site and identify the different communicative resources they are using (i.e., different codes, registers, genres, as well as graphic elements such as emojis and animated GIFs). Analyse how people are using these resources to index aspects of their social identity as well as to manage their communication with different kinds of audiences.

2. Collect examples of memes constructed around a common image or a common catchphrase. Examine how creators of these memes use

---

3 https://knowyourmeme.com/memes/male-tears.

strategies of *recombination* and *recontextualisation*, and the ways these strategies result in reinforcing or altering the meaning of the original images or phrases. Do these memes promote particular attitudes or ideologies? Are they associated with particular social categories or membership in particular online collectives?

3. Collect a sample of data from a social media site of people commenting on or criticising other people's language. Analyse the way these comments work to promote or perpetuate particular language ideologies or to stigmatise or marginalise different groups of people.

4. Identify a specific online community, collective, or affinity space (such as participants in an online forum or Facebook page, players of a particular game, or commenters on a blog or YouTube channel) and try to identify a set of unique communicative resources (such as words, phrases, graphics, styles) that participants share. Think about how these resources function to reinforce their collective social identity.

5 Code Mixing, Crossing, and Translanguaging

PREVIEW

KEY TERMS

code mixing
code switching
conversation
analysis
crossing
double-voicing
linguistic purism
markedness model
metaphorical code
switching
translanguaging
situational code
switching
we-code/they-code

In Chapter 2 we saw that people often creatively use different kinds of resources to communicate different meanings at different times and with different people, and in Chapter 3 we considered different 'varieties' of language associated with different groups of people. In this chapter we will focus on people's practices of mixing together more than one 'language', 'dialect', or register when they communicate and some of the reasons for these practices. We will provide an overview of the different ways these practices of 'mixing resources' have been conceptualised in sociolinguistics, including code switching, crossing, and translanguaging. The focal topic for this chapter is language in education, where we will explore issues around mixing and switching linguistic resources in classrooms.

5.1 Introduction

At around lunchtime at the school complex Alter Postweg in Augsburg hundreds of pupils pour into the tram. A multilingual jumble of voices arises. What reaches my ears is not only German, Turkish, Greek, Russian and other languages, but I can also hear mixed conversations in German and Turkish, German and Greek, or German and Russian, in which languages are switched at breathtaking speed. I listen, amazed by the pupils' virtuosity, until my research interest takes me back to academic soberness, knowing that these adolescents' and kids' linguistic productions are hardly valued, and not at all respected, in the school classes they have just left. Monolingualism and German alone is what counts there. However, the conversations outside the official lessons' discourse literally do speak another language; one that is varied and diverse, mixed, polyphonic and multilingual. This 'language' is ignored and despised by majority society and by the official guardians of the language norm. It is not seen as the logical, and likewise antithetical, outcome of a development that has its roots in the history of recent migration (since the 1960s) and in the consequential emergence of polylingual, polycultural and multi-ethnic areas in many urban centres in Germany (and elsewhere). The linguistic result of this situation is what is nowadays called 'hybrid language'.

(Hinnenkamp 2003: 12–13)

In Chapter 1 we talked about the prevalent and powerful notions that (1) monolingualism is better than multilingualism and (2) there is only one 'standard' and 'correct' way of speaking or writing a particular 'language'. These ideas are not just found in people's everyday discourse, but also in official laws and policies governing things like immigration and education. We called these notions the *monolingual ideology* and the *standard language ideology*. Related to these ideologies is a third ideology that we can call the ideology of **linguistic purism**: the notion that 'languages' should only be used in their 'pure form' and that mixing together 'pieces' of different 'languages' results in 'deficient', 'corrupted', or 'distorted' texts or utterances.

The reality, however, is that, just as there are very few places that are purely monolingual, there are also hardly any examples of 'languages' that have managed to remain 'pure'. Most of the codes that we normally refer to as 'languages' such as English, French, and German, are the result of other 'languages' evolving and merging together, borrowing words from still other languages along the way (see Chapter 9). English, for example, evolved from a number of dialects spoken by Anglo-Saxons, who migrated to what is now the British Isles from what is now Germany, then later was heavily influenced by Old Norse, Latin, French, and Greek, and even today regularly incorporates new words borrowed from languages as different as Chinese and Arabic.

Just as 'languages' are mixtures of other languages, people often mix 'languages' together when they speak. This is especially true of people who are highly competent in more than one code or live in places where multiple 'languages' are spoken. Indeed, scenarios like the one in the example above are common features of everyday life in most places in the world. The facts that (1) 'languages' regularly mix with or borrow from other languages, and (2) in the everyday speech of real people, the boundaries between one 'language' and another are often blurred, show how untenable the ideology of linguistic purism really is and remind us why it is often necessary to use quotation marks when we write the word 'language'.

As people mix linguistic codes, varieties, and other resources they produce 'hybrid' ways of talking and writing. This behaviour is often referred to as **code mixing** or **code switching**. **Code mixing** usually refers to the mixing of linguistic units (e.g., morphemes, words, phrases, clauses) from different 'languages' within a sentence (intrasentential) while code switching usually refers to mixing across sentence boundaries (intersentential). Many linguists simply use the term 'code mixing' to refer to both intrasentential and intersentential mixing.

Consider, for instance, the examples below, which contain lexical items usually associated with English and Spanish:

(1) Do you remember **esta chica**?   (Intrasentential)
    'Do you remember **that girl**?'
(2) Yesterday I went to the shops. **Me compre una falda.** (Intersentential)
    'Yesterday I went to the shops. **I bought a skirt.**'

In the first example, linguistic units from English ('Do you remember') and Spanish ('esta chica') are mixed within the same sentence (intrasentential code mixing). The second example is an instance of intersentential code mixing or 'code switching' because one clause is in English ('Yesterday I went to the shops') followed by a separate clause in Spanish ('Me compre una falda').

Of course, distinctions like this are based on the assumption that English and Spanish are two clearly separate 'languages' and that when people switch, they are always conscious that they are drawing on two distinct codes. These are assumptions that many contemporary sociolinguists have begun to question (see below). Nevertheless, these assumptions have dominated work on linguistic hybridity for a long time, and some of the analytical frameworks that have been built on these assumptions can still be very useful in helping us to understand how and why people mix different resources when they communicate.

Even the acknowledgement that such hybridity exists and that it is something worth studying is a fairly new development. Until the 1970s most linguists regarded this phenomenon as language 'interference' – one language interfering with a person's ability to express themselves in another language – and took it as evidence of some kind of deficit or impediment on the part of speakers. People who mixed different codes were often labelled 'lazy', 'uneducated', or 'confused', unable to form 'correct' sentences or utterances in a given 'language'.

Carol Myers-Scotton (1993: 48), one of the most prominent scholars of code switching/mixing, reports:

[E]ven though I was doing fieldwork intermittently from 1964–1973 on language use in African multilingual communities, I never recognised [code switching] as a special phenomenon until 1972 ... Even when I myself observed language in use, as I often did, I managed to 'ignore' code switching.

This early reluctance to even recognise code switching/mixing as a legitimate communicative practice itself shows how powerful the influence of the ideology of linguistic purism has been, even among linguists.

Eventually, however, sociolinguists started to acknowledge that this kind of linguistic hybridity was not only common but also *purposeful*, and began to turn their attention to trying to understand why people did it. As we said in Chapter 2, whenever people choose particular resources from their communicative repertoires, they do so for a purpose – in order to make some kind of special meaning, to show themselves to be particular kinds of people, to manage their relationships, or to advance some kind of view of the world. Below we will describe some of the frameworks sociolinguists have developed over the years to understand how people *use* code mixing to achieve these different purposes.

5.2 Social Motivations for Code Mixing

One of the earliest studies of code mixing was conducted by linguistic anthropologists Jan-Petter Blom and John Gumperz, who explored the language practices of people living in Hemnesberget, a village in Northern Norway. Blom and Gumperz (1972) observed that in this village people frequently mixed two varieties: Ranamål, the local variety, which is associated with cultural and local identity in Hemnesberget, and Bokmål, the variety used across Norway in education, mass media, and official transactions. They noticed that people who lived in this village regularly and skilfully switched between these two varieties in everyday interactions. For example, a clerk and customer at a bank might use Ranamål to greet each other and talk about personal matters and then switch to Bokmål to conduct their financial transactions.

Based on their observations, Blom and Gumperz argued that there are two different reasons why people might switch from using one code to using a different one (intersentential code mixing or, as they called it, 'code switching'). The first had to do with a change in the situation – either the participants in a conversation change, or the topic changes, or what people are *doing* in the conversation changes. Gumperz (1982) labelled this **situational code switching**. The example we gave above of the bank clerk and the customer switching to Bokmål when they started to conduct 'official business' is an example of this – because they were engaging in a new 'more official' activity, they started using the 'language' usually associated with that activity. Another example would be when two colleagues who are chatting in Urdu are joined by a non-Urdu-speaking co-worker; the presence of this new participant might lead them to switch to English to include this person in their interaction.

The second reason people might switch to a different code is to make some kind of *social meaning*. They might want to show that they have a particular attitude towards the topic they are discussing or the people they are talking to, or they might want to *index* (see Chapter 2) some social group or set of ideas. Gumperz (1982) calls this **metaphorical code switching**. A teacher in an English-medium school in Hong Kong, for example, might switch to Cantonese to try to create a feeling of closeness with her students or to signal that she is angry with them.

Situational code switching is based on the idea that there are certain 'languages' that are 'appropriate' to certain situations. Metaphorical code switching is much less predictable, based on the particular kinds of meanings a speaker in a given situation might want to make, and so sometimes it involves switching to a 'language' that may not be considered the 'appropriate' or expected language in that situation.

Activity: Situational or Metaphorical Switching?

Read the examples below which contain instances of code switching. Using Gumperz's (1982) distinction, consider whether each is a case of situational or metaphorical code switching. In each case discuss the factors that may have triggered the switch.

1. A grandfather in Oberwart (Austria) is calling his two grandchildren to come and help him. He calls them twice in Hungarian, but they ignore him. Then he switches to German.
2. At a restaurant in central London two Italian friends look at the menu and discuss their food choices in English. They also speak to the waiter in English when they place their order. Then they switch to Italian to talk about their day.
3. In a bilingual family in Poland, a 5-year-old girl often switches between French and Polish. She uses French to speak to her French monolingual father but uses Polish to speak to her French-Polish bilingual mother.
4. In a business meeting in Scotland a salesperson uses RP to present a new local product to potential clients. But during the presentation Scottish-accented forms surface when he is emphasising the 'local' character of the product.

Another thing Gumperz noticed in his research both with Blom in Norway and later in other studies in places like India, Austria, and the

United States, was that multilingual people often associate the different codes and varieties they use with their feelings about the different social groups they belong to. Codes or varieties shared by particular ethnic groups, for example, might be used to signal one's affiliation with that group, and to express solidarity or intimacy in 'in-group interactions' (interactions involving members of the same group). Gumperz called these codes **we-codes**. At the same time, other linguistic varieties might be associated with other groups, or larger groups (like the 'nation') that, although people might belong to, they may not identify with as strongly as they do with local groups. Such codes might be more associated with formal contexts or with 'out-group interactions' (interactions with people who belong to a different group). Gumperz calls these **they-codes**. One example Gumperz (1982) gives is Spanish speakers in the US who consider Spanish as their ethnically specific in-group language (i.e., a we-code) and English as the out-group language of the majority population (i.e., a they-code). Depending on the situation, Spanish-English bilinguals might choose to use Spanish in order to invoke the values and identities associated with their in-group, even in cases where English is understood by all of those involved in the conversation. Another example is Cantonese speakers in the Chinese province of Guangdong, who are likely to use Cantonese with other Cantonese speakers even though Putonghua is the 'standard language' of the country and the 'language' used in school and for official functions. The important thing about this distinction, however, is not just that people are more likely to use we-codes and they-codes with certain people or in certain situations, but that they use these codes *strategically* to communicate something about their relationship with others, to create feelings of closeness or to distance themselves from them.

While the we-code/they-code distinction has been adopted by many sociolinguists to explore code switching in different communities around the world, others (e.g., Jørgensen 1998; Sebba & Wootton 1998) have been critical of it, pointing out that social identities are much more complicated than this distinction implies and that the kinds of social relationships associated with particular code choices can change from situation to situation and even within a particular interaction. Speaking Spanish in the US, for example, may not always be a matter of Latino identity; in fact, it could index a number of other identities related, for instance, to someone's gender, occupation, age, or the social role they are enacting (such as being a 'parent'), or signal particular kinds of activities like joking or flirting.

Other linguists have tried to confront these complexities by developing models that focus more closely on how people mix resources in particular situations and how their code choices work to alter those situations. One of these is the American linguist Carol Myers-Scotton, who conducted extensive work in Africa in the 1980s and 1990s. Myers-Scotton observed that in linguistically diverse places, like Kenya, for instance, where more than sixty different languages are used, people often switched between the local variety of their village or town, the inter-ethnic lingua franca of the wider area (e.g., Swahili), and other external languages like English. The we-code/they-code distinction in this context was simply inadequate to effectively explain why people chose a given code from among the multiple codes available to them in different situations.

In order to explain this, Myers-Scotton turned her focus to *social norms*. Norms are sets of expectations about what constitutes 'normal' behaviour. When it comes to communication, norms have to do with expectations about *what to say to whom, when, where, and how*, and so are closely related to Hymes's (1966) idea of *communicative competence* (see Introduction). Different speech situations have different norms associated with them in different societies and social groups. That's not to say that people always follow norms. Sometimes (quite often, in fact) they choose to go against norms, because doing something unexpected is *also* a way of communicating things to others. But norms, these sets of expectations, serve as the *backdrop* against which people make rational choices about what options to choose from their communicative repertoires.

Based on these ideas, Myers-Scotton (1993) introduced what is known as the **markedness model**. When people deploy resources from their repertoires in particular situations which conform to prevailing social norms associated with these situations, these are called **unmarked** choices. In other words, unmarked choices are 'normal' choices. When people make choices that go against the norms, that is, when they say things or speak in ways that are unexpected, these are called **marked** choices. Marked choices serve to signal that speakers are trying to make some kind of special meaning with the way they are speaking. The point that Myers-Scotton is making is that choices about what kind of resource to use in specific local situations take their meaning in part from the wider sociolinguistic *ecology* in which these local situations are embedded. People 'play with' the expectations others have about how they will talk in order to manage their interactional goals and their interpersonal relationships.

To understand how this works, consider the conversation below which took place in Western Kenya between a salaried worker, who is visiting his home village, and a farmer, who wants to borrow money from him. In this conversation, three codes are used: Lwidakho, which is the local language of the village, Swahili, which, along with English, is an 'official language' of Kenya and used as a lingua franca throughout East Africa, and English, which is associated in Kenya with educated elites. In the transcript *Swahili is in italics*, **English in bold** and Lwidakho in normal text.

1	FARMER:	As I live here, I have hunger.
2	WORKER:	(interrupting) *What kind of hunger?*
3	FARMER:	It wants to kill me here…
4	WORKER:	(interrupting again, with more force) *What kind of hunger?*
5	FARMER:	Our children… (said as an appeal to others as brothers)
6	WORKER:	*I ask you, what kind of hunger?*
7	FARMER:	Hunger for money; I don't have any.

8   WORKER: **You have got a land.**
9   WORKER: *You have land [farm].*
10   WORKER: You have land [farm].
11   FARMER: my brother. . .
12   WORKER: I don't have money. **Can't you see how I am heavily loaded?**

(Myers-Scotton 1993: 82–3)

In this example we can see how the two speakers negotiate their social relationship against the backdrop of social norms regarding language use. When the farmer approaches the worker to ask for money, he uses the local code, Lwidakho. This is an *unmarked* choice because both interlocutors share the same ethnic background and the conversation is taking place in a rural, informal context. However, the worker chooses codes not normally associated with this kind of situation – Swahili and English. In other words, his behaviour towards the farmer is *marked*. Of course, in different contexts these two codes could have been the unmarked choices (e.g., Swahili would be unmarked in inter-ethnic communication and English when used among educated elites). In this particular context, however, the choice of these codes carries a special social meaning; by declining the appeal to solidarity implied by the farmer's use of the local variety and instead using Swahili (which is used to talk to people from other places) and English (which is used to talk to people of socio-economic backgrounds different from the farmer's), the salaried worker creates *distance* between himself and the farmer, thereby communicating his reluctance to lend the farmer money.

Some people, however, have criticised the markedness model. They argue that people's choice of which code to use is not always the result of rational choices based on prevailing norms. Sometimes people might have different ideas about what the norms are, and sometimes what motivates code mixing has more to do with managing the contingencies of the conversation at hand than with a focus on social norms.

An alternative way of thinking about the motivations for code switching was proposed by the sociolinguist Peter Auer (1998). Auer argued that code switching may serve various functions in a given interaction, and a single switch may have numerous effects. He also challenged Gumperz's and Myers-Scotton's assumption that language use can always be explained in terms of larger societal and cultural norms. Instead, Auer applied insights from **conversation analysis** to focus on the role of the switches at the local, micro level of a given interaction.

Conversation analysts are mostly concerned with how people construct their turns in conversation based on what their interlocutor has said in the immediately preceding turn and what they want or expect them to say in the next turn. From this perspective, the analyst interested in code switching focuses on how the interaction develops *sequentially*, paying attention to turn-taking and 'adjacency pairs' (kinds of utterances that usually go together such as 'question–answer') and identifying *where* exactly in the turn or the sequence the code switching occurs. Auer explains that switches do not only carry specific social meanings, but also function as tools used by interlocutors to structure and manage their conversations.

This idea is illustrated in the example below, which is part of an informal conversation between young Spanish-German bilingual speakers (W: female; M: male) of South American origin in Hamburg. Spanish is represented in **bold** in this example.

1	W:	**qué hora es?**
		(what time is it?)
2		(2.0)
3	→	wie spat?
		(what time?)
4	M:	zwanzig nach elf
		'twenty past eleven'

(Altenberg 1992; cited in Auer 1998: 23)

Auer explains that in this example, code switching is used in order to organise the conversation. W asks M a question using Spanish. Instead of an answer, this question is followed by a long pause in line 2. In a second attempt in line 3, W repeats the part of the sequence that was not responded to in German (even though the other speaker also understands Spanish), which then elicits the required response. Auer (1984) explains that this is a *discourse-related code switch* because it allows W to 'repair' the turn which failed to elicit the expected response.

Sebba and Wootton (1998) adopted conversation analysis to analyse the linguistic practices of British-born people of Caribbean descent who use two distinct varieties of English: a variety of London English known as 'Cockney' and London Jamaican (a variety of Jamaican Creole). They found that shifting between Cockney and London Jamaican occurred frequently in the everyday speech of their informants. Switches were used for various functions; for example to change topic, check information, comment on how what was said should be interpreted, emphasise something they said, request information, and to repair conversational breakdowns.

The example below illustrates a switch from London Jamaican (in normal font) to Cockney (in bold). B, M, and L are playing a game, where they slam down a domino on the table and call out a word. In line 1, B sets the jocular tone of the interaction by commenting at the beginning of her turn and then laughing. London Jamaican is used during the game up until line 3, where B cannot remember the word called out by the other player. At this point she switches to London English ('what did you say again … what did you say?'). The function of the switch here is to elicit or check information, to enable B to complete her turn.

1	B:	'ear 'im now no! he he
		(you) slap down 'im say ['pin' (0.8) 'im slap down 'im say 'nee[dle
2	M:	[(pin) ha ha ha [ha ha ha
3	B:	'im slap down i **what did you say agai[n**? (0.6)

```
4   M:                                          [eh ha ha ha ha
5   B:   (0.8) what did you say?
6   L:   Crablouse
```

(Sebba & Wootton 1998: 468)

On other occasions, the switch was from London English to London Jamaican. Sebba and Wootton report that instances of this kind of switch were more prominent in their data. In the example below, B and her friends are discussing the length of time it takes to get over a relationship once it's ended. The central theme of the conversation is time; in other words the length of time between relationships. The reference to time in B's turn in line 2 is realised through a switch to London Jamaican. According to Sebba and Wootton, the function of the switch in this case was to 'upgrade' or highlight an important part of the conversation.

```
1   J:   I mean it does take a time ge??in' to kn- find the right person
2   B:   Le? me tell you now, wiv every guy I've been out wiv, it's been a?-
         a whole heap o' mont's before I move with the next one
3   J:   NEXT one, year!
         (1.8)
4   J:   Look how long it's been with me though Brenda
```

(Sebba & Wootton 1998: 475)

Conversation analysis is valuable as it helps us understand the way switches from one code to another function at the local level of a given interaction. At the same time, some sociolinguists are sceptical of this micro-analytical approach, arguing that it might not fully account for the different kinds of *social meanings* that may be associated with code mixing.

5.3 Crossing

The examples discussed above all illustrate the language practices of people who habitually mix codes that they have fairly high competence in, either because they have been raised in multilingual environments or because they have moved to areas where learning additional codes was a necessity. There are also situations, however, where people mix codes in which they have limited competence, in effect, appropriating words or phrases from 'other people's' languages and inserting them into their own.

The British sociolinguist Ben Rampton (1995: 280) calls this practice **crossing**, which he defines as 'code alternation by people who are not accepted members of the group associated with the second language they employ. It is concerned with switching into languages that are not generally thought to belong to you.' Because all of us have *some* competence in a variety of codes (see Chapter 2), crossing is not a particularly unusual phenomenon. Sometimes it has instrumental functions – we might, for example, use phrases in a language we have limited competence in to make ourselves understood when visiting other countries. Often, however, crossing is used to create social meanings, to enact particular identities (see Chapter 6), or to manage our relationships with others.

These more social and strategic functions of crossing were the focus of Rampton's (1995, 1998) ethnographic study of the language practices of multi-ethnic groups of teenagers in London, which included speakers of Indian, Pakistani, Afro-Caribbean, and Anglo descent. In his observations of these teenagers' interactions, Rampton noticed that they frequently adopted the codes and speaking styles of other ethnicities – Indian kids and white kids, for instance, using phrases from Jamaican Creole, and white kids and Afro-Caribbean kids appropriating Panjabi words or adopting accents associated with South Asian English.

Rampton explains that the meaning and social function of crossing is not always straightforward, and it can vary depending on different contexts and people's communicative purposes. In Chapter 2 we referred to the Russian literary critic Mikhail Bakhtin, who said that whenever we use language we are always drawing on and mixing together different 'voices'. But when we do this, we also *position* ourselves in relation to these voices in different ways, a phenomenon Bakhtin refers to as **double-voicing**. Sometimes we appropriate someone else's 'voice' in order to mock, criticise, or distance ourselves from the person whose 'voice' is being appropriated. At other times we may take up someone else's 'voice' in order to affiliate ourselves with the person or people whose 'voice' we are using.

The example below is from Rampton's ethnographic work in London. While Rich (Anglo, male, 15), Ian (Anglo, male, 15), and some other boys were queuing for dinner, they noticed a pupil of Bangladeshi descent breaking the rules and trying to push in. Ian is trying to get the teachers' attention to complain. In lines 7 and 9–11 we see that some of the other boys are using Stylised Asian English (represented in **bold**) to directly address the intruders and urge them to leave. It seems that crossing in this exchange is used to manage conflict as the boys criticise and scold the intruders appropriating the code associated with their ethnicity.

1	IAN:	EH ( ) EM MISS (.) WHERE THEY GOING (.)
2	RICH:	MISS THEY'VE PUSHED IN
3	IAN:	OI (.) LOOK Baker ((a 6th former)) THESE LOT PUSHED IN
4		(.) THEY JUST (OUR DINNER) THEY (BOUGHT IT) (.)
5		GET BACK TO THE BACK
6	RICH:	GED OU'
7	ANON A:	((in exaggerated Asian English)) **OUT:**
8	RICH:	GED OU'
9	ANON A:	((slowly in Stylised Asian English)) **GE:T OU:T**
10	ANON B:	((slow)) **OUT BOY OUT**
11	ANON A:	((slow)) **GE:T OU:T**
12	RICH:	(those others) pushed in

(Rampton 1995: 143)

But crossing can also be used to affiliate oneself with the group from whom a particular way of speaking was borrowed. The sociolinguist Cecilia Cutler (1999), for example, describes the linguistic practices of a white middle-class teenager, who used a number of stylistic elements (pronunciation and slang) associated with African American English in order to align with the urban, streetwise identity he linked to people who spoke this way.

On other occasions, crossing might be influenced by wider social conditions. The example below comes from a study by Dirim and Hieronymus (2003), who explored language use in linguistically mixed adolescent groups in Hamburg (Germany). In particular, they focused on the use of Turkish by non-Turkish youth. The example involves three adolescent girls from different ethnic backgrounds who live in Hamburg. Maike (19 years old) is German, Tanja (17 years old) is Libyan-German, and Aischa (20 years old) is Afghan. None of them has a Turkish background. The conversation took place while Maike visited Tanja. During this visit Aischa phones to say that she is coming as well. Shortly afterwards the doorbell rings. In this example, German is represented in normal font and Turkish is in **bold**.

1	MAIKE:	Tür geklingelt Tanja
		The doorbell rang, Tanja.
2	TANJA:	warte mal das ist Aischa
		Wait a second, that's Aischa.
3	MAIKE:	ja schon so früh? Korrekt
		Really, so early? Yes.
4	TANJA:	**ha Aischa meraba kızım**
		Hello, my dear
5	AISCHA:	**naber kız**
		What's up, girl?
6	TANYA:	**iyi misin**
		How are you?
7	AISCHA:	**iyim**
		I'm fine.

(Dirim & Hieronymus 2003: 52–3)

Here we can see that although none of the three girls comes from a Turkish background, Tanja greets Aischa in Turkish. This choice might initially seem odd, but it can be understood within the context of the migration history of Hamburg. Hamburg is an urban city that has experienced increased migration from various parts of the world and especially from Turkey. Through the years, Turkish has become a well-established language in this city. As young people from different ethnic backgrounds socialise together, different linguistic resources find their way into their linguistic repertoire. Without necessarily gaining full competence in these other languages, these young people have taken to using some words and phrases from them with their peers. These creative language alternations function as identity-marking tools which enable these inner-city young people to integrate, manage their relationships, negotiate identities, and index belongingness.

5.4 'Languaging' and 'Translanguaging'

More recent perspectives on how and why people mix codes when they talk have attempted to go beyond the frameworks of 'code mixing', 'code switching', and 'crossing' that we described above. They criticise these frameworks for being too narrow, for focusing too much on the 'conscious' and 'rational' dimensions of hybridity at the expense of its more creative and intuitive dimensions, and, most of all, for being 'stuck' in a view of language that sees 'languages' as discrete entities separated by clear boundaries. In many ways, these new perspectives reflect the fact that people's communicative repertoires are themselves becoming more diverse as they interact in more *superdiverse* societies (see Chapter 9), and for many people, mixing bits and pieces of different 'languages' has simply become their 'normal' way of communicating. Several different terms have been used to describe this phenomenon, including '**translanguaging**', 'polylingual languaging' (Jørgensen 2008), 'code meshing' (Canagarajah 2011, see below), and 'metrolingualism' (Pennycook & Otsuji 2015). Underlying all of these terms is the idea of *languaging*, a concept originally introduced by the applied linguist Merrill Swain (2006) to capture the creative and dynamic dimensions of communication in which people do not just 'use' language, but also *create* language as they interact with others in real-world situations.

The most popular way to talk about linguistic hybridity nowadays, at least in educational circles, is with the term *translanguaging*, which Li Wei (2018: 9) defines as the 'fluid and dynamic practices that many people engage in when they communicate that *transcend* the boundaries between named languages, language varieties, and language and other semiotic systems'. This conception is very different from the idea of code switching, which applied linguist Ofelia García compares to the language function on a smartphone which allows people to choose either one language or another. In reality, García says, often when bilingual and multilingual people communicate they are not 'switching' between one language and another but rather selecting features from their *entire* linguistic and semiotic repertoires, creating new, original, and complex constructions that cannot be assigned to one or another 'language' (García & Li Wei 2014).

The most important thing about this approach is that it emphasises the *transformative* nature of hybridity – the fact that, by mixing resources from different social contexts together, translanguagers are able to create *new* social spaces and new opportunities for making meaning and enacting social identities. 'Translanguaging creates a social space for the language user,' says Li Wei (2018: 23), 'by bringing together different dimensions of their personal history, experience, and environment; their attitude, belief, and ideology; their cognitive and physical capacity, into one coordinated and meaningful performance, and this *Translanguaging Space* has its own

FIGURE 5.1
Translanguaging on
WhatsApp

transformative power because it is forever evolving and combines and generates new identities, values and practices.'

The WhatsApp interaction in Figure 5.1 illustrates how people work together, drawing upon a range of different resources, to create these unique social spaces.

The exchange is between three Greek-Cypriot friends, Zoe, Chloe, and Tina, who have known one another for many years. Chloe initiates the interaction in lines 1 and 2 by saying that she misses her two friends and that going out for a drink with two other friends was not as fulfilling and fun. She then asks Zoe and Tina to bring some needed 'crazynesss' (sic) to her life. In lines 3–7, Zoe and Tina try to lift Chloe's spirits by mocking her other 'boring' friends and then start to make plans to see Chloe and 'save her sanity'. A closer look at this exchange shows that the three friends seem to cobble together 'pieces' of different codes, namely Cypriot Greek (bold) and (sometimes unconventional) English (normal font). In using Greek, to avoid switching to the Greek keyboard, they use Roman characters. They also combine their text with other resources such as emojis, unconventional punctuation, abbreviations, and creative spellings. This allows the friends to create a humorous ('crazy') tone in their interaction and express solidarity with one another.

Depending on the social media platform, additional modes and resources might be available to people. The post in Figure 5.2 was shared on Facebook by Souma, a young Algerian female who studies food sciences

FIGURE 5.2
Translanguaging on Facebook
(Abdelhamid 2020: 112)

at the Institut National de l'Alimentation, la Nutrition et des Technologies Agro-Alimentaires (INATTA) in Algeria. Souma has competence in both Algerian Arabic and French. She shared an image of a text written in Algerian Arabic which translates to: 'why there is no module called food where we could learn, for example, about food from other countries, and in exams they could bring us dishes to taste and say which country the dish belongs to. We would all pass.'

In her comment which accompanies this image, Souma combines elements from French (bold) and Algerian Arabic (normal font). She writes Algerian Arabic in Roman characters instead of using the conventional Arabic script and also incorporates emojis into her text:

Normalement haka n9raw f **l'INATAA** 😵 mch **zoologique** w **math** w lkhorti 😭

😠 😠

(*Normally* this is what we study in *INATAA*. not zoology and **maths** and the nonsense)

Abdelhamid (2020) explains that by using all these different resources for the production of this post, Souma is able to do various things. Firstly, through French she can project her identity as a student, as this is the language used in the domain of education in Algeria. At the same time, Algerian Arabic allows her to step back from her student identity to express her dissatisfaction with what is delivered in her classes. The use of emojis allows her to express these emotions in a humorous, non-threatening way and to show her identity as a young, hip user of social media. All these linguistic and semiotic resources are creatively combined together in this post to express Souma's feelings, to manage her relationship with both her friends and the institution she attends, and to perform her complex, hybrid identity.

As we've seen in this section, translanguaging is a dynamic practice that enables people to use multiple elements, resources, and modes from their repertoires to create meaning, transmit information, manage relationships, and perform identities. But translanguaging is also a practice that challenges and transforms dominant language ideologies. As we will see in this chapter's focal topic, in many multilingual educational contexts, such practices of mixing are often viewed negatively. This is mostly because of the ideologies of monolingualism, standardness, and linguistic purism that characterise most language and education policies. But many sociolinguists now agree that translanguaging can be beneficial in the classroom, not only because it encourages students to use the full range of their repertoires to communicate, but also because it empowers them to treat their 'natural' ways of communicating as 'normal' and valid.

Activity: Analysing Translanguaging in the Classroom

The concept of translanguaging actually originated in the field of bilingual education and pedagogy, and many scholars who have explored language use in multilingual schools have noted the ways teachers and students often combine different linguistic resources in such settings to facilitate learning. There are those, however, who oppose such practices, arguing that using too many different languages in language classrooms might 'confuse' students and take time away from giving them as much input in the target language as possible. The exchange below is from an English reading class in Singapore. Most children in the class come from Malay families, but some speak Chinese or Tamil at home. Read the exchange and discuss whether or not you think the use of different languages facilitates or hinders teaching and learning. MDMY = Madam Y (teacher, Malay); s = Student

1	MDMY:	I'm going to ask this: Can you remember what do we mean by the 'home so snug'? Yes?
2	MDMY:	No I said what do we mean by the 'home so snug'?
3	MDMY:	What does that mean?
4	MDMY:	Share? What do we mean by home so snug?
5	S4:	So hot? So hot.
6	MDMY:	Do we mean that when I say 'a home so snug' am I talking about the home is very hot, you don't want to live in the home? Or am I talking about in the home it is so comfortable that you would want to stay inside the home?
7	MDMY:	So which is it? Don't want to stay in the home or want to stay in the home?
8	S2:	Stay.
9	MDMY:	Want to stay. So what is the word that we can use in your mother tongue to say that the home is comfortable?
10	S3:	*Rumah. (house/home)*
11	MDMY:	*Rumah. Rumah yang apa?* Home is *rumah* yes correct, very good. But *rumah yang apa? (Which house?)*

12	S2:	(Inaudible)
13	MDMY:	*Rumah yang? (That house?)*
14	S2:	(Inaudible)
15	MDMY:	Again. *Rumah yang tak selesa atau rumah yang selesa?* *(Uncomfortable home or comfortable home?)*
16	S2:	*Selesa. (Comfortable)*
17	MDMY:	*Rumah yang selesa.* Then for the Mandarin if your home is very comfortable how do you say it?

(Vaish 2019: 284)

5.5 Focal Topic: Language Policies and Language Use in Classrooms

The focal topic of this chapter is the tension that sometimes exists between language policies and actual language practices in educational settings. As we have seen in this chapter, multilingual speakers routinely draw upon and mix the different resources they have in their communicative repertoires for all sorts of different reasons. While this behaviour is common in everyday communication, in classrooms, this kind of mixing is often considered unacceptable and discouraged by teachers and, in many cases, even prohibited by official policies which promote the use of one language as a medium of instruction. In such contexts, teachers who allow their pupils to mix different codes in the classroom, what Probyn (2009: 123) calls 'smuggling the vernacular into the classroom', are often accused of sabotaging students' learning.

What these ideologies and policies fail to recognise is that people who have a wider range of linguistic resources are not poorer language users. In fact, their more diverse repertoires can actually facilitate learning. But in classrooms, these resources are rarely acknowledged, and this creates tensions and conflicts between everyday flexible multilingual practices and top-down educational policies.

For many students, the problem with the imposition of a single, dominant code as the medium of instruction is not just that they are prohibited from engaging in practices of translanguaging that are natural to them, but that they are *required* to engage in a different kind of 'code switching', that is, they are required to switch to a code that is very different from what they use in their daily lives and which they may have less access to and mastery over than other students who come from backgrounds where the dominant code is also used at home. In this case, 'code switching' is not a matter of linguistic hybridity but an imposition of linguistic purism, a matter of forcing people to adopt entirely different codes when they enter different situations.

This fact reminds us that people's decisions about which resources to use and how to mix them are often not entirely theirs. They are constrained by policies and expectations about how they are supposed to talk in different situations as well as by the different values assigned to different resources and different ways of using them by the societies in which they live. For some people, the resources that they develop at home or that they use among their friends are also highly valued in school or at work. For others, however, the resources they develop at home and with their friends are devalued in more formal situations such as classrooms, workplaces, and interactions with authority figures such as police officers. For them, whether or not to 'code switch' is usually not a choice. It's an obligation. While it is an obligation that many people manage to meet, there are often serious consequences for those who fail to meet it. At the same time, there are also consequences for those who are successful at switching to the dominant code since they don't have the privilege of using resources that they might consider more 'authentic' for them at school and work, and every time they adopt the dominant code they may feel that they are actually helping to perpetuate the stigmatisation of their own 'natural' way of speaking.

The first article we will summarise in this section is by the American linguist Vershawn Ashanti Young. In it he makes an argument against requiring African American children to avoid using the resources that they use at home in their school assignments and instead stick to 'Standard English'. He insists that making such students engage in this kind of 'code switching' when they move from home to school can disadvantage them, and he suggests that teachers encourage what he calls 'code meshing' (a practice more akin to translanguaging), which would allow students to use a wider range of resources from their communicative repertoires in school.

In the second article Margie Probyn explores the use of translingual pedagogies to teach science in South Africa, where the majority of the pupils speak local indigenous African languages but the language of instruction is English. Probyn believes that the imposition of an 'English-only' pedagogy has a negative effect on pupils' academic achievement. She also argues that enabling teachers and students to use *all* of the resources they have available to them may help students and teachers to break free of the post-colonial monolingual ideologies prevalent in classrooms and give students the chance to develop and celebrate their particular cultural identities.

Young, V. S. (2009) 'Nah we straight': An argument against code switching. *JAC*, 29(1–2), 49–71   In this article Young presents a detailed critique of the practice of encouraging African American students to 'code switch' in school. By 'code switching', he is primarily referring to the 'necessity' for African Americans to adopt the ways of speaking favoured by the majority white population. Although, as we have seen in this chapter, switching from one linguistic variety to another in different situations is something normal that everybody does, Young's argument highlights the fact that code switching often involves different ways of speaking that are valued differently, and so when people are 'forced' to switch to a more highly valued code in order to fit in, it makes sense to investigate why one code is valued over another and what the consequences of this might be on people's status and power in society.

Young begins his article by musing about the media attention that often accompanied President Barack Obama's occasional use of African American Vernacular English (AAVE) in public, noting that the fact that this was seen as something to remark on illustrates the fundamental unfairness of the linguistic marketplace when it comes to black Americans. While Obama's ability to use 'Standard English' with a high degree of competence, and his avoidance of AAVE on the campaign trail and in official appearances may have helped him to win the presidency, the fact that he *had to* code switch is the problem.

Many mainstream educators in the US, Young notes, regard teaching African American children to adopt 'Standard English' while at school as good practice, a way of helping minority students 'transition' from 'home grammar' to 'school grammar' (Wheeler & Swords 2006). 'Code switching', they insist, has nothing to do with race. Young disagrees. He argues that teaching children that their variety of English is unacceptable in school reinforces racial inequality and gives teachers – and, later, employers – an excuse to discriminate against African Americans. Making speakers of AAVE switch to 'Standard English' in school implicitly requires them to acknowledge the 'superiority' of this code and of those who speak it.

Young is especially critical of the 'separate but equal' argument many educators make regarding 'code switching' and their contention that keeping the home variety separate from the school variety does not mean that one is more highly valued than the other; both are 'equal' in their respective settings. This is the same argument, Young points out, that people used to support the racial segregation of schools in the US before that policy was struck down by the Supreme Court in 1954. Forcing students to use one code at school while they use another at home, he argues, results in what the sociologist W. B. Du Bois (1994) calls 'double consciousness'. 'The doubling of one's racial self-consciousness is produced,' Du Bois writes, 'from having to always look at one's self through the eyes of others.'

Young suggests an alternative to this kind of monolingual 'code switching', which he calls *code meshing,* the practice of allowing students to increase the expressive potential of their speech and writing by combining different resources. 'Unlike code switching,' he writes, 'code meshing does not require students to "hold back their Englishes" but permits them to bring them more forcefully and strategically forward.' The focus for schools, he says, should be less on teaching the grammar of the 'standard' variety and more on increasing students' rhetorical skills, something that can be achieved by encouraging them to creatively combine resources rather than 'translate' from one to another. Code meshing not only allows students to enhance their written and spoken expression with resources that they bring from home, but also has the potential to promote real diversity in education and in the society at large, expanding people's ability to understand and appreciate linguistic difference.

Probyn, M. (2019) Pedagogical translanguaging and the construction of science knowledge in a multilingual South African classroom: Challenging monoglossic/post-colonial orthodoxies. *Classroom Discourse*, 10(3–4), 216–36   In this article Margie Probyn explores languaging practices in South African multilingual classrooms, where, she argues, the dominance of English over local African languages may have a negative impact on learning. South Africa, as we mentioned in Chapter 1, has eleven official languages: two colonial languages (Afrikaans and English) and nine indigenous African languages. But English, which is spoken by only 10 per cent of the population, continues to dominate in the political, economic, and educational domains. Despite post-apartheid language policies which aim to uphold principles of equality, access, and social justice in education, the historic linguistic inequalities in South Africa persist.

One of the main challenges within the educational system in South Africa is that there is a wide gap between the achievement of a minority of white middle-class learners who attend well-resourced schools and that of the majority of learners who come from working-class and poor families and attend historically black township and rural schools. The latter, who comprise 80 per cent of the school population, speak predominantly indigenous African languages at home and have little exposure to or knowledge of English. However, when they go to school, the medium of instruction as well as of the examinations is English. This means that these children learn through a medium they do not fully comprehend, which creates barriers to their learning and often results in poor academic performance.

Probyn explains that English-medium educational politics in South Africa originated from the colonial ideology of linguistic hierarchies, where English was valued more than the local indigenous languages. This ideology promoted the supposed superiority of colonial languages over indigenous ones as well as ideas of linguistic and racial purity and superiority. Over time these ideas became normalised and are therefore difficult to change.

In this study, Probyn investigated 'languaging' in eight township and rural schools on the Eastern Cape, one of the poorest provinces in South Africa. The schools she visited lacked the kinds of resources found in middle-class schools; only 3 per cent had stocked libraries and 2 per cent had stocked laboratories, 20 per cent had no electricity, and 19 per cent had no water. Many of these schools had no toilets. In most cases, teachers and learners shared a common home language, isiXhosa, but the official medium of instruction was English. The data for the project consisted of videotapes of science classes in each of the eight schools.

Out of the eight teachers Probyn observed, one (Teacher B) was unique in his willingness to encourage translanguaging in his classroom. He used isiXhosa 53 per cent of the time, compared to the other seven teachers, who used it only between 0 and 13 per cent of the time. Teacher B regarded the students' home language as an important resource for meaning-making, and translanguaging as a practice that would enable them to better understand the content of the science lesson. He used flexible practices according to the learners' needs. For instance, he would elicit a concept in isiXhosa and then ask the students to say it in English, and when learners were struggling to say something in English, he would encourage them to use isiXhosa instead.

Compared to the other teachers, Teacher B was able to get his students to exploit the different resources available to them to construct knowledge. Probyn argues that the translanguaging pedagogical programme adopted by Teacher B, rather than constraining their ability to learn by imposing a monolingual medium of instruction, actually helped students engage more actively in the learning process and to develop self-confidence.

Project Ideas

1. Investigate code switching/mixing in an interaction that involves bilingual/multilingual people. You may record and transcribe a bilingual/multilingual conversation or find data from readily available sources, e.g., TV, radio, YouTube. Clearly indicate instances of switches in your data. Analyse the switches using one of the approaches outlined in this chapter, aiming to identify the social motivations for the switches.

2. Conduct an interview with a bilingual or a multilingual person that you know. Ask them under which circumstances they use different codes. Ask them if they were allowed to use all their languages at school and if yes, under what circumstances. If they have children, find out whether they have chosen to raise them multilingual or monolingual and why.

3. Over the last decade, we have seen the emergence of 'social media influencers'. These are people who create a reputation for themselves based on their knowledge or expertise. Identify an influencer who you think mixes different linguistic and semiotic resources in their posts. Collect five posts and, using ideas you learned in this chapter, analyse the influencer's communicative practices and how they use them to orient to their audiences and construct certain kinds of social identities.

4. Code mixing, crossing, and translanguaging are common phenomena in popular music. The sociolinguist Jamie Shinhee Lee (2011) for instance, has examined the use of AAVE features in Korean Hip-Hop (a practice that is called 'Blinglish') (see Chapter 9), while Luanga Adrien Kasanga (2019) has looked at code mixing in popular music in the Democratic Republic of the Congo, focusing on the mixing of English in Lingala lyrics. Identify other singers or performers (stand-up comedians, actors, etc.) who mix codes or adopt codes from speakers from different backgrounds and consider the reasons why they do this.

CHAPTER

6 Style and Identity

PREVIEW

KEY TERMS

audience design

auditor effect

authenticity

bricolage

Communication
Accommodation Theory

contextualisation

convergence

divergence

identification

performativity

referee

style

styling

stylisation

In this chapter we will talk about how people use language and other communicative resources to show themselves to be 'certain kinds of people'. We begin by discussing the notion of *identity*, arguing that people don't just have one identity, but rather perform different identities in different situations by adopting different styles of speech and behaviour. We will then review the different ways sociolinguists have understood *style*, from perspectives which focus on how people adopt certain styles to fit the people they are talking to, to perspectives which focus on how people actively 'style' their identities in order to align to certain groups or to strategically manage different social situations. The focal topic features a discussion of how people use communicative resources to manage gender and sexual identities.

6.1 Introduction

Back in 2010, Facebook founder and CEO Mark Zuckerberg famously said, 'You have one identity. The days of you having a different image for your work friends or co-workers and for the other people you know are probably coming to an end pretty quickly.' He even went so far as to say that 'having two identities for yourself is an example of a lack of integrity' (Kirkpatrick 2011: 199). What Zuckerberg was really arguing for in this quote was that people should feel comfortable using his platform, which is designed to encourage people to communicate simultaneously to multiple audiences consisting of their friends, acquaintances, co-workers, and family members. But anybody who has been embarrassed when people see things on their social media feed that were not intended for them or gotten in trouble at work for showing a part of themselves online that they normally wouldn't bring to the office knows that there is something deeply flawed about Zuckerberg's philosophy.

The fact is, you *don't* just have one identity. You *do* have a different image for your parents, your boss, your lover, and different groups of friends. There are, of course, lots of things about you that are the same across all of these relationships. But there are lots of things that are different. You might do different things with different people, discuss different topics, dress differently, act differently, and talk differently. There is nothing wrong or dishonest about this. It's normal. What would be strange is if you acted the same way towards everyone, if you, for example, talked the same way to your boss as you do to your lover.

Over sixty years ago the famous American sociologist Erving Goffman compared social life to a performance. The self, he said (1959: 244) is 'not an organic thing ... whose fundamental fate is to be born, to mature, and to die'. Rather, it is 'a performed character', 'a dramatic effect arising diffusely from a scene that is presented'. We go through our lives, playing different kinds of characters in different situations. Sometimes our performances are successful, that is, others take us to be the kinds of people we are trying to show ourselves to be, and sometimes they are less successful.

In order to 'pull off' these performances, Goffman says we make use of various kinds of 'expressive equipment' available to us in our social environments, such as clothing, props, and the décor of our homes or workplaces. But the most important kinds of equipment we have for performing social identities are the *resources* we have in our communicative repertoires, which include different ways of talking (codes, registers, and genres) as well as different ways of dressing, adorning ourselves, gesturing, and handling different kinds of objects. As we said in Chapter 2, whenever we use a particular kind of word (e.g., 'stoked' vs. 'enthusiastic') or speak in a particular kind of accent (such as a 'Geordie' accent), we are signalling to others something about what kind of person we want them to take us to be.

In sociolinguistics, the different ways individuals talk in different situations to enact different identities is called **style**, and the act of picking and choosing resources from our communicative repertoires in order to do this is called **styling**. Penny Eckert (2004), who studied the linguistic styles of different groups at Belten High School, defines style as a person's linguistic performance and a continuous construction of a *persona* (or *character*). In Chapter 3 when we were talking about Eckert's work we were mostly interested in *inter-speaker variation*: the different ways different kinds of people talk. When it comes to *style*, we are mostly interested in *intra-speaker variation*, the different ways particular people might talk in different situations.

Usually when we think of style, we think of styles of clothing or hairstyles, the ways people decorate their bodies to show something about their personalities, to align with different trends, to 'fit in' with their friends, or to stand out in a crowd. Sociolinguistic style is not so different. In fact, many people have used the metaphor of fashion to talk about linguistic style. The sociolinguist Nik Coupland notes that one way to think about a person's communicative repertoire is 'like a closet containing a specified number of clothing items'.

In this conception, speakers select items from their individual clothing (or speech) repertoires. They do this either to match particular situations they find themselves in ... (dressing 'to fit in'), or to deviate to some extent from normative expectations ... (dressing 'to be different').

(2007: 82–3)

Although, as Coupland points out, this metaphor is in some ways an oversimplification, it does provide a useful way to think about what we do when we use language and other semiotic resources to style our identities. Penny Eckert uses a similar analogy when she compares linguistic styling to making particular kinds of fashion choices:

Small stylistic moves, such as the addition of a Mickey Mouse watch to a business ensemble, can tweak an already-existing style and the persona that it presents – in this case perhaps inserting a zest of playfulness. The tweaking, however, is not just about the tweaker, but adjusts the social world around the tweaker. Perhaps the businesswoman wearing a Mickey Mouse watch to a meeting wishes to convey a certain amount of liveliness and independence – not just for the fun of it, but more likely in order to distinguish herself from those that she sees as stodgy and uninteresting. And the nature of this stodginess is specific to the community in which she wears business clothing – it is probably not aimed at her boorish grandfather, but at her colleagues' office or business practices. And with this stylistic act, she puts the distinction on the table for all to see.

(2004: 2)

There are a few important points about style that we can take from Eckert's example. The first is that style is not a matter of the indexical meaning of a single resource (such as the pronunciation of a particular vowel, a particular grammatical feature, or, in this case, a particular fashion accessory) but rather, how that resource is *mixed* with other resources. Eckert says that stylistic practice 'involves a process of **bricolage** by which people combine a range of existing resources to construct new meanings or new twists on old meanings' (2004: 2). The meaning of resources depends as much on how they are combined with other resources as it does their more general social meaning. A Mickey Mouse watch has a different meaning when worn with a business suit than it does when worn with jeans and a tee-shirt.

Another important point about style that we can take from Eckert's example is that style is never entirely individual. Style depends on the *social meanings* that different resources have. Certain kinds of resources are associated with or 'point to' certain kinds of people and certain kinds of social situations. Without some agreement about these social meanings, it would be difficult to make the right stylistic choices. By the same token, we can also say that *identity* is also never entirely individual; we depend upon a range of social expectations, and even 'off the rack' identities in order to perform our individual identities.

Some people, in fact, see identity less as a matter of individual uniqueness and more as a matter of **identification**: the way in which we 'identify with' or distance ourselves from particular social groups and particular 'off the rack' identities. This is the view taken by sociolinguists Robert Le Page and Andrée Tabouret-Keller (1985: 14), who see 'linguistic behaviour as a series of *acts of identity*' (emphasis ours). '[T]he Individual', they write 'creates for himself the patterns of his linguistic behaviour so as to resemble those of the group or groups with which from time to time he wishes to be identified, or so as to be unlike those from whom he wishes to be distinguished' (1985: 181).

Finally, and closely related to the above points is that style always has a *political* dimension, that is to say, it always indexes particular sets of power relationships. One reason for this is that different people have different rights to use different resources and different kinds of access to those resources (see Chapter 2), and because of this, they have access to different kinds of identities. In Chapter 2 we mentioned French sociologist Pierre Bourdieu (1977), who said that people use linguistic (and other semiotic) resources in the context of 'marketplaces' where some resources are more highly valued than others. In later work, Bourdieu (1984) applied this idea of value more generally to the way people use and consume resources, noting that the kinds of stylistic choices we make, from the clothes we wear to the food we eat, become ways in which we create 'distinctions' between ourselves and the social groups we belong to and other social groups.

It is important to point out before we go any further that to say social identity is a matter of *style* is not a way of belittling people's identities or accusing them of being 'fake' or 'shallow'. Sometimes, for instance, people denigrate homosexuality as being a 'lifestyle' and dismiss transgender individuals as 'dressing up'. This is *not* what we mean when we talk about styling identities. When we talk about style, we are not calling into question who people 'really are'. Rather, we are attempting to understand how they *communicate* who they are to others.

6.2 Style as 'Audience Design'

The idea of style in sociolinguistics has changed considerably over the past half century, with different sociolinguists understanding style to mean different things. For many of the early variationist sociolinguists such as William Labov and Peter Trudgill, style is primarily a matter of how much attention a person is paying to the way they speak, which they believe inevitably has an effect on the kinds of linguistic choices they make.

You will recall from Chapter 3 Labov's study in New York department stores in which he elicited the phrase 'fourth floor' twice from shop assistants, the first time by asking where a certain item was located in the store, and the second time by pretending he hadn't heard them clearly and asking them to repeat themselves. The idea was that this second condition, which Labov called the 'emphatic' condition, would show him how people say the phrase when they are speaking more 'carefully' or paying more attention to their words.

Variationist sociolinguists use a variety of ways to try to get people to focus more closely on the way they talk (such as reading 'minimal pairs') or to focus less closely on the way they are speaking (such as engaging them in casual conversation or getting them to tell a story about a traumatic event). The idea is that when they are paying attention to how they are talking, people are more likely to talk the way they think they *should* talk (that is, to produce prestige variants) rather than the way they 'normally' talk. Thus, in conditions where they were prompted to focus on their speech, participants in Labov's study pronounced more post vocalic [r], and participants in Trudgill's study in Norwich (1974) were more likely to say *going* rather than *goin'*. Sometimes people refer to these two styles of speaking as 'formal' and 'casual'. The problem with this view of style, of course, is not just that it is rather limited, but also that it treats stylistic choices as primarily a matter of individual mental functioning (i.e., attention to speech), ignoring the social situations in which these choices are made.

A closer look at Labov's department store study, however, reveals another important dimension of style. You will recall that Labov gathered his data from shop assistants in three different department stores which, for him, represented three different social classes: upper class, middle class, and working class. It is important to remember that he did not elicit speech from the customers in these stores, but from shop assistants whose social class may not have matched that of the customers they were serving. Shop assistants working at the upper-class store, Saks, for example, were likely not upper class themselves, given that they were working as shop assistants. An underlying assumption of Labov's study, then, was not that the way these shop assistants talked was a reflection of their *own* social class, but that it was a reflection of the social class of their customers. In other words, the shop assistants likely *adapted* their speaking styles to match the speaking styles of their customers.

The idea that people change the way they speak when they are speaking to different people is the basis of Allan Bell's theory of style as '**audience design**'. The main idea of this theory is that people 'design' their speech in relation to their audiences. To test this, Bell (1984) analysed the speech of newsreaders for New Zealand's public broadcasting system, where more than one radio station broadcast from the same studio and news readers alternated reading the news for different stations throughout the day. Bell compared the way the same newsreaders read the news for two different stations, one, which he called YA, whose audience was national, and the other, ZB, whose audience was more local. He focused on four variables: (1) [t] voicing – pronouncing [t] like [d] when it occurs in the middle of a word; (2) consonant cluster reduction – e.g., pronouncing [la:st] as [la:s]; (3) determiner deletion – e.g., saying 'prime minister' rather than '*the* prime minister'; and (4) the use of contractions – such as 'won't' for 'will not'.

What he found was that the same newsreaders produced different variants, depending on the station they were broadcasting from. When they were broadcasting to the more 'local' audience, they tended to produce more 'non-standard' variants typically used by members of this audience ([t] voicing, consonant cluster reduction, determiner deletion, and negative contraction). When they were broadcasting to the national audience, they tended to use more 'standard' or 'prestige' variants. Figure 6.1 summarises Bell's results.

In interpreting these results, Bell noted that most of the relevant contextual variables were constant across the two conditions: the speakers, settings, genres, and topics were all the same. There was also no reason to think that the newsreaders were paying more or less attention to the way they talked in either of the two conditions. The only thing that was different was the *audiences* that the newsreaders believed were listening to them.

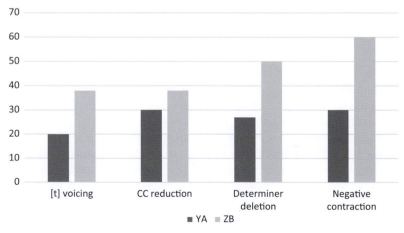

FIGURE 6.1
Newsreaders' production of different variants when reading for radio stations YA and ZB (adapted from Bell 1977)

Based on this, Bell (2001: 141) redefined style as 'what an individual speaker does with a language in relation to other people'. In general, he said, people alter their style to 'fit' their audience. These choices, however, are still based on the kind of sociolinguistic variation we talked about in Chapter 3 – the association of particular linguistic features with particular social groups. Shifts in style based on audience, Bell argued, don't just occur on the level of pronunciation, but can also occur on the levels of grammar and word choice.

One way to explain Bell's findings is through what is known as **Communication Accommodation Theory** (CAT), advanced by social psychologist Howard Giles and his colleagues (Giles & Powesland 1975; Giles & Smith 1979), which predicts that people alter their language in order to manage their relationships with the people they are speaking to. In a range of different experiments they found that speakers changed the way they talked (in terms of things like speech rate, accent, content, and pausing) to make it more similar to the way their addressees talked. Giles and his colleagues called this phenomenon **convergence** and hypothesised that it is a way for people to gain social approval.

Sometimes, however, people may maintain their way of speaking or even alter their speech to make it more *unlike* the speech of their addressees, which Giles and his colleagues refer to as **divergence**. The reason for this might be to distance themselves from the people they are speaking to or even to show hostility towards them. Bourhis and Giles (1977), for instance, found that Welsh speakers of English adopted a broader Welsh accent when speaking with an English (RP) speaker who disparaged the Welsh language, and Jenny Cheshire (1982) found that boys in Reading who disliked school were sometimes more likely to use 'non-standard' grammar and pronunciation when talking with their teachers than they normally would.

The idea that people change the way they speak to adapt to the speech of the people they are talking to also has implications for sociolinguistic research. Peter Trudgill (1981), who studied the speech of people in the British city of Norwich, for instance, found that when he was interviewing his participants, he himself changed the degree to which he produced the kinds of linguistic variants he was studying. For instance, when he was speaking to a person who frequently produced glottal stops (produced by briefly obstructing the air flow through the glottis) for the /t/ variable in the middle of words, he found himself also producing more glottal stops.

Activity: Analysing A Travel Agent's Style

The Welsh sociolinguist Nik Coupland conducted one of the most famous studies to test Bell's theory of style as **audience design**. In his study he recorded the speech of a travel agent named Sue when she was talking on the phone to clients from different occupations (I representing the highest-paid occupations and V representing the lowest-paid; Sue herself belonged to group III). Among the variables he

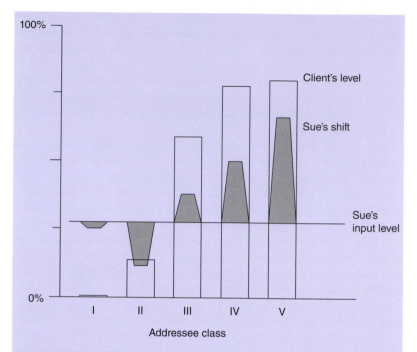

FIGURE 6.2
Sue's convergence on the intervocalic [t] variable across five occupational classes of clients
(adapted from Bell 1984: 165)

looked at were 'h-dropping' (not saying the 'h' sound at the beginning of words), 'g dropping' (saying 'goin'' instead of 'going'), the intervocalic [t] variable, which Welsh speakers sometimes produce as a [d] or a 'flap' (produced by briefly tapping the tongue to the alveolar ridge), and simplifying consonant clusters.

Figure 6.2 shows the amount Sue changed the way she said the intervocalic [t] variable in relation to the different kinds of people she was talking to. Look at the chart and answer the questions below.

1. What does the chart show about Sue's speech behaviour when talking to different kinds of clients?
2. Which social class did Sue converge the most to?
3. Which social class did she converge the least to?
4. What do you think might account for these differences?

Often, however, who actually constitutes the 'audience' of our speech can be complicated. In many situations, for instance, there may be several *different* people present and listening to what we are saying. Bell classified these different listeners as *addressees* (the people to whom our speech is directed), *auditors* (people who are present and listening, even if we are not directly talking to them), *overhearers* (people who are not part of the conversation but might overhear it), and *eavesdroppers* (people who are

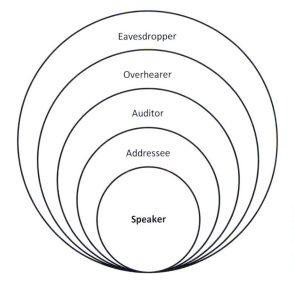

Eavesdropper

Overhearer

Auditor

Addressee

Speaker

FIGURE 6.3
Different kinds of listeners in a speech situation (adapted from Bell 1984: 159)

secretly listening in). He pictured these different kinds of listeners placed at different distances from the speaker, as depicted in Figure 6.3, and predicted that the 'further away' from the speaker the listener is, the less they would affect the speaker's style, with eavesdroppers not affecting it at all, since the speaker would normally not be aware that they are listening. Bell called the effect that listeners *other* than the addressee have on a speaker's speech the **auditor effect**.

A number of studies have confirmed this hypothesis. The Cypriot sociolinguist Maria Christodoulidou (2013), for example, studied the ways Cypriot university students altered their pronunciation of Greek in casual conversations (e.g., at dinners, parties) when different people were present in the conversation. Not surprisingly, she found that, when talking to people from Greece, the students tended to use phonological variants more associated with 'standard Greek' rather than those associated with the local Cypriot variety. But she also found that, even when talking with fellow Cypriots, the students used more 'standard Greek' variants when Greeks were present as auditors in the conversation, though the shift was not as pronounced as it was when Greeks were addressees.

The idea that even 'third parties' such as auditors and overhearers have an effect on how people talk also has implications for sociolinguistic research, demonstrating that even when researchers are not the ones conducting interviews, just their presence might affect the speech of participants.

It also has implications for understanding the kinds of social media interactions we talked about at the beginning of this chapter, where there are typically lots of different kinds of 'listeners': those for whom our posts are intended, those whom we might not be addressing directly but assume are 'part of our conversation', those who simply 'overhear' our conversations by virtue of their presence in our social network, and even 'eavesdroppers', people who may not be part of our social network but might be 'stalking' us on Facebook or Instagram. This merging of lots of different people from different social contexts (home, work, school) into one big audience on social media is known as 'context collapse' (Marwick & boyd 2010).

Digital media scholar danah boyd (2012), who studied the privacy practices of teenagers using social media sites like Twitter, found that young people deal with the problem of context collapse in various ways. They might, for example, alter the style or content of messages intended for their friends in order to hide their intentions from their parents who might also be reading their Twitter feeds. But she also found that Twitter users sometimes compose messages in ways that *position* certain members of their friend groups as 'overhearers' in order to make them feel excluded.

Media sociolinguist Jannis Androutsopoulos (2014), whose work we mentioned in Chapter 4, says that one thing that sometimes complicates the problem of context collapse is that people's online social networks are often even more diverse than their offline social networks, consisting of friends in different countries who might have different levels of competency in different resources. The people he studied, for example, were immigrants to Germany from China and Greece whose social networks included people who understood Chinese or Greek but not German, or who understood German and English but not Chinese or Greek. In examining the kinds of linguistic choices his participants made, Androutsopoulos noticed that his participants altered the language of their posts based not just on who they were addressing, but sometimes also on others in their social networks that they thought might be interested. For example, using English could be used as a way of including both German friends who did not understand Greek and Greek friends who did not understand German.

The most important thing that we can learn from Androutsopoulos's study is not just that people design their Facebook posts by adapting their linguistic choices based on who they think their audience is, but also that they actively use their linguistic choices in order to design their audiences, to 'hail' certain users and to include or exclude others.

6.3 Style as 'Speaker Design'

Along with 'receptive' style shift – people altering their speech style based on their audience – Bell argues that sometimes people shift styles even in the absence of audience members associated with these styles in order to *index* (see Chapter 2) being members of particular groups. He called this kind of style shifting 'referee design'. A **referee** is a person or group that people 'refer to' in their heads when they are speaking. For instance, your mother might have taught you to speak in a certain way, to say 'please', for example, when making a request because that's what 'polite people' do. Later, you start to say please even when your mother isn't there, not because you think your mother might be listening, but because you want other people to think that you are a 'polite person'. In such cases, style is not so much a way of accommodating to your audience, but a way of *performing* a particular social identity by talking in a way that references certain groups or certain kinds of people. In contrast to style as audience design, we might call this 'style as speaker design', because speakers are designing their utterances based on what kind of speaker they want others to take them for.

Some of the most dramatic examples of using style to perform social identities can be seen in actual performances by entertainers or politicians. Peter Trudgill (1983), for example, studied the pronunciation that the Beatles used in their songs from early in their careers to the last days that the band performed together, and he found that in most of their early songs they used American pronunciation (especially when it came to pronouncing postvocalic [r], voicing the [t] sound in the middle of words like 'little', pronouncing the diphthong /ai/ in words like 'life' as an [a], and replacing the rounded British [ɒ] in words like 'hot' with the unrounded American [ɑ]). They might have been doing this, of course, to try to accommodate to the pronunciation of their American fans, but it's more likely that they were doing it to align themselves with American rock and roll singers like Elvis Presley and Buddy Holly who influenced their music. Interestingly, Trudgill found that as their careers progressed, the Beatles gradually began to adopt a more British style, possibly because British bands had become more trendy.

The interesting thing about the 'American' variants that the Beatles adopted (and many other non-American singers still adopt) is that they are associated with *different* varieties of American English, and it would be unlikely for all of them to occur in the actual speech of an American (Simpson 1999). In other words, rather than a 'real American accent', this is a **stylisation** of an American accent, a hybrid of features associated with speech patterns in the American Midwest and the Southern states, as well as African American Vernacular English.

Another example of stylisation in the performance of entertainment identities is the widespread adoption of stylised African American Vernacular English by hip-hop singers around the world. At the same time, sometimes *not* adopting an expected style can also be a way of performing certain identities. Australian sociolinguist Renae O'Hanlon (2006: 202), for instance, observes that, while most singers of other pop genres in Australia adopt stylised American accents, Australian hip-hop artists tend to sing in local Australian accents as a way of 'keeping it real'.

Most singers, of course, (like most people) have available to them a varied repertoire of styles, and they often mix different styles when they sing in order to highlight certain aspects of their personas or locate themselves in particular musical genres. Lisa Jansen and Michael Westphal (2017), for instance, argue that the Barbados-born international pop star Rihanna not only adopts different styles as she switches genres (for example, reggae, hip-hop, R&B, and electro dance music) but even sometimes mixes styles in a single song. In their analysis of Rihanna's single 'Work', they show how she strategically combines phonological and grammatical features from Caribbean English Creole – mostly Jamaican Creole and Bajan – 'standard' American English and, to some extent, African American Vernacular English, adopting different styles in different parts of the song. In describing this hybrid style, Jansen and Westphal invoke Eckert's notion of bricolage (see above), arguing that Rihanna skilfully draws from multiple linguistic resources in her repertoire to perform different aspects of her identity in different passages of the song.

Activity: Stylisation in Music

Choose a singer that you are familiar with and try to describe the style/s they use when they are singing. Try to point to particular features (such as particular grammatical constructions or the way they pronounce certain words).

1. What do these features tell you about the identity or persona that the singer is trying to perform?
2. Does the singing style of the singer match their speaking style, or is it different? Are there features in their singing style that are associated with groups (ethnic, regional) that the singer does not belong to?
3. Do you think the genre of the singer's music (e.g., hip-hop, country-western, dance hall) has anything to do with their stylistic choices?
4. Does the singer change their style from one song to another, or even within a single song? What is the effect of this?

So far, we have been talking about the way people use different styles to perform identities in the context of what Coupland (2007) calls 'high performance', namely events that are planned, rehearsed and performed to audiences either onstage or broadcast through various media. Coupland draws on the work of the anthropologist Richard Bauman (1977) to argue that the thing that distinguishes such performances is that they create a special kind of situation in which more attention than normal is paid to *how* people talk (or sing) and in which performers are more likely to produce *stylised* performances (involving, for instance, 'putting on' particular accents). At the same time, Coupland (2001: 50) also argues that 'it would be apt to invoke performance as a quality of most and probably all styling'. In other words, the kind of 'multivocal performances' (Jansen & Westphal 2017; see Bakhtin 1981) that we see from performers like Rihanna are not all that different from the way normal people perform identities in everyday life. In our everyday interactions we also mix and match resources from our communicative repertoires in order to create different personas, and sometimes we even engage in stylisation, imitating the ways of speaking of other people or other groups.

Often people use these different stylised voices in their everyday talk in order to *position* themselves in relation to particular reference groups in the societies in which they live. The sociolinguist Elaine Chun (2001), for example, discusses how a Korean American teenager uses features from African American Vernacular English in order to distance himself from 'white' identity and to perform a 'masculine' identity. In other words, by adopting a particular style, along with its associations with certain kinds of racialised and gendered stereotypes, he is able to construct for himself a particular kind of male Korean American identity.

In Chapter 5 we talked about Ben Rampton's observations of *crossing* in a multicultural group of teenagers in London – how, in their interactions, they sometimes adopted the language or speaking styles of other ethnic groups, white kids, for example, using features from Jamaican Creole or black kids sometimes speaking in stylised South Asian accents. Sometimes, Rampton notes, this practice served to blur the social and ethnic boundaries between speakers, but sometimes it actually strengthened these boundaries. For Rampton, crossing is part of a complex and dynamic process of identity performance in which people signal their orientations towards the different 'voices' they adopt.

Finally, it's important to remember that style and stylisation are not just a matter of deploying linguistic resources. They are also a matter of the way people use their bodies (gestures, facial expressions, the way they walk) as well as the clothing people wear, their hairstyles, bodily adornments, and even the places where they go and the kinds of people they surround themselves with. The styles of the Jocks and Burnouts that Eckert studied at Belten High (see Chapter 3) were not performed simply by the way they pronounced vowels, but also by the kinds of jeans they wore and where they hung out both in school and out of school. At the same time, however, these configurations of resources don't always fit together in predictable ways. Sometimes people perform different styles with their voices, facial expressions, gestures, and clothes to index multiple, even contradictory, identities. Linguistic anthropologists Marjorie Goodwin and H. Samy Alim (2010) call this 'transmodal stylization', giving the example of how white girls on a playground bully an African American girl by simultaneously adopting a speech style associated with wealthy 'Valley girls' and performing gestures stereotypically associated with African Americans.

6.4 Style in Interaction

So far we have talked about the way people use stylistic choices to accommodate to their audiences (style as audience design) and to perform particular social identities by indexing groups of people that may not be present in the interaction (style as speaker design). But people also use style to 'design' the social situations in which they are interacting, to signal, for example, what they are doing and how they feel about it.

The anthropologist John Gumperz, whom we mentioned in Chapter 2, argued that linguistic styles can serve to create contexts for our communication, a process that he called **contextualisation**. You might, for example, put on some stylised accent when insulting a friend in order to signal that you are joking, or speak in a more 'formal' style to signal that you are having a 'serious discussion'.

In Chapter 2, we used the word *register* to refer to the different ways of talking associated with different activities or different kinds of people, noting for instance, that 'talking like a doctor' (i.e., using particular terminology, and even a particular tone of voice) is one way for someone to show that they are a doctor. But doctors don't always speak like doctors, even when they are *being* doctors. One of the most famous studies demonstrating how people use different styles (registers) to contextualise their utterances is research done by linguists Deborah Tannen and Cynthia Wallat (1987) in which they analyse the speech of a doctor as she is examining a young patient in the presence both of the patient's mother and of a group of medical students she is supervising. Throughout the interaction, the doctor shifts her style according to whom she is addressing, using what they call a 'teasing register' with the child, a 'reporting register' with the medical students, and a 'conversational register' with the mother:

[Teasing register]

DOCTOR: Let's see. Can you open up like this, Jody. Look. [Doctor opens her own mouth]
CHILD: Aaaaaaaaaaaaah.
DOCTOR: [Good. That's good.
CHILD: Aaaaaaaaaaah.

[Reporting register]

DOCTOR: /Seeing/ for the palate, she has a high arched palate
CHILD: Aaaaaaaaaaaaaaaaaaaaaaaaaah.
DOCTOR: but there's no cleft,

[maneuvers to grasp child's jaw]

[Conversational register]

… what we'd want to look for is to see how she … moves her palate. … Which may be some of the difficulty with breathing that we're talking about.

(Tannen & Wallat 1987: 209)

In this situation, the doctor is not just accommodating to different addressees, but she is actively changing the 'frame' or context to signal that she is doing different things in the interaction.

6.5 The Politics of Styling

It should be clear by now that the way styles are used to perform identities affects and is affected by the relationships of power and the status of different groups of people within a given situation and a given society. In other words, style always has a *political* dimension.

One reason for this, as we noted in Chapter 2, is that access to different resources is unequally distributed across societies – some people don't have the opportunities to perform certain identities because they don't have access to or the chance to gain competence with particular resources. As we also said in Chapter 2, some resources are considered more valuable than others in particular societies or in particular contexts of communication (just as different items of clothing in your closet are more valuable than others or more appropriate for different occasions).

And so, the idea that we can simply choose different styles the way we choose different items of clothing from our closet is a bit simplistic. Our choices are always constrained not just by what resources we have available but also by what other people think are appropriate styles (and appropriate identities) for 'people like us'. One important consideration when it comes to style is the issue of **authenticity** – which is not so much about whether we are being 'honest' or 'genuine', but rather whether other people think the style we have adopted 'fits' and that we have the 'right' to adopt it. Of course, sometimes we're not trying to be authentic – that is, we might adopt a style in a mocking or ironic way that deliberately distances us from the identity we are performing. At other times, however, we might adopt a style mainly as a way of showing that we *are* authentic ('keeping it real'), as with the Australian hip-hop artists that O'Hanlon (2006) studied (see above).

If others think that the style we are adopting is somehow not suitable for us or does not reflect our 'true' identity, they might regard us as 'fake', spoiling our performances. One example of this can be seen in Dennis Chau's (2021) observation that Hong Kong Chinese who adopt features of American English in their speech are sometimes referred to by other Chinese as 'Fake ABCs' (ABC is an acronym meaning 'American-born Chinese'). Because of their perceived linguistic inauthenticity, such people are accused of being insincere and pretentious. Interestingly, this type of judgement is mostly directed at women, and, in such cases, accusations of inauthenticity help to reinforce stereotypes of women as devious, shallow, and materialistic (since it is presumed that one reason they are doing this is to attract a 'rich foreign boyfriend').

This brings us to the most important political dimension of style – the fact that styling identities (and especially engaging in the kinds of *stylisation* of the speech of different groups that we talked about above) always, to some extent, draws upon and perpetuates *stereotypes* about the way particular kinds of people talk and act. As Chun (2001: 61), who studied the use of African American Vernacular English by Korean Americans (see above), puts it, 'an understanding of the social force of language in performances of identity also entails a critical examination of the dominant discourses that contextualize these performances'. What she means by this is that all acts of styling take place within and depend upon societal assumptions not just about the value of different kinds of styles, but also about the value of different kinds of people (e.g., different races, genders, social classes). Styling doesn't just depend on stereotypes, it *enacts* and perpetuates them.

Another way to say this is that we don't just perform styles and identities, but that style is in itself performative. The notion of **performativity** comes from a branch of linguistics called *speech act theory*, which concerns itself with how people 'do things' (such as make requests and issue apologies) with words. In this theory, a 'performative' is a kind of speech act which *enacts* the action that it names (such as *sentencing* someone to a prison term or *pronouncing* two people to be married). The American philosopher Judith Butler (1988) extended this idea to thinking about the way we enact social identities. By behaving in certain ways, including saying certain things and adopting certain kinds of styles, we don't just perform identities, but we also create realities in which these identities are a part. She gives as an example the performance of gender identities. Whenever people adopt particular behaviours or styles associated with being a man or being a woman in a particular society, they further strengthen the associations between these behaviours and styles with masculinity and femininity, so that the next time they want to 'act like a man' or 'act like a woman', they have little choice but to adopt these behaviours and styles. To put it more succinctly, just as we perform identities, identities also perform us.

6.6 Focal Topic: Performing Gender and Sexuality

The focal topic of this chapter is how people perform identities associated with gender and sexuality, and how these performances are constrained by societal stereotypes about what it means to, for instance, talk or act 'like a man' or 'like a woman'. Much of the work in sociolinguistics that took place in the twentieth century was based on assumptions that gender and sexuality are bipolar *categories* that people could be assigned to – people were either 'men' or 'women', 'gay' or 'straight', and a lot of attention was paid to trying to describe the features of the talk of people who were placed into these different categories. Variationist sociolinguists such as Trudgill (1974), for example, observed that women produced more 'standard' variants than men. Later, however, ethnographic studies like those conducted by Eckert (2000) and Bucholtz (1999) showed that the kinds of variants women produced sometimes had more to do with other social groups they belonged to (such as 'Burnouts' or 'nerds') than with their gender.

One of the earliest attempts to describe what it means to 'talk like a woman' was that of the American linguist Robin Lakoff (1975), who said that women's speech (at least in the North American context in which she was working) tends to be characterised by things like (1) more 'standard' pronunciation and grammar, (2) hedging and indirectness, (3) more 'polite' forms and a greater tendency to apologise, and (4) the use of what Lakoff called 'empty adjectives' (such as 'adorable' and 'gorgeous'). Lakoff was not saying that women 'naturally' talk this way, but that this is the way society *expects* women to talk, and that when they do talk this way, unequal power relationships between men and women are reproduced and perpetuated. Later scholars debated whether these features in 'women's speech' are mostly the result of socialisation (women are taught to talk this way from early childhood) or mostly the result of unequal power relationships (women talk this way because they are often in subordinate positions and these features – such as hedging and apologising – are characteristic of people in more subordinate positions). Similar approaches were taken when it came to language and sexuality, with scholars trying to isolate, for example, the distinctive features of 'gay speech'.

More recent work on language and gender, as well as on language and sexuality, does *not* assume that gender and sexuality are stable categories, but that they are identities that people perform in lots of different ways in different circumstances. This perspective owes a lot to the work of Judith Butler, whom we talked about above. Butler's idea that identities are *performative* means that things like gender and sexuality are *socially constructed* through the way people talk and act. Although people's performances of gender and sexuality are constrained by society's expectations, there also exist opportunities for people to challenge these expectations and create new kinds of identities associated with gender and sexuality.

The two articles reviewed in this section show how speech styles associated with gender and sexuality (as well as gender and sexuality themselves) are more fluid and dynamic than once thought, and how these styles are sometimes used strategically to achieve particular interactional goals. The first article focuses on phonological features of the voices of transgender speakers as they transition from one gender to another. It demonstrates that there are not always clear links between certain features and certain gender identities, but that people often mix different features together to perform different kinds of gender identities. The second article provides a detailed description of the way a female high school student in a sex education class strategically shifts styles to perform her identity when talking with other students about issues of gender and sexuality.

Zimman, L. (2017) Gender as stylistic bricolage: Transmasculine voices and the relationship between fundamental frequency and /s/. *Language in Society*, 46(3), 339–70 In this article, sociophonetician Lal Zimman explores the complex ways speech style indexes gender, and, in doing so, highlights some of the inadequacies of conventional ways of understanding style, as well as conventional ways of understanding gender. He focuses on certain phonological features in the speech of trans men, people who have transitioned from a female gender assignment to a male one.

Examining the way transgender speakers adopt new stylistic features in their speech to index their new gender identity provides unique insights into societal ideas about what it means to 'talk like a man' and 'talk like a woman'. It also brings together some of the important ideas about what drives people's stylistic choices which we talked about in this chapter.

Perhaps more than most people, transgender speakers, especially in the early days of their transition, pay particular attention to the way they speak, consciously attempting to style their speech in ways that, in their minds, conform to their new gender identity. At the same time, they also pay particular attention to the ways other people *perceive* their speech. Transgender speakers 'whose voices mark them as audibly transgender', Zimman says (p. 340), 'often find that speaking is the act that prevents them from having their self-identified gender recognized and affirmed by others'.

Interestingly, what Zimman found in his study was that the way trans men style their voices does not always conform to social expectations about what it means to 'sound masculine', but instead involves speakers combining a range of features, some usually associated with masculinity, and some usually associated with femininity, to perform a variety of *different kinds* of 'masculine voices'.

Of course, not all of the changes in the voices in transitioning trans men are the result of styling. Typically, trans men undergo testosterone therapy, which results in physiological changes, including a thickening of the vocal cords. And so, trans men undergoing hormone therapy will experience a lowering of the overall pitch of their voices (a feature usually associated with 'male voices') without having to consciously try to lower their pitch. At the same time, there are other features, such as the way certain sounds are pronounced, that they *do* have control over and often try to manipulate to make their voices sound more 'masculine'. One of these is the pronunciation of the /s/ sound, which studies have found women usually produce with a longer duration and at higher frequency range than men. Interestingly, longer and higher pitched /s/ sounds have also been linked to whether or not people think men 'sound gay'.

In his study, Zimman followed fifteen trans men over the course of a year during their first months of hormone therapy. He regularly measured the overall pitch (known as 'fundamental frequency') of their voices throughout the study as well as the pitch and duration of their /s/ sounds. He also talked to them about their feelings about their own voices and their experiences with the reactions of other people to the way they spoke.

Not surprisingly, he found that the pattern of downward change in overall pitch was consistent across all of the speakers as they underwent hormone therapy. At the same time, however, he found that the adoption of a more 'male sounding' /s/ sound was not consistent, with some speakers making their /s/ sounds shorter and lower and others retaining longer higher pitched /s/ sounds. He even found that the duration and pitch of /s/ sounds among some speakers *increased* even as their voices got lower. Several of these participants talked about feeling more comfortable incorporating more traditionally 'feminine' characteristics into their speech as they started being perceived more consistently by others as men.

One reason for these differences, Zimman argues, is that gender is not a simple binary categorisation, and that the different men he studied themselves had different understandings of gender. For example, those who identified as 'men' or 'trans men' tended to produce more 'male sounding' /s/ sounds, and those who identified themselves as 'genderqueer' or some other non-binary gender identity tended to retain more 'female sounding' /s/ sounds. Zimman notes that there were also other factors that affected his participants' gender performances and the way others perceived them. One participant, for instance, a Filipino with a British accent, reported that even with his lowered voice and 'male sounding' /s/ sounds, people still perceived him as female more often than he would have liked.

Based on his study, Zimman (p. 361) argues that it is a mistake to think about gender as 'a unidimensional scale with femininity on one end of a continuum and masculinity on the other'. 'Instead,' he says, 'gender is constituted by numerous overlapping and sometimes even conflicting sets of practices that can be combined and recombined in a huge variety of ways'. He writes:

gender fundamentally operates like other facets of identity: constructed through a process of bricolage (see above) that draws on both material and symbolic resources, emerging contextually in concert with multiple intersecting identities, and remaining open to change in the ongoing process of articulating the self. (p. 365)

This research challenges traditional binary notions of what it means to 'sound like a man' or 'sound like a woman', demonstrating that trans men don't just 'switch' from a 'female sounding' to a 'male sounding' voice, but instead different people use their voices to perform gender in different ways, depending on their experiences, their understandings of gender, other aspects of their identities, and the social contexts that they find themselves in. This is an insight, of course, that is just as relevant to understanding how cisgender people perform gendered identities.

King, B. W. (2018) Hip Hop headz in sex ed: Gender, agency, and styling in New Zealand. *Language in Society*, 47(4), 487–512   This article explores how people use style shifting in a more interactive way to manage gender- and sexuality-related aspects of their identities in the ongoing flow of interaction. King describes the talk of a female teenager of Pacific Islander descent named Luana as she participates in a sex education class in a New Zealand high school. His analysis focuses on how Luana uses different speech styles, including hip-hop style, to challenge a range of fixed identity categories (man, woman, gay, straight) in order to deal with an uncomfortable interaction with another student.

King recorded Luana and her classmates as part of a larger ethnographic study about sex education. The particular lesson he analyses in this article involved students asking and answering questions that are stereotypically asked to sexual minorities (such as: 'Are you offended when a straight person of the opposite sex comes on to you?'). Students in the class were meant to move around the room, asking these questions of different partners. At one point, Luana was paired with a boy named Liam, who transformed the question above to 'would YOU be offended if I came onto you right here?' What King is mostly concerned with in his analysis is how Luana used style to cope with having been put into an uncomfortable position of being treated by Liam as a sexual object.

One of the main stylistic resources she draws upon, according to King, is the 'voice' of Hip-Hop Nation Language (HHNL, see Chapter 9). Hip-hop, he explains, has been an important form of cultural expression for Māori and Pasifika people in New Zealand since the late 1970s, partly because of the sense of marginalisation they share with other participants in hip-hop such as African Americans in the US. Many of the stylistic features of hip-hop language as it was used in this community indexed stances of 'swag' and 'braggadocio', and this style was mostly associated with Māori and Pasifika boys, with the exception of Luana, who sometimes adopted this style in a gender-nonconforming way.

When Liam positions Luana as a sexual object in the context of this activity, Luana responds by shifting to a hip-hop style, lengthening her vowels and expanding and contracting her syllables in a manner approximating African American English, and loudly accusing Liam of being a 'buzz killer'. King argues that the 'masculine' stance indexed by her hip-hop styling allowed her to resist being positioned as an object of Liam's sexual attentions and to regain a position of agency in the interaction.

Resisting being positioned as a sexual object by projecting a stance of 'masculine swagger' indexed by her hip-hop style, however, created a new kind of identity problem for Luana in respect to her classmates: later her sexuality was called into question by another boy in the class, making it necessary for her to resist this new positioning by loudly proclaiming how much she 'LOVES boys'.

King points out that the management of gender- and sexuality-related identities can be particularly awkward in groups of adolescents in which certain expressions of gender and sexuality might be stigmatised. Girls in particular, he says, must deal with the risk of being called a 'slut' or a 'dyke' based on the way they respond to the sexual advances of boys, a product of powerful patriarchal gender stereotypes in the society.

The bigger point that King makes in his paper is that identities around gender and sexuality need to be constantly negotiated in the context of particular situations and based on the kinds of stereotypes and values that dominate those situations. People draw upon norms of masculinity and femininity in strategic ways depending on their needs and the contexts they find themselves in, using styling to assume different kinds of stances and project different kinds of identities.

Project Ideas

1. Record yourself or another person talking in different situations and to different people (you might, for example, record the way you talk when you are giving a presentation in class and when you are talking to your friends). Transcribe the two recordings and see if you can identify differences in the pronunciation, grammar, and word choice.

2. Collect a corpus of songs from a singer that you like and analyse them for stylistic features related to pronunciation (such as those related to a stylised American accent described above). See if you can find any differences in the way the features are used in different songs, different genres of song, or whether the way they are used changes over the course of the artist's career.

3. Collect data of people engaging in explicitly gendered performances (such as the performances of 'drag queens' and 'drag kings' – *RuPaul's Drag Race* is a good source of data for this). Attempt to isolate the kinds of stylistic features that you think index gender. Also notice if and when the performers adopt other kinds of stylised 'voices' (such as stylised African American English). Do a close analysis of the speech of one or two performers, focusing on how and why they shift styles.

4. Replicate Androutsopoulos's (2014) study. Collect some multilingual interactions from Facebook posts (for ethical considerations in relation to collecting data from online sources please see Appendix A.3). Observe how people design their Facebook posts and how they adapt their linguistic choices depending on who they think the audience is. Do they include or exclude certain people and how?

CHAPTER

7 Language Attitudes, Mocking, and Appropriation

PREVIEW

KEY TERMS

appropriation
citizen
sociolinguistics
covert
language
attitudes
folk
linguistics
language
mocking
matched
guise
technique
overt
language
attitudes
stereotypes

Throughout this book we have talked about how different resources ('languages', 'dialects', 'styles') are *valued* differently in different societies. The value assigned to different resources manifests not just in structural inequalities (see Chapter 2), but also in the pervasive everyday *attitudes* people have about particular 'languages' and ways of using language, and the acts of 'othering' and aggression that sometimes result from these attitudes. In this chapter we will focus on the study of language attitudes, exploring how and why people respond to other people's communicative practices in negative or positive ways. The focal topic explores how the linguistic practices of certain groups of people are represented, mocked, and appropriated in ways that perpetuate racism and marginalisation.

7.1 Introduction

Love Island is a reality TV show featuring single people who travel to an exotic island hoping to find love. The show was first broadcast in the UK in 2005, but now, because of its popularity, versions have been produced in different countries around the world. The contestants, known as 'Islanders', live in a luxury villa in isolation from the outside world and are constantly under video surveillance. To remain in the game, contestants must couple up and win the hearts of their prospective partners as well as the support of the public, who ultimately decide who stays on the show and who is dumped.

The Islanders tend to attract considerable attention from fans on social media, and viewers often comment on their appearance, behaviour, body language, knowledge, and the ideas they express on the show. The contestants' language use is also sometimes a focus of fans' attention. In 2018, Hayley, a young model from Liverpool in north England, was one of the contestants. Being from Liverpool, Hayley had an accent that was rather different from the rest of the Islanders, who spoke with more so-called 'standard' southern British accents. Shortly after she arrived on the island, comments about Hayley's way of speaking began to emerge on social media. Below are some examples from Twitter:

a. Hayley's accent makes my skin crawl #LoveIsland @LoveIsland
b. Ngl it's so difficult listening to Hayley speak … what level of education does this girl have #LoveIsland
c. #loveisland Hayley is an absolute snake. She's so fake and completely vile and has now been found out haha. Girl is thick as a pig shit and can't even speak actual sentences properly. Go get yourself an education your embarrassing.
d. OMG seriously?!?!! Finally get rid of Hayley and her annoying voice and now we're getting Ellie who sounds 1000000 times worse. Who knew that was even possible??? #LoveIsland

What is striking about these comments is that viewers' negative attitudes towards Hayley's accent are linked with negative attitudes towards Hayley *as a person*. Her accent is seen as evidence for a lack of education and a lack of sincerity. What is also striking is how aggressive the language of these tweets is, and how viscerally the viewers respond to Hayley's way of speaking ('[it] makes my skin crawl').

As we said in Chapter 1, because of the power of the 'standard language ideology', people often complain or denigrate people whose linguistic practices deviate from the 'standard'. This kind of behaviour is also seen in viewers' comments about other contestants. For instance, one Islander named Niall from Coventry was criticised for his frequent use of the word 'like'. Ironically, those who complain about other people's language often exhibit 'non-standard' features in their own language, such as tweet C's use of '*your* embarrassing' for 'you're embarrassing', and tweet B's and D's use of non-standard abbreviations ('ngl' meaning 'not gonna lie' and OMG meaning 'Oh my God').

What's going on here, however, is much more than just a matter of *verbal hygiene* (see Chapter 1). Viewers' attitudes about Hayley's speech are not just 'linguistic' judgements, but also involve judgements about class, gender, and about different regions of the country. This is perhaps the most important thing to remember about language attitudes: that the attitudes that people express about the way people talk often have their source in other kinds of attitudes. In fact, expressing negative attitudes about the way people talk is often a more 'socially acceptable' way of expressing other kinds of negative attitudes (about, for instance, someone's race or where they came from).

7.2 Overt and Covert Attitudes

Sociolinguists have been interested in people's attitudes towards different language varieties since the 1960s. One of the first to address language attitudes was William Labov, whose work we talked about in Chapter 3. In his study of the speakers on the island of Martha's Vineyard, Labov found that people had different feelings about the way people talked, associating one way of pronouncing words (like 'light' and 'nice') with 'islander identity' and another way with 'mainlander identity', and they used their own choices about pronunciation as a way of showing loyalty to one group or another. As with the example above, the feelings that people had about the way people around them talked were not just feelings about vowel sounds, but feelings about different kinds of people.

When studying people's attitudes towards language (or, for that matter, their attitudes towards anything), it's important to remember that people do not always express their attitudes directly, and sometimes they may not be entirely conscious of their own attitudes, that is to say, they may have *unconscious biases*. Figure 7.1, drawn by sociolinguists Nancy Niedzielski and Dennis Preston (2007: 2), attempts to capture this complexity. 'What people say' (a) is put on the top (the narrowest) part of the

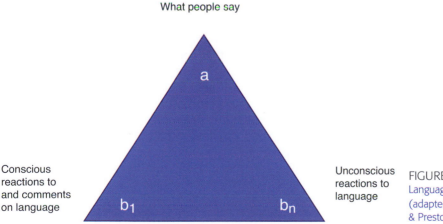

FIGURE 7.1
Language attitudes (adapted from Niedzielski & Preston 2007)

triangle, whereas what people *think* (their 'reactions to language') is represented by the base, metaphorically expressing the fact that what people say about their attitudes represents only a small part of what they think. One side of the base of the triangle represents their *conscious* reactions (b_1), and the other side their *unconscious* reactions (b_n), represented as a continuum from *conscious* to *unconscious*.

Another way of thinking about this is to distinguish between *overt* and *covert* language attitudes (Labov 1966/2006). **Overt attitudes** are evaluations which are consciously felt/thought and explicitly expressed. The attitudes about Hayley's accent in the tweets above, for example, can be classified as overt attitudes. It is also possible for language attitudes to be less explicit and less obvious, even to those who hold these attitudes. **Covert attitudes** are those that people do not express, either because they think it would be somehow wrong to express them or because they are not completely aware of them themselves. They are often expressed *indirectly* through behaviour, such as avoiding people who speak a certain way.

This distinction highlights one of the main complications of studying language attitudes: the fact that directly asking people what they think or how they feel about different language varieties will never reveal the full picture. Other, more *indirect*, methods need to be used to understand their covert attitudes.

That is not to say that overt attitudes are not important; in fact studies that have used a more direct approach have yielded some interesting findings. The simplest way to do this is by asking people to explicitly articulate their evaluations with questions such as: 'Do you like speaking Geordie?', 'Should children learn to speak Welsh?', 'Do you think isiXhosa should be used in schools in South Africa?', 'Do you like the sound of Australian English?' and so on. Perhaps a better way to do it is to design a questionnaire. The advantage of questionnaires is that people can fill them out without the researcher watching them, and their answers can be analysed using inferential statistics (see Appendix A.2), which can help us to find statistically significant patterns in people's responses.

MacKinnon (1981), for example, used a questionnaire to ask people in Scotland about their attitudes towards Gaelic. The questionnaire contained sixteen questions on whether Gaelic should be officially recognised, whether people should be allowed to use it in official public events and at school, and whether speaking Gaelic was important for their everyday lives and for expressing their identities. Interestingly, although the number of people who actually speak Gaelic is relatively low according to census figures, most of the people who completed the questionnaire reported positive attitudes towards Gaelic.

More recently, Coupland and Bishop (2007) explored contemporary British language attitudes using an online questionnaire. Thirty-four different accents in the UK were evaluated, including major regional British accents, accents associated with other countries, and global varieties of English. Participants were presented firstly with audio spoken samples (or 'guises') and then conceptual labels for the accents. They were asked to evaluate each accent on a scale from 1 (low) to 7 (high) based on the questions: 'How much prestige do you think is associated with this accent?' and 'How pleasant do you think this accent sounds?' In total, 5,010 participants from different geographical regions across the UK completed the questionnaire. The results revealed that accents associated with 'standard' speech like 'The Queen's English' and 'Standard English' were strongly favoured in terms of prestige and social attractiveness. However, urban accents like those in Birmingham and Liverpool, as well as foreign accents like Asian and German, were consistently downgraded. Coupland and Bishop (2007) explain that these findings demonstrate that standard language ideologies are still pervasive in contemporary Britain. Interestingly, there was not always a correlation between how 'prestigious' people thought an accent was and how pleasant they thought it sounded. Regional accents such as Scottish, Cornish, and Southern Irish, and some non-British English accents such as Australian and New Zealand, for instance, were scored higher on the pleasantness scale than they were on the prestige scale.

Activity: Attitudes Towards Multilingualism

Language attitudes include not just people's attitudes towards specific language varieties, but also their attitudes towards larger sociolinguistic phenomena such as 'multilingualism'. Jaworska and Themistocleous (2018) used an online questionnaire to ask people in the UK their attitudes towards living in a multilingual society. While some of their questions used a scale like that in Coupland and Bishop's questionnaire, for others they elicited more 'open-ended' responses. One of the questions, for example, was: 'Overall, would you say that lots of languages being used is a positive or negative thing? Please give your reasons for your opinion.' Below is a sample of some of their answers:

PARTICIPANT 2: I'm ambivalent! A good mix of cultures and languages is a positive thing but sometimes I walk down Friar Street and don't hear any English. I feel rather indignant!

PARTICIPANT 21: I believe diversity is a good thing and multiculturalism can strengthen a community. The flip side to this is that if there is a distinct language barrier between communities then it can cause those communities to become isolated.

PARTICIPANT 47: Only people with native English must work in call centres, nurseries, any public service where it's necessary to speak to customers. Sometimes when I call NHS people with a strong Indian accent reply. I hardly can understand them.

PARTICIPANT 54: They steal jobs and are annoying.

PARTICIPANT 57: They need to learn the language of the country they are in instead of making us feel like we are abroad.

PARTICIPANT 68: It shows that people are more aware of diversity and able to perceive other people's traditions and cultures (i.e., bring mutual respect and understanding between nations and bring peace and healthy co-existence).

PARTICIPANT 90: Many languages enriches the cultural landscape making us a more tolerant society.

PARTICIPANT 132: I think coming into contact with different languages and different cultures on a daily basis can only be a good thing for people. However, I do believe there can be difficulties when people come to live here from other countries and do not try to learn English.

PARTICIPANT 171: It denotes an open-minded society which respects different people. More importantly, it is more creative at all levels (economy, education).

- Discuss these responses with your peers and categorise them based on whether they express positive, negative, or mixed attitudes.
- Identify the themes that emerge in the participants' responses. What are some of the reasons they brought up to justify their attitudes? What kinds of *assumptions* about languages and speakers can you detect in their responses?
- Do you think there might be other, more 'covert', factors that might have influenced people's attitudes? Explain.

The benefit of direct approaches is that they can provide researchers with the respondents' conscious perceptions of their attitudes and, as demonstrated in Jaworska and Themistocleous's (2018) study, they can also include opportunities for respondents to reflect on the *reasons* why they might have such attitudes.

At the same time, direct approaches have limitations. Sometimes, for example, it is difficult to separate out people's attitudes towards the 'label' a particular accent is given and the accent itself. People also can be reluctant to express negative attitudes towards a group of speakers, not wanting to seem prejudiced, and so might choose to give a more 'socially appropriate' response to make them appear open-minded, unprejudiced, democratic, rational, or well-adjusted (Garrett 2010).

More indirect approaches seek to avoid these limitations. One way is to ask people to make judgements about *particular* speakers rather than about groups of people and the way they speak. A popular technique with which to do this is called the **matched guise technique**, pioneered by Lambert and his associates in the 1960s while they were studying the attitudes of bilingual people in Montreal towards French and English. Participants in the study were asked to listen to recordings in French and English produced by four male bilinguals, each of whom read French and English versions of the same passage. The recordings were then presented in alternating English–French order to English-speaking and French-speaking participants who were asked to evaluate them. What is important is that the participants were not aware that they were

Good looks	1	2	3	4	5
Sense of humour	1	2	3	4	5
Ambition	1	2	3	4	5
Leadership	1	2	3	4	5
Intelligence	1	2	3	4	5
Self-confidence	1	2	3	4	5
Sociability	1	2	3	4	5
Religiousness	1	2	3	4	5
Character	1	2	3	4	5
Likability	1	2	3	4	5

FIGURE 7.2
Semantic differential scale (adapted from Lambert et al. 1960)

evaluating the same person twice, once speaking in French and the second time speaking in English. Since the French and English versions were made by the same speakers, the chance that participants' judgements would be affected by other aspects of the speakers' voices (such as pitch or voice quality) was minimised. Participants were asked to rate the person who was speaking in each of the guises on fourteen attributes (such as looks, ambition, and self-confidence) on a scale from 1 (lowest) to 5 (highest). A sample of the 'semantic differential scale' Lambert and his colleagues used is reproduced in Figure 7.2.

Lambert and his colleagues found that, while participants who spoke primarily English rated English guises higher on most of these attributes, participants who spoke primarily French *also* rated English guises more favourably. Even more surprising was that the French-speaking participants judged the French guises (i.e., those in their 'own' language) less favourably than the English speakers did. Lambert and his colleagues (1960) concluded that these patterns are a reflection of community stereotypes in Canada in relation to English and French in which English tends to be more highly valued, and that they also indicate a 'minority group reaction' (p. 51) on the part of the French speakers (a phenomenon where members of a minority group internalise negative opinions about them held by the majority group).

Language attitudes play a significant role in many real-life decisions in domains such as law, education, health, and employment, sometimes with serious consequences for people. People's attitudes towards the way people speak, for example, can make them more ready to judge them negatively in contexts such as courtrooms. Psychologist John Dixon and his colleagues (1994) employed the matched guise technique in a study in South Africa where they asked white English-speaking South Africans who also knew Afrikaans to listen to audio recordings of an exchange between a male English-speaking interrogator and a young male suspect. In the guises, the suspect responded to the interrogation either in English with lapses into Cape Afrikaans or completely in Cape Afrikaans. The respondents were asked to rate the speaker's likelihood of being guilty of one of two crimes: violence against another person or passing fraudulent cheques. Suspects who used English were rated significantly less guilty than those who used only Cape Afrikaans, leading Dixon and his associates to conclude that there is a link between non-standard varieties, social attractiveness, and attribution of guilt.

This kind of discrimination has also been observed in employment. Studies by Rey (1977) in Florida, Kalin and Rayko (1980) in Canada, and Giles, Wilson and Conway (1981) in the UK all demonstrate that speakers with non-standard or foreign accents are often considered inappropriate for executive jobs. More recently, Professor of Human Resources Andrew Timming (2017) examined the effect of foreign accents on job applicants' employability in the US. Five different accents were selected for inclusion in this experiment: American, Chinese, Indian, Mexican, and British. For each accent, two male and two female voices were digitally recorded to simulate a telephone job interview. Managerial respondents in the study seemed to discriminate against applicants with foreign accents and to deem them more appropriate for non-customer-facing jobs. British-accented speakers, however, were rated more favourably.

The matched guise technique has proven very popular among sociolinguists as a way of uncovering covert language attitudes. At the same time, the technique does have limitations. One of the main criticisms of the matched guise technique is that the speech recordings are contrived. This means that respondents are not expressing their attitudes towards 'authentic' language but instead towards artificially produced samples. Another problem with this technique is that it is not always clear what they actually measure. Do the participants rate guises based on regional or social features they identify, based on other qualities of the speaker's voice, or because the voices on the recordings remind them of someone they like or dislike? Finally, indirect methods cannot explain why people have the attitudes they do or the underlying assumptions they have about languages and their speakers.

7.3 What People Say about Language

In the late 1990s American sociolinguist Dennis Preston developed a new, more ethnographic approach to language attitudes which he called **folk linguistics**. Folk linguistics is basically the study of people's everyday beliefs about language and language speakers, elicited with minimal input from researchers – that is, no labels, leading questions, or matched guises. The aim is to find out how *people themselves* talk about language.

One way Preston and his collaborator, Nancy Niedzielski, did this was to give people blank maps of the US and ask them to label what they thought were the main speech regions in the country and what they thought they should be called (Niedzielski & Preston 2003). They also asked them to rate on a ten-point scale all the states of the US for language 'correctness' and 'pleasantness'. One group of participants were from Michigan in the northern part of the US, and another from Alabama and South Carolina in the south. When people filled in their maps, they used labels that were often very different from those that linguists use, and these labels often revealed either subtle or overt attitudes towards the ways they thought people in different regions talked, labels like: 'the worst English in America', 'Southern – Hillbilly', 'snobs', 'twag', and 'nasal'. Niedzielski and Preston also, predictably, found that the Northerners and the Southerners in the study had very different attitudes about the way people in different parts of the country (including themselves) spoke. The Michigan respondents had a great deal of linguistic confidence, rating their own way of speaking to be the most 'correct'. They considered the English spoken in New York City and in the south as the least correct. On the other hand, the Southerners gave themselves low marks for correctness, but high ratings for pleasantness. Niedzielski and Preston theorise that this focus on pleasantness may be linked to linguistic insecurity: areas with greater insecurity focus on pleasantness to project a local, unique identity. However, those who are linguistically secure (i.e., those who think they use 'correct' language) do not need to do so, since their status is already secure.

The studies by Preston and his colleagues have been replicated in other contexts. Instead of using a map of the whole country, for example, Betsy Evans (2002) focused in one particular state in the US: Washington. Her aim was to investigate where Washingtonians perceive differences in English in their state to exist and how they feel about these differences. Figure 7.3 shows a map completed by a 44-year-old female respondent from Seattle (Evans 2002: 272). As we can see, eight cities are circled and short labels are provided near them. The respondent used labels that expressed cultural associations (e.g., 'fishing town', 'sounds like farmers', 'rednecks'), as well as labels indicating linguistic features or sounds (e.g., 'ain't', 'yoo').

Overall, folk linguistic studies are very useful because they provide insights about how dialect regions exist *in people's minds*. This kind of information enables researchers to understand what people are judging and how they are judging it on their own terms. Respondents generate their own labels instead of having to fit their attitudes into the pre-set

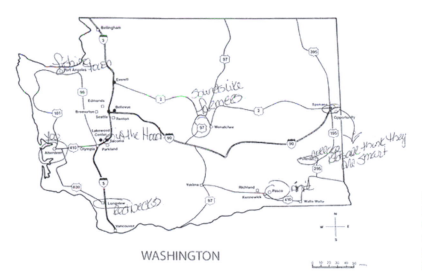

FIGURE 7.3
Hand-drawn map by a 44-year-old female respondent from Seattle (adapted from Evans 2002)

labels used in questionnaires. These labels are not just descriptive, but also tend to have strong negative or positive connotations, helping us understand how attitudes about language come to be embedded in the very language people use to talk about it.

In addition to the kinds of interviews conducted by scholars like Preston and Evans, there are also other ways that we can obtain laypeople's views about language. In fact, as we saw in the tweets about Hayley on *Love Island* that we presented at the beginning of this chapter, people often express their attitudes about the way other people speak over media, social media, and in their everyday conversations. In Chapter 4, for example, we talked about how commenters on YouTube and producers of internet memes evaluated the way a young white girl spoke on television, questioning her upbringing and her education, and accusing her of inauthenticity for appropriating features of African American English (Aslan & Vásquez 2018).

This kind of everyday talk about language that is shared freely in daily conversations and on YouTube, Twitter, and other social media sites can offer valuable insights into people's language attitudes. The sociolinguist Betsy Rymes calls the study of this kind of everyday talk about language **citizen sociolinguistics**, which she defines (2020: 5) as 'the study of the world of language and communication by the people who use it and, as such, have devised ways to understand it that may be more relevant than the ways professional sociolinguists have developed'. By participating in conversations about language, people share knowledge, views, and opinions which can help sociolinguists understand how social values, norms, and **stereotypes** are created and consequently how language actually works in people's lives. At the same time, they also participate in spreading, reproducing, critiquing, and challenging attitudes about language in the societies in which they live.

Rymes (2020) gives as an example the pronunciation of the word *croissant*. Some people in the US might pronounce the word using a French-sounding pronunciation like 'kwuh-SAHN', others a more American pronunciation, like 'kruh SANT'. Still others might use a 'super-American' pronunciation like 'CREscent' or 'CROYscent'. Rymes set out to explore the subtle rules behind these different pronunciations using citizen sociolinguistics. She started with a simple internet search by typing into Google the question 'How should I pronounce 'Croissant'?' The Google query came up with different results. One woman from an English language website confidently explained that Americans should say 'kruh SANT'. A YouTube video featured the same pronunciation, and a response on Yahoo Answers attempted to advise people on how to reproduce a French accent: 'Phonetically – 'Kwar-sor' – spoken fast... Haha, best way I can describe a French accent in type!' Rymes (2020) moved on to obtain more everyday stories from students and friends, asking about their own experiences and their views about how the word should be pronounced. This question was received with bemusement, chuckles, and even more possible pronunciations. She then asked a Parisian friend: 'What do you think when an American says, in the midst of a Ham and Cheese type sentence, *kwar-sor* with that super-French pronunciation?' The answer was, 'I think it sounds *cute*.' Not 'correct', 'exquisite', or 'magnifique'. Simply 'cute'. This example illustrates Ryme's point, that the way 'ordinary people' talk about and understand language is often very different from the way linguists do. Listening to them she argues, can be a way of uncovering nuances about language and language use that are invisible to the more formal frameworks of understanding that linguists often use.

7.4 Language Mocking and Appropriation

Another way to understand people's attitudes towards different ways of speaking and different kinds of speakers is to examine not how they talk about other people's language, but how they *represent* it. Mass media, for example, constantly provides representations of people's language use in ways that sometimes reinforce stereotypes about certain kinds of speakers. Perhaps the most famous example of this is Rosina Lippi-Green's 1997 (2nd edition, 2012) analysis of language representations in Disney animated films in which she found that heroes and heroines usually speak in 'Standard American English', villains often have foreign accents (including British accents), and that characters who speak African American English are almost always animals. Based on her analysis, she argues (2012: 85) that animated films don't just entertain children, but also teach them 'to associate specific characteristics and lifestyles with specific social groups, by means of language variation'.

Other studies have also looked for patterns of language stereotyping in television shows and movies. Lene Lundervold (2013), for instance, analysed the accents of characters in the television series *Game of Thrones*, finding that most of the 'bad' characters spoke with RP accents, whereas most of the 'good' characters spoke in regional accents, especially Northern English accents, echoing the findings from Coupland and Bishop's (2007) study discussed above that sometimes in the UK regional accents are associated with friendliness. What is important about media representations of language use is that they not only reveal the stereotypes in society about the relationship between certain ways of speaking and certain character traits or behaviours, but they also contribute to reproducing and perpetuating these stereotypes. In fact, along with the family and school, the media is among the most important sources for people's attitudes about language.

It is also not unusual, as we said in Chapter 6, for people to produce *stylised* versions of the language varieties used by other people, often as a way of showing affinity with the people who speak that way, but also as a way of distancing themselves or even ridiculing speakers of these varieties. Perhaps the most common place we can see examples of such stylisations is in the media. In Chapter 6 we gave some examples from popular music. Other kinds of performances such as stand-up comedy and drag are also places where language stylisations are common. Sebba (2003), for instance, discusses the stylised London Jamaican accent employed by comedian Sacha Baron Cohen when performing his character Ali G, and Chun (2010) talks about how the Korean American comedian Margaret Cho produces stylised versions of 'Asian English' to make fun of the way white people think Asians talk.

Sometimes practices of **language mocking** become pervasive features of particular societies and mechanisms for the everyday reproduction of racism and other forms of discrimination. This is the case in the US with what the sociolinguist Jane Hill refers to as 'Mock Spanish'. Hill has spent decades documenting examples from the mass media, advertisements, product names, tee-shirt and souvenir slogans, and the everyday talk of Americans of the humorous appropriation of Spanish words into English or the addition of supposedly Spanish features to English words. Examples include the addition of -o at the end of English words, sometimes along with the use of the Spanish definite article *el* (e.g., 'el cheapo'); the use of Spanish words in humorous or negative contexts (e.g., *nada* to mean 'less than nothing'); the use of sexualised Spanish words in the place of English equivalents (e.g. *cajones*); and parodic mispronunciation or misspelling of Spanish (e.g., 'Fleas Navidad' on a Christmas card) (Hill 1998: 682–3).

Hill argues that Mock Spanish in the US constitutes a practice of 'everyday racism' by marking public space as 'white' and portraying Spanish as a deviant form of communication which does not deserve to be taken seriously. When white people use Mock Spanish, she says, they are often trying to index congeniality and humour, but do so at the expense of perpetuating negative stereotypes of Spanish speakers. When they use Mock Spanish to Spanish speakers (see the summary of the article by Barrett in the focal topic at the end of this chapter), it serves as a strategy of condescension – a way of asserting power over them.

There are also other examples of mock varieties prevalent in the US and elsewhere, such as 'Mock Asian' (Chun 2010) – the stylised representations of Asian accents (e.g., 'flied lice') or of Asian languages (e.g., representing them as gibberish with sounds like 'ching-chong-ching-chong'), made even more racist by its failure to make any effort to differentiate different Asian languages or Asian speakers – and 'Mock Ebonics' (Ronkin & Karn 2002) – derogatory stylisations of African American English, referred to by Bucholtz and Lopez (2011: 680) as 'linguistic blackface' or 'linguistic minstrelsy', evoking the racist minstrel shows of the nineteenth and early twentieth centuries in the US and UK. In all of these cases, the circulation of mock varieties serves not just to denigrate speakers of the language variety that is being mocked, but also to reinforce racialised notions of language and to assert the 'normativity of white language and culture' (Bucholtz & Lopez 2011: 684).

Closely related to practices of language mocking are those of **language appropriation**, which is basically a matter of imitating the way other people speak, not for the purpose of mockery, but for the purpose of personal gain or profit. Of course, not all acts of appropriation are necessarily exploitative or racist. In Chapter 6 we gave examples of people – from famous performers like the Beatles to ordinary people – appropriating communicative resources associated with people from backgrounds different from their own as a way of performing certain kinds of identities.

But sometimes acts of linguistic or semiotic appropriation can be offensive. Several scholars and commentators (e.g., Matamoros-Fernandez 2020; Parham 2020) have used the term 'digital blackface' to describe when white people appropriate the voices, music, and movements of African Americans in genres like internet memes, animated GIFs and TikTok videos. TikTok is an especially good place to find examples of appropriation, and many black TikTok creators have criticised white creators for capitalising on cultural styles created by African Americans. In the case of TikTok, however, what is considered 'appropriate' appropriation and what is not is often unclear, especially since the practice of reusing soundtracks from other people is one of the main affordances of the platform. Jones (2021b) argues that this makes it necessary for creators and fans to negotiate the acceptability of different forms of appropriation on a case-by-case basis by commenting on, critiquing, and creating 'duets' with other people's videos.

Activity: Justin Bieber and 'Mock Spanish'

'Despacito' is a song by Puerto Rican singer Luis Fonsi featuring Puerto Rican rapper Daddy Yankee which was released in January 2017. In April 2017, the smash-hit remix featuring the famous Canadian singer Justin Bieber was released, topping the charts in forty-seven countries for weeks. 'Despacito' was ranked among the best Latin songs of all time.

In the remix version Bieber sings in both English and Spanish, despite the fact that he is not a competent Spanish speaker. In one of his live performances Bieber forgot the lyrics of the Spanish chorus of the song and used instead random Spanish words, singing: 'blah, blah, blah, burrito, dorito, and poquito' to imitate the sound of Spanish (see www.youtube.com/watch?v=ZrwMeslmeRY). Some fans criticised Bieber for employing 'Mock Spanish'. One blogger, for instance, wrote, 'Hey Bieber, if you can't sing in Spanish – that's fine, but don't mock us' (lola 2017). The originator of the song, Luis Fonsi, however, defended Bieber, saying, 'I've done songs in other languages, I know how hard it is' (Moreno 2017).

1. Search the Internet for other people's opinions about this case. Why were some people offended by Bieber's behaviour and others more willing to forgive him for it?
2. Do you think this is an example of language mocking?
3. Is there anything problematic about Bieber appropriating the Spanish language in the first place or his attitude towards this appropriation?
4. What forms of privilege might Bieber enjoy as a white Canadian singer that singers of other backgrounds may not enjoy?

7.5 Focal Topic: Language and Racism

In this section we will explore in more detail the ways practices of language mocking and appropriation can perpetuate racism and discrimination. We will focus on two studies, one dealing with the use of 'Mock Spanish' in a Mexican restaurant, and the other examining the appropriation of African American English by the Australian rapper Iggy Azalea.

In the first article, sociolinguist Rusty Barrett describes the interactions between English-speaking Anglo and monolingual Spanish-speaking employees in an Anglo-owned Mexican restaurant in Texas. He observes how Anglo managers frequently use English mixed with Mock Spanish when communicating with Spanish-speaking employees, even though they are able to communicate in Spanish, which often results in misunderstanding for which the Spanish speakers are usually blamed. This use of Mock Spanish, he argues, reflects the broader language ideologies in US society and perpetuates racial segregation and inequality in this particular workplace.

The second article, by Maeve Eberhardt and Kara Freeman, presents a sociolinguistic analysis of the use of African American English by the white rapper Iggy Azalea, which reveals that her use of AAE features exceeds that of other white rappers such as Eminem. They argue that Azalea's appropriation of African American English, and her ability to capitalise on it to advance her career, is an example of the linguistic and social privilege that whiteness affords in contemporary society.

Barrett, R. (2006) Language ideology and racial inequality: Competing functions of Spanish in an Anglo-owned Mexican restaurant. *Language in Society*, 35(2), 163–204   This article focuses on the way language attitudes and language practices can operate to perpetuate racism and inequality in the workplace. It describes an ethnographic study of an Anglo-owned Mexican restaurant in Texas which the author conducted while he was working as a bartender there. The managers and most of the serving staff at the restaurant were white, while nearly all of the kitchen staff were Mexicans or Guatemalans, many of them monolingual Spanish speakers. Barrett's status as an English–Spanish bilingual gave him access to a wide range of interactions in the restaurant and different perspectives on what was going on there.

Barrett discusses a range of overtly racist practices engaged in by the Anglo managers and servers, such as disparaging Latinx customers and giving them bad service and excluding non-Anglo staff members from social events. The main focus of the article, however, is on how linguistic practices contributed to the marginalisation of the Spanish-speaking employees.

The main practice Barrett examines is the use of 'Mock Spanish' by managers when giving directives to the kitchen staff, even though many of them were competent enough in Spanish to speak a more 'standard' variety. Usually, this involved the substitution of single Spanish words into otherwise English sentences ('There's *agua* ['water'] on the *piso* ['floor']'; Did you *limpia* ['clean'] the *baño* ['bathroom']?). Sometimes this practice made the directives from managers difficult for the Spanish-speaking staff to understand, and when this resulted in them not carrying out a task they had been asked to do, they were accused of being 'lazy'.

Barrett gives two possible reasons for this practice. First, this way of speaking showed that the managers were unwilling to make an effort to communicate more clearly to the Mexican and Guatemalan staff: 'The general irrelevance of Spanish grammar for Anglo speakers', he says (p. 182), 'reflects an ideology in which Spanish speakers themselves are viewed as inconsequential'. This attitude extended to Anglo staff who were less proficient in Spanish and sometimes jokingly made-up Spanish words and expressions, as in the following exchange:

SERVER: Will you ask Luis to refill the ice bin?
BARTENDER: OK… How do you say 'ice'?
SERVER: I don't know? Ice-o? (both laugh)
BARTENDER: (to busser who is passing through the wait station): *Mas ice-o, por favor.*
BUSSER: *¿Qué?* (What?)

(p. 182)

In this case, the 'Spanish' is entirely for the benefit of the Anglo speakers' own amusement, and the actual Spanish speaker is marginalised in the interaction, even though it supposedly involves an attempt to communicate with him.

Second, the use of 'Mock Spanish' allowed managers to convey a certain kind of attitude associated with this way of talking, one that indexed both friendliness and superiority. Barrett cites the work of Jane Hill (1998), noting how 'Mock Spanish' is seen as a way of constructing 'congeniality', even though what it actually does is perpetuate racist stereotypes of Spanish speakers and assert the dominance of English over Spanish. Despite the fact that this way of speaking was both difficult to understand and condescending, the assumption was that the Spanish-speaking employees would eventually 'get used to it', and although the managers recognised that their directives were sometimes not understood, they chose to fall back on racist stereotypes (e.g., the 'laziness' of the Spanish speaker) when they were not followed.

At the same time, Barrett also observes how Spanish-speaking staff used the situation to perform acts of resistance. Since Anglo employees usually made little effort to make themselves understood, Spanish-speaking employees could sometimes pretend not to understand. Contrary to the assumption of Anglo managers, Barrett says, they rarely if ever used this strategy to avoid their actual work responsibilities but rather to avoid conflict in cases where an Anglo employee asked them to do things that violated workplace rules.

The use of 'Mock Spanish' in this workplace, Barrett concludes, does not just reflect the Anglo workers' attitudes towards Spanish (and Spanish speakers), but also helps to maintain unequal power relationships in the workplace. He writes:

Language ideology both reflects and enacts racial inequalities. In Anglo–Anglo interactions, Mock Spanish may function as a form of symbolic revalorization, reproducing derogatory racial portrayals of Latinos for Anglo amusement. When used in interactions with Spanish speakers, Mock Spanish serves to exclude Spanish speakers from interactions in which they should be active participants. The failure to listen to the needs of Latinos and the failure earnestly to attempt to communicate with Spanish speakers are not forms of symbolic revalorization but are basic components of racial subordination.

(2006: 201)

Eberhardt, M., and Freeman, K. (2015) 'First things first, I'm the realest': Linguistic appropriation, white privilege, and the hip-hop persona of Iggy Azalea. *Journal of Sociolinguistics*, 19(3), 303–27   While the article by Barrett described above deals primarily with language mocking, this article takes up the issue of linguistic appropriation through a close examination of the language used by white Australian rapper Iggy Azalea to construct a 'marketable hip-hop persona' (p. 309). Eberhardt and Freeman argue that Azalea's 'overzealous' (p. 303) use of features of AAE in her music (features that she does not use when she is speaking in other contexts) constitutes an appropriation of African American language and culture ultimately made possible by the privilege her whiteness bestows on her.

Throughout history there have been ample examples of whites co-opting black cultural forms (e.g., jazz and blues) and then enjoying more profit from them than those who originally created them. Eberhardt and Freeman quote Jane Hill (2008) in arguing that such practices are at the centre of white privilege:

The constitution of White privilege, achieved by recruiting both material and symbolic resources from the bottom of the racial hierarchy, Color, to the top, Whiteness, is one of the most important projects of White racist culture.

(Hill 2008: 158)

At the same time, as we will discuss in Chapter 9, hip-hop, although it has its roots in African American urban culture of the late 1970s and 1980s, has become a global phenomenon, with artists from places as far afield as Malaysia and Japan appropriating various aspects of the art form, including some features of African American English. Such appropriation, however, has its limits. As Cutler (2003) observes, non-African Americans who are at the core of hip-hop culture usually adopt fewer AAE features and instead try to incorporate features of their own linguistic repertoires into hip-hop forms. As Cutler puts it:

there is perhaps also a sense that trying to sound too black might actually make one less 'real' because one is trying to be something one is not; that is, respecting ethnolinguistic boundaries is an essential part of 'keeping it real' because it is an acknowledgement that one is not trying to be black.

(Cutler 2003: 226)

Eberhardt and Freeman give a number of examples of white hip-hop artists, such as Macklemore, who use a considerable amount of AAE in their music, and have subsequently been criticised for their 'race mockery' (D'Addario 2013), and others who use almost none, such as Eminem (who actually grew up in a context in which AAE was spoken), and are praised for their authenticity.

The study Eberhardt and Freeman conducted consisted of analysing forty-eight of Iggy Azalea's songs as well as five radio interviews. The analysis of Azalea's music revealed ample use of phonological and grammatical features associated with AAE such as:

- monophthongal /ai/ (rhyme [rɑːm]);
- /r/-lessness (mister [mɪstə]);
- glide weakening of /ɔɪ/ (boy [bɔə]);
- fortition of /z/ before nasals (business [bɪdnɪs]);
- multiple negation (I don't want none);
- 3rd person singular -s absence (she go);
- copular ain't (If it ain't high class);
- remote past BEEN (got money, BEEN had it);
- habitual be (My chat room be poppin');
- copula absence (She not here).

Eberhardt and Freeman focused in on copula absence as an iconic feature of AAE, comparing Azalea's use of this feature with the African American rappers Eve and Juvenile, as well as with (white) Eminem. What they found was that Azalea uses this feature as much if not *more* than the black rappers, while Eminem hardly uses it at all. At the same time, they found that Azalea *never* uses this feature when she is speaking in interviews. Such a dramatic shift in her style when performing, they argue, shows how carefully constructed her hip-hop identity is, and the fact that she exceeds even black artists in her use of this iconic feature is a case of 'hyper-performance', which may be responsible for some people regarding her music as a mimicry of blackness.

Based on their analysis, Eberhardt and Freeman contend that Iggy Azalea's wholesale appropriation of AAE, as well as the stereotyped notions of blackness embedded in the content of her lyrics (e.g., hyper-sexuality, lavish displays of wealth), make her 'a particularly salient example of a white hegemony that views black cultural resources as ripe for the strategic picking' (p. 305). Her appropriation of AAE fuels her own success and monetary gain while at the same time perpetuating essentialised ideas about race.

Project Ideas

1. Use the BBC voices website (www.bbc.co.uk/voices/) to find five recordings of people from different parts of the UK. Design your own semantic differential scale (see, for example, Figure 7.2) and play the recordings to people to obtain their attitudes towards the varieties in the five recordings. Compare their answers.

2. Replicate Niedzielski and Preston's (2003) study. Give people a blank map either of a whole country or a specific area. Ask them to draw lines and circles around places where they think people's language sounds different. Next, ask them to write down what they'd call that way of talking, if they can think of a label for it. They can also give an example of what's different there, for instance a word or pronunciation people use or a special way of talking. What do these findings tell us about your respondents' perceptions and attitudes towards the varieties they identified on the map?

3. Conduct a small citizen sociolinguistic investigation to explore people's perceptions and understandings about language. Find a debate about language on social media. YouTube, Facebook, and Twitter are good sources to use. Collect comments that people have posted and analyse them. What do these everyday conversations reveal?

4. Compile a collection of TikTok videos in which people appropriate the voices and/or movements of an ethnic group that they are not a member of. Also pay attention to the way other people have commented on or remixed these videos. Explore the factors which might contribute to these appropriations being considered acceptable or unacceptable.

8 Language in the Material World

PREVIEW

KEY TERMS

bottom-up signs

code preference system

corporeal sociolinguistics

embodiment

emplacement system

ephemeral signs

ethnolinguistic vitality

geosemiotics

inscription system

linguistic landscapes

public signs

semiotic landscapes

top-down signs

transient signs

walking-tour interviews

This chapter focuses on the relationship between language and the material world. The material world includes public spaces and built environments, our bodies, and the objects that we use on a daily basis. We will start by exploring different kinds of public signs that are displayed in the physical environment, showing how things like posters, notices, billboards, advertisements, street names, and graffiti both reflect sociolinguistic realities and serve as resources for enacting those realities. We will then turn our focus to the relationship between language and the body. The ultimate aim of this chapter is to demonstrate that our bodies and the world around us are as important for performing social identities and managing social relationships as the words we speak. At the end of this chapter, in the focal topic, we will explore the significance of signage and embodiment in situations of conflict and political protest.

8.1 Introduction

Every era has its defining moments. For our era one of those moments has been the outbreak of the novel coronavirus, which was first reported in China in December 2019 and which by January 2020 had begun to spread globally. In an attempt to contain its rapid spread, governments imposed lockdown restrictions which limited the movement of millions of people.

The COVID-19 pandemic is just the kind of wicked problem that we talked about in the introduction to this book, a problem that involved many of the issues we have focused on here: inequality, identity, meaning-making, and the ways people and resources (and, as it turns out, viruses) travel from one context to another, and a problem that required input from lots of different kinds of people: politicians, doctors, epidemiologists, and even sociolinguists (Jones 2021a). One of the biggest issues around the pandemic was communication: how to convince people to do things (some of which were difficult to do) that would slow the spread of the disease, and how to counter the pandemic of misinformation that was spreading as quickly as the virus. Nearly every action people took in response to the pandemic became an act of communication and, as with all acts of communication, a way of performing social identities and showing allegiances to particular groups and particular ideologies. In some places, deciding whether or not to wear a face mask, for example, became a matter of identity not so different from the linguistic choices we have discussed in previous chapters, such as choosing to pronounce your vowels in a certain way or to appropriate a particular style of speech.

The pandemic also changed the way language was inscribed onto our material environments. As COVID-19 lockdown restrictions were implemented, the streets and public squares of towns and cities around the world suddenly filled with signs telling people what to do, how to act, and sometimes even what to think or feel about what was going on. Figures 8.1 and 8.2, for instance, are signs that appeared in downtown Reading (UK) where we live. 8.1 was produced by the National Health Service (NHS) and the British government, and 8.2 was produced by a private company to thank the NHS.

Like the mural painted on a remaining piece of the Berlin Wall that we discussed in Chapter 2, these signs consist of combinations of different resources: language, logos, images, and understanding them requires a certain configuration of *competencies*. For example, to understand Figure 8.1 it would be useful not just to know English, but also to know that older people were particularly vulnerable to the disease and were at risk of catching the virus from younger people. To understand Figure 8.2 it would help to be familiar with the symbolic meaning of the rainbow and how, in the context of the pandemic, it had become *enregistered* (see Chapter 3) as an expression of gratitude to healthcare workers who were working to save people's lives, an indexical meaning that started in the UK but quickly spread to other countries. But, as we said in Chapter 2, it is not essential to have full competence in all of these resources: it is perhaps

FIGURE 8.1
Official COVID-19 sign
(author's photo)

FIGURE 8.2
'Thank you NHS' sign
(author's photo)

possible to get the message about the dangers of COVID-19 in Figure 8.1, even if you don't read English, and to understand the meaning of Figure 8.2, even if you don't know the meaning of the rainbow.

The more important point is the way the pandemic changed the communicative environments in which people operated, giving rise to new meanings and new ways of speaking and writing. Of course, not all of the public signs about COVID-19 in the UK used English, and not all of them were produced by government bodies or big companies. Figure 8.3. for instance, is a sign produced by the Council for Voluntary Services in Salford (a city next to Manchester in the UK) about the precautions people should take to stop the spread of the virus, which includes both English and Kurdish Kurmanji (Northern Kurdish), along with a number of icons

FIGURE 8.3
Bilingual poster from the Salford Council for Voluntary Services

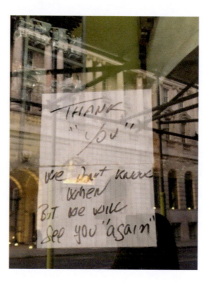

FIGURE 8.4
Sign on a shop in London (adapted from Zhu Hua 2021: 40)

depicting handwashing, mask wearing, and social distancing. Of course, it is unlikely that this sign was posted all around Salford: it was probably placed mostly in areas where Kurdish migrants might have been living. Another interesting thing about the sign is that the English bits appear on top of the Kurdish bits. This might seem like a small thing, but it is a subtle reminder that, in the UK, English is the dominant 'language'.

The sign in Figure 8.4, posted on a shopfront in London, is very different from the others, written in a very different *style* (both linguistically and typographically), and so performing a very different kind of identity for the author and enacting a very different kind of relationship with readers. Applied linguist Zhu Hua (2021) notes that handwritten messages like this were used by shopkeepers to express sincerity and solidarity with their customers in the context of communicating the message that their shops were closed. She also points out that 'we will see you "again"' is a reference to the wartime song 'We'll Meet Again', which was quoted by Queen Elizabeth in her message to the nation about COVID-19. In other words, just by putting 'again' in quotation marks, the author of this sign was able to index feelings of nationalism, resilience, and a common purpose.

Looking at signs like this is interesting because it highlights the extent to which language and other semiotic resources are embedded in our physical environments and affect the way we experience the material world, sometimes in very obvious ways and sometimes in more subtle ways. These particular examples also demonstrate how the linguistic or semiotic aspects of our environments are always changing in response to physical, social, political, economic, and even sociolinguistic changes. In this chapter we will explore in detail the more material dimensions of language use and how they can shed light on many of the issues of meaning, identity, inclusion, and exclusion that we have talked about throughout this book.

8.2 Linguistic Landscapes

The study of language and other semiotic resources on written signs displayed in public space is known as **linguistic landscapes** research. This new approach to sociolinguistic research emerged in the 1990s with the work of Rodrigue Landry and Richard Bourhis, who wrote: 'The language of public road signs, advertising billboards, street names, place names, commercial shop signs, and public signs on government buildings *combines to form the linguistic landscape* of a given territory, region, or urban agglomeration' (Landry & Bourhis 1997: 25, emphasis ours).

As we've seen in the examples above, all sorts of signs can make up the linguistic landscape of a particular place. Early scholars in the field classified signs into two categories: **top-down** and **bottom-up** (Ben-Rafael et al. 2006). **Top-down** signs are official messages produced by public institutions, like the government, councils, and municipalities. They include things like street name signs and road and direction signs, and they often contain official (institutional) information like regulations, public announcements, and official designations. **Bottom-up** signs are created by commercial and other private organisations and include shop signs or notices in offices, factories, and companies.

With the development of the field, the notion of what constitutes linguistic landscapes has expanded to include more ephemeral things such as posters, stickers, receipts, graffiti, and street art. These kinds of signs are called **ephemeral** because they tend to be less permanent. They are often created by members of the public, and their emplacement in specific locales usually involves less conscious planning. Other sociolinguists like Mark Sebba (2010) and Alastair Pennycook (2010) have explored **transient** signs. These include *moving* signs such as advertisements on buses, trains, and taxis and people's clothing (like the tee-shirts we looked at in Chapter 2). Pennycook says that even sounds, like music, and smells (such as those coming from street stalls or markets) should also be considered part of linguistic landscapes as they have the potential to communicate meaning and contribute to the social construction of a given place. As we will see, all these different kinds of signs and semiotic objects work together to represent the sociolinguistic reality of a place, generating configurations of meanings that index identities, power relations, and ideologies.

The first wave of linguistic landscape studies focused almost exclusively on the different kinds of 'languages' that were found on signs in multilingual communities. In their ground-breaking study in the 1990s, for example, Landry and Bourhis (1997) investigated the visibility of French and English on public and commercial signs in Quebec City, the capital of Canada's Quebec Province, where French is widely spoken. They hypothesised that the amount the different languages appeared on signs could tell us something about the **ethnolinguistic vitality** of a particular language, that is, the ability of a group to maintain its way of speaking as an emblem of its culture and identity. They found that the language on signs did indeed correlate with other measures of ethnolinguistic vitality, and that it even had an effect on the language that people spoke when they were in particular places.

Numerous studies followed, investigating the linguistic landscapes of various places in the world. The majority of these early studies categorised signs as top-down or bottom-up and focused on which languages were visible on them. For instance, Backhaus (2007) presents a detailed study of the linguistic landscape of Tokyo, where he counted and categorised the languages visible on signs and then documented their geographic distribution and territorial presence on a map. Table 8.1 shows the languages he found in the linguistic landscape of Tokyo.

As you can see from the table, in addition to Japanese, fourteen other languages were identified in Tokyo's linguistic landscape. What is perhaps most interesting is that English rather than Japanese was found to be the most frequently used language on signs in Tokyo. Other relatively popular languages were Chinese (2.7%) and Korean (1.7%), but most of the other languages appeared on fewer than twenty signs in the sample. Backhaus (2007) also found that while English was prevalent in the linguistic landscape of Tokyo, it was more likely to be used on bottom-up (commercial) signs, whereas Japanese predominated on top-down (official) signs. There are lots of possible reasons for the prevalence of English in the linguistic landscape of Tokyo, but it is unlikely that the prevalence of English speakers is one of them: indeed the number of English speakers among the local population in Tokyo is relatively small compared to other Asian cities (such as Hong Kong and Singapore). A more likely explanation is that English was often used to express *indexical meanings* rather than *semantic meanings*, not to communicate information, but to communicate

Table 8.1 Languages on public signs in Tokyo

Language	Contained	% of cases[*]
Japanese	1674	72.1
English	2266	97.6
Chinese	62	2.7
Korean	40	1.7
French	20	0.9
Portuguese	12	0.5
Spanish	8	0.3
Latin	6	0.3
Thai	5	0.2
Italian	4	0.2
Persian	2	0.1
Tagalog	2	0.1
German	2	0.1
Arabic	1	0.0
Russian	1	0.0
Total cases	**2321**	**100**

* Note that the percentages do not add up to 100 as many signs were multilingual.
(adapted from Backhaus 2007: 71)

a certain mood, or lifestyle (see Chapter 2). Backhaus argues that the majority use of Japanese in top-down official signs was designed mainly to express and reinforce feelings of authority and solidarity, while bottom-up signs used more foreign languages to create a more modern 'global' image for the companies that used them.

Activity: Signs in a 'Buffer Zone'

The island of Cyprus has been divided by a UN-controlled 'buffer zone' since 1974, due to the long-term conflict between Greek-Cypriots and Turkish-Cypriots. Themistocleous (2019) explored the visibility of the two official languages, namely Greek and Turkish, as well as other languages in the linguistic landscape near the dividing line that separates the capital Nicosia.

Table 8.2 shows the prevalence of different languages Themistocleous found in the neighbourhoods close to the dividing line and in the UN-controlled buffer zone.

Table 8.2 Languages on public signs in Nicosia, Cyprus

Language(s)	Greek-Cypriot community		Border and UN-controlled buffer zone		Turkish-Cypriot community	
	N	%	N	%	N	%
English	514	56.36	18	38.30	86	41.75
Greek	198	21.71	6	12.77	1	0.5
Turkish	-	0	4	8.5	64	30.97
English & Greek	180	19.73	4	8.5	-	0
English & Turkish	1	0.11	6	12.76	47	22.85
Greek & Turkish	1	0.11	3	6.4	3	0.99
English, Greek & Turkish	1	0.11	5	10.63	4	1.94
English & other language	6	0.66	-	0	-	0
English, Greek, Turkish, & other language	-	0	-	0	1	0.5
English, Greek, & other language	6	0.66	-	0	-	0
Other language	5	0.55	1	2.14	1	0.5
Total	**912**	**100**	**47**	**100**	**207**	**100**

(adapted from Themistocleous 2019)

1. Which languages are most visible in the linguistic landscapes of each area?
2. Which languages are *excluded* from the linguistic landscapes of each area?
3. What does the visibility/exclusion of languages in written public signs tell us about the sociolinguistic composition and language boundaries in Nicosia?
4. What do you think this tells us about the social and political conditions in the different areas and the opinions and ideologies of the people who control those areas?

By investigating the visibility of languages in multilingual spaces we can obtain information about the sociolinguistic composition and language boundaries of a given community. In other words, by looking at the languages that are included in the public signs around us, we can understand something about who lives in that area and what language(s) they speak (though, as the example of Tokyo showed, the relationship between the language on signs and language speakers is not always straightforward). The important point is that the code choice on public signage is neither neutral nor random; it is *a symbolic practice* which communicates not just information but also ideologies. The visibility or exclusion of languages in the public arena, for example, can provide some insight into which languages in a given community are supported by society and its language policies and which ones are marginalised.

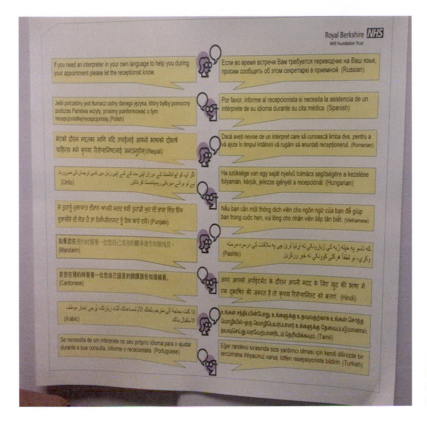

FIGURE 8.5
Multilingual public sign in a hospital
(author's photo)

Consider, for instance, the sign in Figure 8.5. It was found in the waiting area of the outpatient ward at a hospital in Reading. The sign informs patients that if they need the help of an interpreter during their appointment with the doctor, they should inform the receptionist. This message is written in English as well as seventeen other codes, including Urdu, Chinese, Russian, Pashto, Portuguese, Arabic, and so on. We can see that this sign that was produced by an official institution (namely the Health Authority in Reading) prioritises English, the dominant and official language of the UK, because that's the one that appears first. But the choice of the other seventeen languages is also interesting because these languages seem to represent the dominant ethnic groups that live in the town. We can say that this sign is inclusive because it addresses speakers of various languages. It also indexes that Reading is an ethnically and linguistically diverse place. But we should also consider which languages are missing from this sign. For instance, even though Reading has a large Greek-speaking community, the Greek language does not feature on this sign. Another question we can ask is about the order of the other seventeen languages that appear on this sign. Why, for example, is Polish presented after English? Does that mean that this language, and consequently its speakers, have more prominence in Reading compared to let's say Turkish and its speakers, which appears last?

Understanding how to answer questions like this requires an approach to linguistic landscapes that goes beyond simply counting languages, one that examines how different resources (both verbal and visual) are arranged on signs, how the way that signs are placed in the physical environment affects their meanings, who creates signs and why, who uses them and how, and how signs relate to the history, culture, and politics of a given community. This more expansive approach to linguistic landscapes will be the subject of the next section.

8.3 Discourses in Place

As we said above, counting languages alone cannot provide adequate insights into how signs socially construct our material world and function as communicative resources by the people who make them and the people who use them. The sociolinguists Ron Scollon and Suzie Wong Scollon, in their ground-breaking book *Discourses in place: Language in the material world* (2003) attempt to address these inadequacies by proposing a more qualitative framework known as **geosemiotics**. According to this framework, when we analyse signs in the material world, we need to take into consideration three important 'systems':

1. **The code preference system**
   This system has to do with which 'languages' appear on signs and, if they are multilingual, which one comes first. The fact that languages on multilingual signs cannot be displayed simultaneously in the same position creates a choice system. The language that is prioritised (as we saw in Figure 8.5) indexes its prominence, prestige, and status. Consequently, this choice can project ideological stances relating to power relations within a given community.
2. **The inscription system**
   Here we need to analyse in detail the more multimodal aspects of signs (see Chapter 4), including use of fonts, colours, images, and the kind of material that was used to produce the sign (e.g., paper, metal, laminate). The non-linguistic aspects of signs are just as important as the words written on them in helping us to understand both the intentions of those that created the signs and how they might be interpreted and used by different kinds of people.
3. **The emplacement system**
   For this aspect we need to pay attention to *where* in the physical world a given sign is located. The location of the sign can tell us a lot about its meaning and what the sign makers are trying to achieve. The same sign can have different meanings when placed in different locations. The Scollons (2003) remind us that signs always have *indexical meanings* that they create by 'pointing to' aspects of the physical environments in which they are placed (as well as 'pointing to' aspects of the social environments of the societies in which they are found).

FIGURE 8.6
Top-down warning signs
in Cyprus
(author's photo)

These three systems, the Scollons say, *work together* to create meanings and socially construct public space, but also to perform certain identities for the people who have created the sign and project certain identities onto the people who are meant to read it. In this way, linguistic landscapes don't just construct our immediate social environments but also function to reproduce (or sometimes challenge) ideologies and relationships of power in the wider society. Consider, for instance, the sign in Figure 8.6.

In the activity above we explored the different languages that are included or excluded in the linguistic landscape of central Nicosia, a capital that as we said is divided into two separate communities due to the long-term conflict between Greek-Cypriots and Turkish-Cypriots. The sign in Figure 8.6 is a permanent, top-down sign that was found near the Turkish-Cypriot checkpoint.

A geosemiotic analysis of this sign would need to take into account the following aspects:

Code preference: This sign is multilingual, containing three different codes: Turkish, English, and Greek. At first glance, we might think that this sign is inclusive because it addresses speakers of all these codes. However, if we pay closer attention to the order that the codes appear on the sign, we can see that Turkish is prioritised, followed by English, while Greek appears last. English is displayed second despite the fact that it is not an official language in Cyprus, like Greek and Turkish. The Turkish phrase 'Polis Genel Müdürlüğü' ('Police General

Directorate') at the bottom right is not translated into English or Greek, restricting the audience of this part of the sign to Turkish speakers only.

Inscription system: The main text which sets out the immigration rules is written in black capital letters. The use of the capital letters creates an authoritative, official, and almost intimidating tone, which is typical of these kinds of immigration warning signs. This formal tone is further emphasised through the display of red capital letters at the top for the word 'warning'. Red is often associated with danger as well as power, and the combination of the word 'warning' and the red colour functions as an attention-getter. Another visual element includes a Turkish insignia at the top, which shows a red star and crescent, creating associations with the Turkish flag.

Emplacement system: The sign is located close to the Turkish-Cypriot checkpoint. People who want to visit the Turkish-Cypriot community move from the Greek-Cypriot checkpoint through the UN-controlled buffer zone and finally arrive at the Turkish-Cypriot checkpoint where this sign is located. This is therefore one of the first signs someone sees when they enter the Turkish-Cypriot community. It is worth mentioning that the top-down sign behind it is also a warning sign, but that one includes only Turkish and English, excluding Greek altogether.

All three systems work together to tell us something about the power relations between the two communities, the ideologies they have about each other, and the identities they want to project. As the two communities are in conflict, the code of the 'other' (in this case Greek) is displayed last on the front sign and completely excluded on the sign behind. Turkish, the dominant language in the Turkish-Cypriot community, is given priority. This choice not only informs the audience that they are entering a Turkish-speaking area but also shows that Turkish has more prominence, status, and prestige in that area. Greek is given less status. The insignia on the sign works together with the monolingual phrase 'Police General Directorate' at the bottom as well as the prioritisation of Turkish on the sign to indicate that its creators are the local Turkish-Cypriot authorities. The emplacement of this sign in this particular locale serves two functions: (1) informative: it informs the audience about the immigration rules they need to follow upon entering this space, and (2) ideological: it indicates the language boundaries between the two communities. In doing so, it represents the power relations between the two and the fact that they are in conflict and also, by omitting or placing Greek at the end, projects a strong nationalist ideology.

As we have seen in this example, geosemiotics offers an analytical framework which enables us to delve deeper into signs and the way they work in the contexts in which they are placed. It allows us to move beyond a simple categorisation into top-down vs. bottom-up or monolingual vs. multilingual and instead explore how linguistic and other semiotic resources work together to generate meaning, socially construct the material world and project discourses in public space. Taking these ideas further, Jaworski and Thurlow (2010) introduced the term **semiotic landscapes** to account for the diversity of resources other than language which create meaning in the material world.

Activity: 'Don't Feed the Pigeons'

The sign in Figure 8.7 was nailed to a tree in a local park in the UK. It is made of cardboard and handwritten in Hindi with a black marking pen. The text translates to:

Please don't feed rice to the pigeons.
The pigeons cannot digest it.
Rice also attracts rats.
"Thanks"

Use the geosemiotics framework we talked about above to analyse this sign. Consider the following aspects:

- Who do you think produced this sign?
- What is the purpose of this sign?
- Who is the target audience?
- What can you say about the language choice on the sign? Is this sign inclusive or exclusive?
- What kind of other resources/materials were used to create this sign? How does this affect how you interpret the sign?
- Why do you think it was placed in that particular location? How does the emplacement contribute to the meaning? How does its emplacement relate to the sign on its right?

FIGURE 8.7
Sign in a local park in the UK
(author's photo)

Another important development in the field of linguistic landscapes has been the application of more *ethnographic approaches* to the investigation of public spaces. As we said in Chapter 3, conducting ethnography usually involves immersing oneself in the community under investigation, getting to know the people and studying how they communicate in the 'real world'. Combining methods like observations and interviews with the analysis of signs themselves enables us to understand more about how linguistic landscapes come to be the way they are and how the people who inhabit them *experience* and use them. In other words, ethnographic approaches attempt to understand linguistic landscapes not from the point of view of researchers, but from the point of view of the ordinary people who live, work, shop, and travel in a given area.

One study which used this approach was Jackie Jia Lou's (2016) investigation of the linguistic landscape of Chinatown in Washington, DC. By engaging with people who lived and worked in the neighbourhood, Lou was able to uncover the different historical, social, and cultural factors that shaped the linguistic landscape of this traditionally ethnic area. More importantly, she was able to understand how economic forces, such as the increasing replacement of residential properties and small businesses with corporately owned commercial properties, was affecting both the linguistic landscape and the lives of the people who lived there.

In her work, Lou has used a variety of innovative methods to gather data about the way people experience their physical environments. In her Chinatown study, for example, she asked people to draw maps of the neighbourhood, including any landmarks that they thought were important, and then she used these maps as the starting point for interviews with these people. In another study, this one exploring the linguistic landscapes of three markets in Hong Kong (2017), she used the same map-drawing method combined with **walking-tour interviews** in which she walked with her participants through parts of Hong Kong and observed how they interacted with the public signs and other semiotic resources around them. According to Lou, the walking-tour interviews offered three types of information: (1) the participants' perceptions of the areas they walked through and the signs that attracted their attention; (2) the kinds of activities they did in these public spaces; and (3) their attitudes and their everyday language practices within the linguistic landscape. Overall, Lou (2017) demonstrates the importance of engaging not just with linguistic landscapes but with how people experience and use these landscapes in their day-to-day lives.

Ethnography can also highlight another important characteristic of linguistic landscapes: the fact that they are not static. Linguistic landscapes are dynamic and constantly change over time as new shops emerge, new buildings are built, and whole areas are developed and redeveloped. Using ethnographic approaches in linguistic landscape research enables us to unveil changes in public space and the ideologies and identities that are projected through these changes.

The Belgian sociolinguist Jan Blommaert was one of the first to highlight the importance of ethnography for better understanding linguistic landscapes. In his book *Ethnography, superdiversity and linguistic landscapes* (2013b) he examined written public signs in his old neighbourhood, Oud-Berchem, in Antwerp, Belgium. Being a long-term resident in this area, Blommaert was able to identify how globalisation had brought people from an array of linguistic and cultural backgrounds into close contact with one another. In the course of time, these changes transformed the linguistic landscape of the Oud-Berchem neighbourhood. Blommaert observed that, while Dutch was the most common language on written public signs, as the language of the most traditional residential population and the lingua franca used between the different ethnic groups who came later, Turkish was also prominent, as the language of the most established immigrant community and it often appeared in bilingual public signs along with Dutch. Cantonese, Spanish, Polish, Arabic, and Portuguese were also found in the linguistic landscape of Oud-Berchem and they represented the languages of newly established immigrant communities. Overall, Blommaert's approach enabled him to observe the emerging *superdiversity* of his neighbourhood (see Chapter 9).

8.4 Mobile Linguistic Landscapes

In the previous section we saw how linguistic landscapes change over time as different people move into and out of areas, and also how these landscapes are constructed through the lived experiences of people who engage in different activities and linguistic practices in them. But the dynamism of linguistic landscapes can also be seen on shorter timescales, since many aspects of linguistic landscapes are themselves mobile. Examples of mobile signs include things like advertisements and warning signs on buses, lorries, and trains, handbills and flyers people hand out on the street, banknotes, tickets, product labels, and the writing on people's tee-shirts. Even take-away coffee cups from shops like Starbucks can be considered part of these mobile linguistic landscapes.

As these parts of the linguistic landscape move across time and space, their messages travel with them. Bumper stickers on cars, for instance, don't just express the driver's loyalty to a particular political candidate or sports team, but also promote that message in the places through which the car travels. Sometimes the message is commensurate with other signs in the linguistic landscape, and sometimes it is less commensurate, as, for instance, when a car sporting a NY Yankees decal drives through Boston, perhaps inspiring other drivers to honk their horns or shout obscenities.

Siebetcheu (2016) has shown how sporting banners and attire dramatically illustrate the ways mobile signs can alter linguistic landscapes. When football fans carry banners and dress themselves in hats, tee-shirts, and scarves with the colours, symbols, and logos of the football club they support, they not only express their identities as supporters of that club, but also position themselves in opposition to those who support other clubs (who similarly may display their support through wearing different colours and carrying different banners). As these fans move across space, from meeting points to pubs, and eventually to the stands of stadia, the meanings of the signs they carry can change (depending, for instance, on whether they represent the local club or the opposing club). Through this movement, then, these signs transform these various places into sites of competition, rivalry, triumph, and loss. Sometimes these mobile signs, when interpreted as being 'out of place' by others, can even inspire verbal or physical conflicts.

The power of mobile signs to transform linguistic landscapes can also be seen in the signs and art that people carry during political protests. During protests, public spaces are appropriated as sites of resistance through various communicative practices which include the display of posters, banners, stickers, and certain kinds of clothing, as well as embodied communicative practices such as shouting slogans and marching. All these practices function as tokens of allegiance to a particular cause and generate a strong sense of solidarity among protesters. In doing so, they discursively appropriate and transform the public space, redefining it as a space of transgression where different viewpoints and alternative ideologies are expressed. But these signs also travel beyond the original protest sites as they are reproduced in newspaper images of the protest or in photos that protesters post on social media platforms like Facebook, Twitter, and Instagram.

Themistocleous (2021), for example, showed how digital images of protest signage in Cyprus helped organise and mobilise protests, made activists' voices stronger, maintained protesters' morale, and allowed them to share 'real' news. They also provided trajectories for counter-discourses to continuously circulate beyond the physical space of the protest site and reach wider audiences, locally and globally. At the same time, however, the affordances of digital media also enabled other individuals with opposing views to engage with protest signs shared online, resemiotise and change their original meanings, and consequently use them to argue against the protesters' cause.

This last point highlights the fact that linguistic landscapes are no longer just physical; people can also transform space through their digital practices, and these physical and virtual spaces often intersect and interact with each other in interesting ways as linguistic and semiotic resources travel between them. In Chapter 4, for example, we talked about how the mural of Trump and Putin kissing in Vilnius transformed the Keule Ruke hamburger restaurant into a tourist attraction where couples went to photograph themselves kissing underneath the two leaders and uploaded these photos onto social media; the more these images circulated online, the more popular the mural and the restaurant became. Similarly, linguistic practices that begin online can also find their way into physical spaces. Jones and Chau (2021) for instance, report on how the practice of writing Cantonese in Romanised script (rather than Chinese characters) that started on internet forums as a transgressive way of asserting a unique Hong Kong identity during the 2019 protests in Hong Kong eventually found its way onto signs that protesters carried on the street during demonstrations.

8.5 Embodiment

No discussion of the materiality of language would be complete without considering the materiality of the human body and how bodies function as resources for communication and as carriers of linguistic and semiotic messages, referred to as **embodiment**. In Chapter 3 we saw that, while early studies on language variation focused mostly on aspects of speech (pronunciation and grammar), later studies, like those by Eckert (1989) and Mendoza-Denton (2008), also considered other embodied aspects of variation, such as the way people dress and move, the activities they engage in, and the places they hang out. In her study of Belten High School, for example, Eckert (1989) pointed out a range of resources apart from language that students used to perform their identities as either Jocks or Burnouts. This is how Eckert (2000: 1) described the embodied self-presentation in the two groups:

In the centre of Belten High School there is a courtyard. Between classes and during lunch hour, the courtyard comes to life. There are boys wearing flared or bell-bottomed jeans, running shoes, rock concert T-shirts, parkas, jeans jackets. A few have chains attaching their wallets to a belt loop; a few wear black jackets with DETROIT on the back. Many of them have long hair, and stand slightly stooped, leaning somewhat confidentially towards their companions. Many hold cigarettes in their mouths. There are girls with virtually the same clothes, a number with long straight hair, toes pointed inward, holding cigarettes before them between extended fingers.

Around the corner in front of the cafeteria, people who look quite different pack into a small area waiting for the bell to ring. These people are wearing slacks or jeans with the currently more fashionable or straight-legged cut. Some of the girls are wearing dresses or skirts. Many sport designer labels, carefully feathered hairdos, and perfectly made-up pastel faces. Postures are straight and open, faces are smiling.

From this example, we can see that identifying oneself as a Jock or a Burnout involved much more than just pronouncing vowels in a certain way; it also involved how students dressed and wore their hair, and the spaces that they occupied during the lunch break (i.e., cafeteria vs. courtyard).

In Mendoza-Denton's (2008) study, which we reviewed in Chapter 3, we also saw how girls in the two Latina gangs exhibited different embodied practices to index their identities; the Norteñas wore red, had feathered hairdos and wore deep red lipstick whereas the Sureñas wore blue, had vertical ponytails and wore brown lipstick. Different methods of applying eyeliner were also crucial for each Latina gang's identification. These bodily semiotics of style and self-presentation in conjunction with linguistic practices (e.g., the pronunciation of vowels and the use of negative concord in the case of the Jocks/Burnouts and the use of 'Th-Pro words' in the case of Latina gang girls) functioned as emblems of identity and affiliation to different social groups.

Apart from things like clothes and make-up, people also use their bodies themselves in everyday interactions to generate meaning. For example, people can change the direction of their gaze and twist their torsos to address different people within a group. They also use hand gestures and facial expressions to make meaning. Norris (2004) calls these 'embodied modes'. In dynamic interactions, embodied modes unfold and work together with language. Examining the moment-to-moment sequential progression and coordination of embodied modes and language enables us to understand how small movements like raising an eyebrow, pointing a finger, or leaning towards someone enable people to convey meaning and perform social actions.

Gestures, for instance, are important communicative practices which can contribute to an utterance's semantic and indexical meaning. In a recent study, Kira Hall, Donna Goldstein, and Matthew Ingram (2016) examined how Donald Trump used gestures during his political campaigns. They found that Trump carefully coordinated his vast gestural repertoire with his linguistic strategies to accomplish his communicative purposes, which were mainly to critique the political system, caricature his opponents, and promote his own plans and ideological stances. Trump's embodied performances allowed him to create a comedic political style that accrued entertainment value, partly because it was so different from the styles of other candidates whom Trump denigrated as 'boring' and 'low energy'.

Another example of embodied communicative practices comes from a study conducted by Lal Zimman and Kira Hall (2010). In the 1990s Hall explored language and sexuality in Varanasi, a city in northern India. She focused on how language and embodiment can express gender by studying the communicative practices of *hijras*. Hijras are transgender and intersex people who wear clothes, jewellery, and make-up that is traditionally associated with Indian women. This means that their aesthetic conduct is feminine. However, they often use sexually crude speech as well as a special kind of hand clap produced with palms flat and fingers spread wide. Extreme cursing and loud clapping are often considered to be unfeminine and inappropriate for women, at least within the middle-class context of India. Therefore, the hijras' communicative practices and bodily semiotics of style and self-presentation helped them align themselves with that particular social group and assert their identities as 'neither men nor women'.

Other studies have highlighted how bodies can act as carriers of messages in the form of clothing or tattoos. Amiena Peck and Christopher Stroud (2015) refer to messages that people carry on their skin as 'skin-scapes'. Just like other signs in public space, tattoos on people's skin can generate a range of meanings; they can say something about that person, their group affiliation, their identity, their emotions, and perhaps their personality, as well as communicate something about the neighbourhood or area they are occupying.

When the Rugby World Cup took place in Japan in 2019, New Zealand and Samoan players as well as rugby fans were urged to cover up their

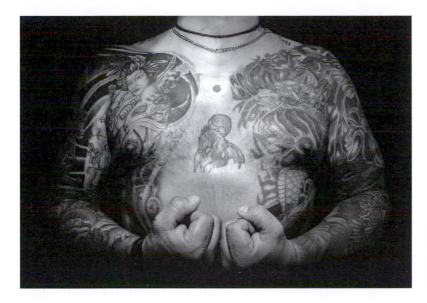

FIGURE 8.8
Skinscapes in Yakuza
(photo credit: Eneas
licensed under CC BY 2.0
license)

tattoos to avoid offending some people in the country. This is because in Japan there is an association between tattoos and Yakuza, a mafia-like group which has operated there for hundreds of years. Tattoos in this group (which can cover almost the entire body; see Figure 8.8) do not just signify that someone is part of a gang, they also depict scenes from the Yakuza member's life, or something symbolically important to them. The tattoos are used to initiate members into the group. Members do not choose when to do a tattoo; it is the tattoo master who decides whether a member is ready to have a tattoo. Tattoos are stigmatised in Japanese society, so the Yakuza tend to keep their tattoos covered up in public. Tourists are also advised to cover up their tattoos in swimming pools (BBC 2018).

Peck and Stroud (2015) carried out an ethnographic study in a tattoo shop in Cape Town for seven months, conducting interviews, making observations, and composing field notes. In addition, they used an innovative method to collect their data by placing a camera on the tattoo artist's helmet in an attempt to capture the moments when a tattoo is created. This study shows how the tattoo artist and the tattooed client work together as co-architects of the *corporeal landscape*. A similar study was conducted by Roux (2015), who analysed the tattoos of female students at three universities in South Africa. This study focused on the kind of semiotics that female students draw on when getting their tattoos, and also on which part of their body they choose to place them. Roux's findings showed that women are mindful of their female identity when they choose the designs, sizes, and emplacement of tattoos on their bodies. More specifically, women seemed to negotiate their femininity by choosing traditionally feminine tattoo designs, which were relatively small in size. Also, tattoos were created on parts of the body where they could be concealed easily. Roux argues that this practice contrasts with male tattoo designs, which tend to be bigger and more visible.

8.6 Focal Topic: Conflict and Politics in Linguistic Landscapes

The focal topic of this chapter explores the dynamics of linguistic landscapes as sites of conflict, rebellion, and political opposition. Conflict can unfold in different forms, ranging from peaceful protests and rallies to violent riots and looting, from the tension in post-war conflict zones to full-scale war.

In this chapter we saw that the linguistic landscape often both reflects and shapes our sociolinguistic realities as it functions to propagate different kinds of ideologies and index identities and power relations among different groups of people. Shohamy (2006) argues that linguistic landscapes are inevitably arenas where political and social battles take place. The role of linguistic landscapes in situations of conflict is particularly crucial, as they can be used as tools to either exacerbate or quell tensions (Rubdy & Ben Said 2015). The linguistic landscape can present affordances to allow local communities to challenge authorities and their hegemonic ideologies, to enable alternative voices and viewpoints to be expressed, and to promote the visibility of marginalised groups who are fighting for social justice, economic or political survival, peace, or equality. People's public semiotic practices have the potential to transform public spaces temporarily, or even more permanently, into sites of transgression. These practices include the display of signs, the actions people perform with their bodies, the clothes they wear, and the ways they move through space.

In this section we will summarise two articles that highlight the role of linguistic landscapes in political conflicts. The first study is by Christiana Themistocleous, who investigates the linguistic landscape of an area in Cyprus which, due to war, remains abandoned and uninhabited. Unlike other studies which explore public signs that are displayed in major urban centres, cities, or rural areas and, in general, in places where some kind of social activity takes place, this study explores a UN-controlled buffer zone that divides two communities in conflict. The focus is on how this contested and neutralised space enables former enemies to display multilingual signs that challenge dominant nationalist ideologies and promote progressive ideologies of unification and peace.

The second study by Dimitris Kitis and Tommaso Milani focuses on embodied performances during 'anarchic' and 'anti-authoritarian' protests in Greece. They argue that, while other fields like sociology and anthropology have investigated the political role of the body and its actions, the field of linguistic landscapes has yet to adequately address this. This study is therefore important because it moves away from static analysis of public signage and instead captures the dynamics of spatial semiotics and the performativity of the body. In other words, instead of exploring spoken or written language, the focus is on the interaction between bodies and the built environment and how people's bodies 'speak' politically during protests.

Themistocleous, C. (2020) Multilingual voices of unification in 'No man's land': Evidence from the linguistic landscape of Nicosia's UN-controlled buffer zone. *Linguistic Landscape*, 6(2), 155–82 Cyprus is mainly inhabited by two ethnic groups: a Greek-Cypriot majority and a Turkish-Cypriot minority. While the two ethnic groups have lived peacefully together in the past, political disagreements in 1974 led to a Greek military coup, a Turkish invasion, and an eventual war between the two sides. After a ceasefire agreement, a buffer zone, known as the 'Green Line', was established by the United Nations to supervise the ceasefire and conduct humanitarian activities. Up until today, public access to the buffer zone is restricted, all commercial activities in it are prohibited, and all the buildings there lie abandoned. The buffer zone runs across the entire island and divides Cyprus and its capital, Nicosia, into the Greek-Cypriot community in the south and the Turkish-Cypriot community in the north. The two communities have lived in complete separation for thirty years, and because of this division, multilingualism in Greek and Turkish is scarce. A decision in 2003 to rebuild the links between the two communities saw the establishment of seven crossing-points across the buffer zone, enabling people to cross into each other's communities for the first time since 1974.

In this study, Themistocleous explores the use of Greek, Turkish, and English in the linguistic landscape of one of these crossing-points. The area is interesting to investigate because, on the one hand, it is a contested space that divides the two communities, but on the other hand, it is a *portal* that connects them. At the same time, it is a neutralised space that is controlled by external forces, namely the United Nations. All these factors have contributed to the transformation of the linguistic landscape of this abandoned area since 2003.

Adopting the geosemiotics framework, Themistocleous provides an in-depth qualitative analysis of the code preference system, the inscription system, and the emplacement system of ephemeral signs like posters and stickers. The creators and target audiences of these signs were also taken into account. In contrast to the linguistic landscapes of the two communities on either side of the buffer zone, in which the language of the 'former enemy' is hardly visible (Themistocleous 2019), the data for this study showed that the linguistic landscape of the buffer zone is multilingual, with many of the ephemeral signs displayed on the walls of the abandoned buildings incorporating both Greek and Turkish as well as English; the latter functioning as a lingua franca.

These multilingual signs in the buffer zone were produced and displayed by ordinary people and grassroot organisations, not governments or international bodies. Some signs were created by Greek-Cypriot organisations and others by Turkish-Cypriot ones. They exhibited three main functions: (1) to promote rapprochement by advertising social events to which both Greek-Cypriots and Turkish-Cypriots were invited; (2) to enhance shared values, highlight similarities between the two ethnic groups, and promote common goals (e.g., finding people who have been missing since the war); and (3) to promote new ideologies of forgiveness, unification, and peace.

Themistocleous (2020) argues that the neutralised character of the buffer zone enables the creation of a new 'imagined community' that consists of social actors from both sides who come to this shared space to display these ephemeral multilingual signs that contain the language of the former enemy. The fact that these signs were not found beyond the buffer zone suggests that the neutralised character of this area allows people to express alternative ideologies which go against dominant nationalist discourses. There is nothing to indicate that the social actors who display these signs in the buffer zone know each other. They don't live in the same communities. However, these former enemies come to the UN-controlled buffer zone to 'do community', and their public doings express a common Cypriot identity, encourage the future development of social ties, and promote a narrative of mutual belonging.

Kitis, D., and Milani, T. (2015) The performativity of the body: Turbulent spaces in Greece. *Linguistic Landscape*, 1(3), 268–90   In this study Dimitris Kitis and Tommaso Milani analyse the ways in which bodies 'speak' politically during protests. The two scholars seek to contribute to the expansion of linguistic landscape research into what Peck and Stroud (2015) call **corporeal sociolinguistics**. The focus of this study is the *body*, more specifically, how people use their bodies to move through space and interact with texts and other material artefacts in the linguistic landscape.

To collect their data Kitis and Milani used a large corpus of digital videos and photographic stills that they found on the Internet. The stills and videos show rallies, sit-ins, mass demonstrations, and riots that occurred in Greece between 2003 and 2012. These protests were carried out by a heterogeneous group of people consisting of leftist activists, students, pupils, the unemployed, migrants, hooligans, thrill-seekers, and *agents provocateurs*. Kitis and Milani acknowledge that the way they collected their data was very different from traditional linguistic landscape methodologies, which typically involve researchers conducting fieldwork to collect photos of signs in public space. They argue, however, that obtaining data from the Internet enabled them to obtain an 'eyewitness perspective' of protests that occurred in the past. At a later stage, they also organised visits to the sites where the protests took place and conducted interviews with people who were involved to gain a better understanding of what had taken place.

Taking the body and its actions as their units of analysis, Kitis and Milani analyse three specific events that took place during the protests: (1) the smashing of CCTV cameras and supermarket expropriations (i.e., when groups raided supermarkets and took food which they later distributed to other people), (2) transformations of the built environment with graffiti or clothing, and (3) confrontational body encounters with police. The analysis reveals that a number of tactics were used that included different kinds of embodied and material practices. For example, protesters wore black clothing and covered their faces with scarves, gas masks, or motorcycle helmets. They carried protest signs or batons. They fought with the police and attacked international organisations, state institutions, banks, and other symbols of authority. Protesters also spray-painted graffiti at different locales, disseminating different messages and inscribing their transgressive messages onto the built environment of the city.

Kitis and Milani argue that all these embodied and material practices enabled protesters to produce *spatial turbulence* in the linguistic landscape. Bodily movements and their interaction with texts and other material artefacts challenged authorities and appropriated, reconfigured, and transformed sections of city. This study demonstrates how, in the context of protests, the way people use their bodies to 'speak politically' both makes use of and changes the linguistic landscape.

Project Ideas

1. Explore multilingualism in your school, institution, or workplace. How many languages are visible on signs? Which is the most dominant? In what order do the languages appear? Which language comes first, second, and last? What does this tell us about the status of different languages in that particular context? What kind of recommendations can you make for language policy in that context?

2. Conduct walking-tour interviews to explore how people experience, react to, evaluate, and understand the linguistic landscape of a particular area. For example, walk with two or three people in an ethnically diverse area where multilingual public signs are visible. Discuss with them how they experience the multilingual linguistic landscape.

3. George Floyd was an African American man killed in May 2020 during an arrest in Minneapolis. Almost immediately protests erupted across the US and around the world, igniting discussions on racism and colonialism. Conduct a Google search or a YouTube search to find images and videos from the Black Lives Matter protests. Observe the kinds of signs people carried during the protests, their clothing, the symbols they used, and their bodily movements. What kind of communicative practices (linguistic, semiotic, etc.) were used during these protests?

4. Ask different people about their tattoos. Try to obtain information about their choice of tattoo, and if it has any symbolic or emotional meaning for them. Discuss with them the emplacement of the tattoos on their bodies. Why did they choose to create the tattoo on that particular part of their body? Ask who the intended audience for the tattoos is. Then analyse the tattoos themselves, focusing on their textual and visual aspects.

CHAPTER

9 Mobility, Contact, and Flows

PREVIEW

KEY TERMS

borrowing
contact linguistics
creole
decreolisation
deterritorialisation
dialect levelling
diglossia
flows
globalisation
koineisation
language shift
mobility
pidgin
scales
superdiversity

This chapter focuses on the *mobility* of communicative resources and the way they interact with and are influenced by different resources they come into contact with as a result of this mobility. It explores the different ways sociolinguists have addressed mobility, from more traditional approaches that focus on 'language contact' to more contemporary ones which attempt to trace the trajectories along which people and resources 'flow' through global networks. It then examines the communicative practices of global hip-hop artists as a case study in language and globalisation. The focal topic for this chapter is migration, specifically the communicative challenges migrants face and the strategies they deploy when they move from one place to another.

9.1 Introduction

Throughout this book we have been talking about how people assemble *communicative repertoires* as they move through their lives, travelling across different kinds of borders (physical, political, social) and through different communities and social contexts, drawing on and (re)mixing *resources* from their repertoires strategically in different situations. We have also talked about how the meaning of and value accorded to different resources changes as people move from one social context to another. The underlying theme of these discussions has been **mobility**, the fact that people and resources (as well as meanings and values) are never static. They are always in motion, and understanding this mobility is key to understanding the relationship between language and society. The sociolinguist Jan Blommaert, in fact, insists that the notion of *mobility* should be what *defines* the study of sociolinguistics. We need to get away from the view that sees language as a set of static abstract systems, he says, and 'replace it with a view of language as something that is intrinsically and perpetually mobile, through space as well as time, and made for mobility. *The finality of language is mobility, not immobility*' (Blommaert 2010: xiv, emphasis ours).

The fact of mobility, both of people and of communicative resources, is perhaps more evident today than ever before in human history. Of course, people have always been mobile, and many other eras in history have seen massive waves of mass migration. But never before have so many different kinds of people been moving to and from so many different places at the rate they are today. Much of this movement is spurred on by economic development, but much of it is also the result of things like war, famine, and the ravages of climate change.

There's reason to believe, however, that what we are witnessing today is not only greater in scale but likely to grow because of political forces and environmental disruptions. The United Nations High Commission for Refugees (UNHCR), in fact, reports that the number of people displaced by conflict has never been higher; at the end of 2019 an estimated 75.9 million people (about one out of every 103 humans on the planet) were either refugees, asylum seekers, or internally displaced people.

At the same time, the world itself seems to be shrinking. New technologies have not just enabled people, goods, and cultural artefacts (signs, sounds, images) to move across the globe at dizzying speeds, they have also helped to create a world that is increasingly economically, politically, and culturally interconnected. The word we usually use to describe this interconnectedness is **globalisation**. One problem with this word is that for many people it implies *homogenisation* (things becoming more the same in different places) and *domination* (where one particular country, culture, or ideology exercises power over others). And, to some extent, both of these things are aspects of globalisation. But globalisation involves much more complex forms of interconnectedness, more complex movements of people and resources in multiple directions, and more complex relationships between the 'global' and the 'local' (Appadurai 1990). One need only to think of a singer like Rihanna, whose song 'Work' we talked about in Chapter 6, who moved from the Caribbean to the US, and now travels the world promoting a music that incorporates resources from a range of places (such as Caribbean Creoles and African American English), music which itself has become a kind of global commodity, influencing the language of other artists all around the world.

To understand the centrality of mobility to the study of language and communication, we need to consider the way mobility works to define communicative resources and repertoires, and even to define the places and spaces where people deploy them. Because of mobility, for instance, it is more and more difficult to subscribe to the belief we talked about in Chapter 1 that resources like 'languages' *belong* to particular places, and that places are defined by the 'languages' that are used there. 'Languages' and other resources have become **deterritorialised**, unmoored from any fixed 'country' or region, and defined not by particular localities, but by the 'translocal trajectories' (Blommaert 2010: 46) along which they move. As they move along these trajectories they accumulate different kinds of meanings and associations and influence and are influenced by resources originating from different places, sometimes forming new resources. But 'languages' and other resources are not just shaped *by* mobility. They are also shaped *for* mobility, for it is access to and competence with these different resources that allow people to move around in the first place (Blackledge & Creese 2017).

Mobility also defines people's communicative repertoires. Blommaert and Backus (2011) argue that people's repertoires are basically *records* of mobility. Examining repertoires, Adrian Blackledge and Angela Creese (2017: 35) say, enables us 'to document in great detail the trajectories followed by people throughout their lives: the opportunities, constraints, and inequalities they were facing; the learning environments they had access to (and those they did not have access to)'. Finally, mobility defines the *contexts* in which people deploy these resources and repertoires. Rather than static places with fixed sets of features, contexts for communication are dynamic, always changing as different kinds of people and resources 'flow' through them.

In the remainder of this chapter, we will explore the different ways sociolinguists have addressed this issue of mobility, from more traditional approaches that focus on 'language contact' to more contemporary ones which attempt to trace the trajectories along which people and resources 'flow' through global networks.

9.2 Contact

Traditionally, for sociolinguists, the most important questions arising from the kind of mobility that we discussed above have focused on the effects it has on 'languages'. The idea is that when 'languages' (or more accurately, *users* of languages) come into contact with one another, they end up influencing and changing one another in various ways. The study of how 'languages' influence each other when they come into contact is called **contact linguistics**. But research on how communicative resources change as they come into contact with other resources can also provide insights into the nature of group relations, group identities, and human creativity.

'Language contact' occurs when, for one reason or another, different codes, varieties, registers, and even genres come into contact, leading to a range of possible results. It can affect the linguistic behaviour of the people who use these resources – they might, for example, mix different codes when they speak or switch between one code and another in different situations (see Chapter 5) – and it can also affect the resources themselves – lexical items from one code, for instance, might be incorporated into another (a phenomenon known as **borrowing**), or two or more codes might merge together to form a new code. Changes in linguistic resources, however, cannot really be separated from changes in the linguistic behaviours of the people who use these resources, since it is through the way language users *use* resources that change comes about. History is full of examples of 'languages' changing as a result of coming into contact with other languages. One example of such a change was the large-scale incorporation of words from French into English after the Norman Conquest in 1066.

There are all sorts of reasons for 'language contact'; it can be caused by migration, trade, war, colonisation, and even mass media. Contact often results in changes in the sociolinguistic situation in a particular place. At the very least, it might make that place more linguistically heterogeneous or 'multilingual'. In some cases, the different resources that have come into contact come to take on different functions in the society, one 'language' or variety, for instance, being used in more formal and 'official' contexts, and the other being used in more informal, everyday contexts. The American linguist Charles Ferguson (1959) used the word **diglossia** to describe such situations. Diglossia is when two or more 'languages' or varieties are used for different things in a society, with one considered the 'high' (H) variety, and the other considered the 'low' (L) variety. Examples include Putonghua (H) and Cantonese (L) in Southern China, and 'Standard' German (H) and Swiss German (L) in Switzerland. But even in situations where such clear functional distinctions do not occur, communities often develop highly regular patterns of code alteration based on who they are talking to and what they are doing (see Chapter 5).

In some cases, when two different codes or varieties come into contact with one another, especially when the speakers of one code or variety have more political, military, or social power than the speakers of the other, one of them can supplant the other, in a process known as **language shift**. In extreme cases, language shift can lead to one code or variety dying out altogether.

Activity: Language Shift and Gender

The linguist Susan Gal (1978) studied what appeared to her to be a case of 'language shift' (from Hungarian to German) in the Hungarian town of Oberwart, located on the border between Hungary and Germany. In order to test her hypothesis, she asked people about the frequency with which they used German in different situations, and she also determined what their main social networks were: did they mostly associate with peasants or did they mostly associate with people who worked in shops and factories. Figure 9.1 shows the percentage of the situations in which informants in three different age groups reported using German (or a mixture of German and Hungarian). The chart also divides informants according to whether or not they were part of peasant or non-peasant social networks.

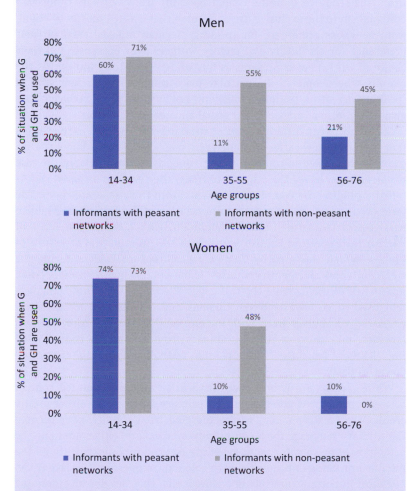

FIGURE 9.1
Percentage that informants with peasant and non-peasant social networks in three different age groups used German (or a mixture of German and Hungarian) (adapted from Gal 1978: 10)

1. What is the difference between the amount of German used by people of different ages? Does this support the hypothesis of a shift towards German in the community?
2. What is the difference between the amount of German used by people with different social networks? What do you think is the reason for this difference?
3. Are there differences in the amount of German used by men and women of different ages and with different social networks? Can you come up with a theory that might explain these differences?

A good example of language shift can be seen in Susan Gal's study of the Hungarian town of Oberwart (see Activity). Gal interprets her findings from this study to indicate a language shift from German–Hungarian bilingualism to the exclusive use of German that was led mostly by young women, whose preference for speaking German indexed their broader preference for the lifestyle of factory workers over peasants (and their choice of workers over peasants as husbands). This study shows that the reasons why people in a particular place might change their way of speaking are often complex, involving not just 'contact' between 'languages' but also a range of other social and economic factors.

Contact between different ways of speaking can also lead to the formation of entirely new varieties. Sometimes, when people who do not share a common code need to communicate frequently (for example, in the case of colonisation or for the purpose of trade) they develop a shared code – called a **pidgin** – by combining elements from their separate codes. The term originates from a Chinese pronunciation of the English word 'business' associated with 'Chinese Pidgin English', a simplified form of English incorporating English words into the grammatical structure of Chinese which was used by Chinese and Europeans traders during the eighteenth and nineteenth centuries. Some pidgins involve a more equal mixture of elements from the two codes. Russennorsk, a trade language that used to be used between Russians and Norwegians, for instance, employed vocabulary from both Russian and Norwegian. Most pidgins, however, take most of their vocabulary from one of the codes (called the 'lexifier language'), usually the code belonging to the more powerful party.

While pidgins are hybrid codes used in situations of limited contact between groups but not spoken as a primary language by either group, **creoles** are languages that, while emerging from contact, later become the primary language for a community of speakers, either gradually by being passed on to subsequent generations, or more quickly through the forcible uprooting of people through colonial conquest or the slave trade. The most important thing about creoles is that they develop an autonomy that pidgins don't have, coming to index particular social identities and distinct communities.

Creoles themselves can change when they come into contact with other languages, or 're-connect' with their 'lexifier languages'. Sociolinguist

Mark Sebba (1993) argues that a variety he calls 'London Jamaican' (see Chapter 5) arose in London and other British cities such as Birmingham as the English-based creoles brought to the UK by migrants from Guyana, Jamaica, Dominica, Barbados, and Trinidad came into contact with the English spoken in Britain and underwent a process of **decreolisation**. By the early 2000s, this way of speaking had become part of a broader variety (also influenced by the English spoken by other migrant groups such as Bangladeshis) spoken by mostly working-class young people in British cities known as Multicultural London English (Cheshire et al. 2011). Partly because of the worldwide popularity of music genres such as Grime, features of this way of speaking have spread globally to places like Australia and the Netherlands (*The Economist* 2021).

Studying pidgins and creoles can highlight how dynamic and unstable the notion of 'languages' really is. As Sebba (1997: 289) puts it, pidgins and creoles force us to 'stop conceptualising language as a *thing*, an *object* which can be captured and put under a microscope and dissected using a set of tools developed by linguists'. At the same time, the terms pidgin and creole can also be problematic. Like most ways of speaking used by minority populations, pidgins and creoles have generally been stigmatised as linguistic 'mongrels', 'impure' and defective mixtures of different 'languages' rather than 'languages' in their own right. More and more linguists, however, recognise that creole formation is a universal phenomenon, and that the kind of hybridisation associated with it is a natural part of the evolution of all 'languages'.

Linguists interested in language contact are also interested in what happens when mutually intelligible varieties associated with the same code come into contact with one another. In such cases, these different 'dialects' sometimes merge to form a new 'dialect' through a process known as **koineisation**, and sometimes, over time, the distinctive features of different 'dialects' get 'washed out' in a process called **dialect levelling**. The British sociolinguists Paul Kerswill and Ann Williams (2000), for example, studied what happened when people from all over the UK moved into a newly created town called Milton Keynes starting in the 1950s. They found that, while parents retained features in their speech associated with the different places they had come from, their children began to lose many of these features and to speak in a more uniform way in an accent that seemed to have been influenced by 'Estuary English' (a variety spoken in areas of the estuary of the River Thames).

9.3 Flows and Scales

More recently, sociolinguists have begun to move away from the metaphor of 'contact' to adopting other ways of talking about the complex ways that different ways of speaking interact with and influence one another. One reason for this shift is the rise of what is known as **superdiversity**, especially in urban centres around the world, brought on by globalisation. Superdiversity is a term coined by the anthropologist

Steven Vertovec to describe the unprecedented diversity of people from different backgrounds that find themselves living in proximity to one another as a result of increased mobility. He defines it as:

[A] term intended to underline a level and kind of complexity surpassing anything. . . previously experienced . . . a dynamic interplay of variables including country of origin . . . migration channel . . . legal status . . . migrants' human capital (particularly educational background), access to employment . . . locality . . . and responses by local authorities, services providers and local residents.

(Vertovec 2007: 2–3)

The idea of superdiversity, however, is not just a matter of lots of different kinds of people being gathered in one place, but also of the increased *connection* between places made possible by digital technologies. Migrants, for instance, more than ever before, are able to maintain close ties with people in the places that they came from (as well as people who have migrated to other places). These connections create complex networks along which ideas, cultural products, and communicative resources can 'flow' rapidly around the world in sometimes unpredictable ways.

The metaphor of **flows** attempts to capture this fluid and dynamic way cultural and communicative resources move around the world and affect one another, less constrained than before by political and social boundaries. The notion of flows comes from the work of the famous globalisation scholar Arjun Appadurai (1990), who argued that, rather than homogenisation (cultures becoming more similar) or the domination of one culture over another, globalisation is characterised by a back-and-forth movement of resources in which, as resources 'flow' to different places they are influenced by other resources in those places, becoming 'localised', and then often 'flow' outward, sometimes influencing the places where these resources originated. The example of features from Caribbean creoles, themselves a product of British colonialism, flowing back to the UK, and then outward in the form of Multicultural London English, illustrates this dynamic.

Appadurai identified a range of different kinds of flows: the flow of people, of technologies, of money, of media products, and of ideas and ideologies. All of these different kinds of flows affect the kinds of communicative resources available to people, the kinds of meanings these resources take on, and the kinds of values they are assigned in different contexts. One of the main effects is that resources have become deterritorialised, less defined by their association with particular places and cultures and more defined by their *mobility*.

To understand how these resources interact with one another both globally and locally in actual situations of communication, sociolinguists have employed yet another metaphor, that of **scales**. All interactions occur on multiple scales of time and space. For example, you may be reading this chapter in your dormitory in preparation for a class tomorrow, but this reading is taking place within the wider scales of the course you are taking and the university you are attending, which are situated within wider scales of your degree programme, your academic career, the broader field of sociolinguistics and of academic study more generally, the city and country that your university is located in, and larger global political and economic systems, and all of these different scales can affect your reading of this chapter. What this act of reading 'means' to you depends on which of these scales you are attending to, whether, for example, you are just focused on passing tomorrow's quiz or on your future career as a sociolinguist, and how you read can be affected by things occurring on all of these scales, whether it be the noise of people partying in the room next to you or a global pandemic that has kept you isolated in your dorm room for months.

Whereas the idea of 'flows' is a horizontal metaphor, envisioning resources moving *across* contexts, the notion of scales is a *vertical* one, envisioning resources occupying multiple contexts simultaneously. These contexts are not just layered, but they are also hierarchical, which means that different sets of values or *orders of indexicality* (see Chapter 2) determine how particular resources are treated on different scales. For example, different 'languages' or varieties may seem to exist 'side-by-side' in a community, such as English and Spanish in some places in the US, but they also exist within layered scales. On the level of a particular home or neighbourhood, Spanish may be highly valued, but on the level of the state or nation, Spanish is ranked lower than English in relation to social prestige and language policy. So, when a person moves from a more local space to spaces where these higher-scale orders of indexicality are dominant, the value of Spanish and what they are able to do with it changes. As Blommaert (2007: 12) puts it:

> Forms of language use that are sanctioned by the State ... develop in relation to ... upscaled variet[ies], and are often predictably downscaled ... This form of downscaling takes the form of disqualification: particular linguistic resources are defined as not appropriate, valid or acceptable in a particular (State controlled) context. Upscaled language varieties, in contrast, are varieties of entitlement and enfranchisement in relation to the State's sociolinguistic regime. They allow for [a] kind of exportability ... where discourses and language forms became emblematic of elite identities and roles – carrying validity and value across a wide range of contexts.

Since scales exist simultaneously, sometimes people can use linguistic resources strategically to frame their communication in the context of one scale or another, indexing the values associated with these different scales. Blommaert (2007: 6) gives the example of a conversation between a tutor and a PhD student:

S: I'll start my dissertation with a chapter reporting on my fieldwork.
T: We start our dissertations with a literature review chapter here.

Here the student starts out operating on the scale of their particular dissertation and how they want to write it. In order to refute the student's plan, the tutor 'upscales' the conversation, invoking the broader scale of institutional academic norms ('we' do things this way), and in doing so exerts power over the student, asserting that the set of values on this 'higher' scale supersede the set of values the student is operating with.

Applied linguists Suresh Canagarajah and Peter De Costa (2016: 3) propose that we treat scales not as static hierarchies, but as a category of *practice*. They write:

> It is not scales themselves (as perhaps containers of social and communicative life) that are of interest, but scaling practices … This notion of scale as a verb rather than a noun gives importance to constructs such as rescaling, scale jumping, and scale differentiation – all relating to the ways scales are practiced in social life.

The use of the metaphors of flow and scale can help us to get a clearer picture of how communicative resources can connect together different contexts, how they circulate, and the ways they are used in particular situations. They help us see how different resources are distributed horizontally in different places, but also how they are distributed hierarchically in ways that reveal social inequalities and relationships of power and subordination.

9.4 Hip-Hop

Perhaps nothing illustrates the concepts of flows and scales that we discussed above better than the global phenomenon of hip-hop. In fact, hip-hop is so interesting to sociolinguistics that 'hip-hop linguistics' has become a recognised subdiscipline in the field.

Although hip-hop began within African American communities in the US, its musical styles and communicative practices – such as tagging (graffiti), b-boying (break dancing), MCing and rapping – have spread throughout the world to places as far afield as Europe, Australia, Japan, Malaysia, and Fiji. But the hip-hop in Japan or Australia is not the same as that in America; as it has taken root in different places, hip-hop has become *localised*, incorporating the interests, styles, and linguistic resources of these different places. At the same time, these different 'hip-hops' are still connected through a range of common ideologies, identities, and communicative resources; they all 'belong' to what sociolinguist H. Samy Alim (2006) calls the 'Hip-Hop Nation', which Alim and Pennycook (2007: 90) describe as a 'multiethnic, multilingual … postmodern "nation" with an international reach, a fluid capacity to cross borders, and a reluctance to adhere to the geopolitical givens of the present'.

The main question to ask as a sociolinguist, then, is how hip-hop artists in these different locales use multiple resources – global, local, and 'glocal' – to negotiate both their unique local identities and their membership in this larger 'Hip-Hop Nation', at the same time connecting themselves to and contrasting themselves with (even competing with) other artists in their own countries and regions and across the globe.

One way to approach this question is with the concept of global flows. Globalisation is in part what has made hip-hop possible, and all of the kinds of flows Appadurai (see above) talks about have contributed to its development and evolution, including flows of people, of media products such as streaming music files and music videos, of money, of technologies that allow young people not just to connect with one another online but also to engage in the kinds of remixing that are central to the genre, and, most important, of ideologies and identities. Alastair Pennycook (2007), in fact, argues that hip-hop might be one of the best things that scholars can look at to understand the dynamics of globalisation.

From a linguistic point of view, hip-hop highlights many of the arguments about 'languages' and other communicative resources we have been making throughout this book – especially their dynamism, fluidity and adaptability. Alim (2009: 114) says that 'the language remixes involved in the creation of global Hip Hops cause us to remix the very notion of language'.

Examples of this can be seen in Pennycook's (2003) analysis of the language used in hip-hop in Japan. Below, for instance, is a quote he provides from a song by the Japanese hip-hop group Rip Slyme, rendered in what Japanese young people call 'freaky mixed Japanese' (a transliteration of the lines is given in *italics* and a translation is given in **bold**):

Yo Bringing That, Yo Bring Your Style 人類最後のフリーキーサイド
Yo Bringing that, Yo Bring your style Jinrui saigo no furiikiisaido

Yo Bringing That, Yo Bring Your Style The last freaky side of the human race

(Pennycook 2003: 515)

Just this one line, Pennycook points out, creatively brings together multiple communicative resources, including features associated with African American English ('Yo'), 'Standard English', Japanese *kanji* and Japanese *katakana* (used for a phonetic rendering of the English word 'freaky' in *furiikiisaido*). Even the name of the band, Rip Slyme, combines different resources, meant to imitate the stereotyped Japanese pronunciation of the English words 'Lips Rhyme', a move that is both 'funny' and challenges the values of 'global English' which 'downscales' local varieties like Japanese English.

Of course, this kind of remixing is not limited to language but extends to musical phrases, clothing, movements, dances, and other global and local musical genres. And often these 'glocalised' remixes flow outward, connecting with and influencing musical artists working in different genres. The Korean girl band Blackpink (written BLΛϽKPИИK) is a good example of the way these multi-ethnic, multilingual glocal remixes of music and culture can become global phenomena. Composed of four girls, two Koreans, one Thai, and one New Zealander, the group mixes hip-hop styles with K-pop, and has recorded songs with famous American artists such as Selena Gomez and Lady Gaga.

Just as hip-hop illustrates complex global flows of communicative resources, it can also shed light on how resources get valued differently on different scales. Of course, on many scales, especially those dominated by governmental or educational institutions, hip-hop is severely down-scaled, its linguistic creativity denigrated as linguistically impure or 'gibberish'. But hip-hop has its own scales. The two most basic are the scale of the 'Global Hip-Hop Nation', with African American hip-hop as the most salient point of reference, and the various local scales, with values on the former influencing local practices and vice versa. But it is not always a matter of the global scale valuing more global, US-inspired communicative resources over local ones. In fact, perhaps the most powerful value of the 'Global Hip-Hop Nation' is authenticity, or 'keepin' it real', a value that facilitates local artists to deploy resources in ways that distinguish them from global hip-hop styles. As Pennycook (2007: 14) puts it, authenticity in hip-hop 'is not a question of staying true to a prior set of embedded languages and practices but rather an issue of performing multiple forms of realism within the fields of change and flow made possible by multiple language use'.

But the linguistic practices in hip-hop, as we saw with the naming of Rip Slyme above, can also challenge values on other more institutionally controlled national or global scales. Tope Omoniyi (2008), for example, describes how the ideological stance in the lyrics of Nigerian MC 2-Shotz, who raps mostly in Nigerian pidgin, distances him from local artists who rap in English and, more generally, challenges the local dominance of 'Standard English' (referred to in Nigeria as *foné*, derived from 'phonetics') as a marker of education and social status:

You speak *foné* / I choose to speak Pidgin / For all my people to understand me / Dat na the main reason / I rap for my people hear and feel me / If dat no be *keepin it real* / a beg mek somebody explain to me / You no fit yarn *foné* pass American / So I choose to do am Naija style / All the while.

You speak standard English (foné, derived from phonetics, meaning posh or RP English) / I choose to speak Pidgin / For all my people to understand me / That is the main reason / I rap so my people can hear and feel me / If that ain't keepin it real / Then somebody please tell me what is / You can't speak standard English better than an American / So I choose to do am Naija style / All the while.

(quoted in Alim 2007: 120)

The global circulation of hip-hop culture and the resources associated with it, and the ways these resources are recontextualised and (re)mixed with other resources on the local level, can teach us a lot about globalisation and the impacts of mobility on language and communication. Hip-hop also highlights the inadequacy of thinking about 'languages' as bounded, static things and demonstrates the utility of concepts like 'flows' and 'scales' in helping us to understand how meanings, values, and identities are created and transformed as a result of the mobility of communicative resources.

Activity: Whose Hip-Hop?

Search YouTube for examples of hip-hop performances from around the world (e.g., 'Indian hip-hop', 'Chinese hip-hop'). Choose an artist from a place or region that you are familiar with (perhaps a place you have lived or visited) and analyse how they (re)mix global and local resources. Pay special attention to how they use language, but also pay attention to other communicative resources such as musical styles, movement, and clothing.

1. What resources do they use that index their membership in the 'Global Hip-Hop Nation'? In other words, what makes their performances recognisable to you as hip-hop? How do they change or adapt these resources to their local situations?
2. What resources do they use which index their local contexts? How do they combine these local resources with more global resources? What does this tell you about the relationship between the global and the local?
3. What kinds of values and ideologies do you think are expressed in their performances, including ideas about politics, economics, social relationships, and the relative values assigned to particular communicative resources?

9.5 Focal Topic: Migration

The focal topic for this chapter is migration. When we think of migration, we usually just think about the mobility of people, but migration also involves the mobility of communicative resources and ideologies about language and communication both *from* and *back to* the places from which people have migrated. As these resources move from place to place, they take on different kinds of meanings and are assigned different values.

Migration is often framed as a 'problem' by politicians and commentators in the press, and the way migration and migrants are *represented* can have a dramatic impact both on the immigration policies of governments and on what people think about migrants and how they treat them. In thinking about migration, it is important to separate these 'discourses' about migration and migrants from what is actually happening, including the reasons people move from one place to another and the kinds of circumstances they face when they do so. At the same time, it is important to understand how these discourses affect the ways migrants are treated, their access to different kinds of communicative (and material) resources, and how the resources they bring with them are valued in the societies they move to.

The two articles summarised here challenge some of the assumptions that people might have about migrants and their language use. The first article, by Jenna Ann Altherr Flores, Dongchen Hou, and Wenhao Diao, challenges the assumption that migrants normally use the dominant language of the societies that they move to when communicating to other migrants with different linguistic backgrounds. They examine the experiences of two different communities of migrants in a US border town, revealing how people renegotiate linguistic hierarchies by engaging in linguistic practices that involve neither solely English nor their first languages.

The second article, by Adrian J. Bailey, Suresh Canagarajah, Shanshan Lan, and Devereux Gong Powers, deals with the scalar politics involved in the linguistic practices of South Korean professionals living in Hong Kong. They show how their use of and attitudes towards different languages (especially different Englishes) is characterised by various sets of tensions between competing language ideologies and how they navigate these tensions in different situations.

Both of these articles use ethnographic methods involving interviewing and observing how people use language in real life, highlighting the fact that understanding processes of globalisation requires that we focus not just on broader political and social processes, but also on the lived experiences of actual people as they navigate their trajectories through various local and transnational contexts.

Altherr Flores, J. A., Hou, D., and Diao, W. (2020) *Lingua francas* beyond English: Multilingual repertoires among immigrants in a southwestern US border town. *International Journal of Multilingualism*, 17(2), 107–33 It is often assumed that when migrants from different backgrounds and with diverse communicative repertoires move to a particular place the dominant code in that place (such as English in the US) naturally becomes the lingua franca among these migrants. Embedded in this assumption, of course, is a monolingual ideology that references the scale of the 'nation' to assign a higher value to the 'national language', ignoring the values that might be attached to other languages on other scales associated with, for example, families, neighbourhoods, and institutions like churches and schools.

In this article Jenna Ann Altherr Flores and her colleagues seek to challenge this assumption by showing how, in the US, languages other than English sometimes serve as lingua francas among immigrants. The site of their investigation is a town in the US state of Arizona called Deserton, which is close to the border with Mexico. Some 12.7 per cent of the town's population are immigrants, and while most, as might be expected, are Spanish-speaking migrants from Mexico and other Latin American countries, there are also populations of migrants from other places who speak a variety of other languages, such as Mandarin (Putonghua), Cantonese, Tagalog, Vietnamese, Hindi, Nepali, Somali, Swahili, Kinyarwanda, and Farsi.

The article consists of two case studies, one of the Deserton Mandarin Christian Church, whose parishioners come primarily from Mainland China, Hong Kong, Taiwan, and Singapore, and the other of an apartment complex inhabited by resettled Lhotshampa refugees, who were originally from Myanmar (formerly Burma) but lived since the 1980s in refugee camps in Nepal before being resettled in the United States.

Another assumption that people sometimes have is that migrants of the same ethnicity will share a common language, but this is often not true, as these two cases illustrate. Migrants, just like everyone else, have access to diverse repertoires of 'truncated' resources (see Chapter 2), some of which they share with others of the same ethnicity, and some of which they don't. In the case of the Chinese churchgoers, for example, these resources included Putonghua, Cantonese, and a variety of other Chinese languages, as well as different ways of writing Chinese: (1) the simplified script used in Mainland China and Singapore, (2) the traditional script used in Hong Kong and Taiwan, and (3) *pinyin*, a Romanised way of writing Chinese used by Chinese learners. Different people in the church had different configurations of competencies with these different resources. In the case of the Lhotshampa refugees, resources included Nepali and other Nepali and Bhutanese languages like Magar, Tamang, Limbu, Hindi, and Dzongkha. Again, different people in the apartment complex had different levels of competence in these different languages. Of course, included in these repertoires were the more dominant languages spoken in Deserton: English and Spanish.

In their investigation of the Chinese church, Altherr Flores and her colleagues found that Putonghua, rather than English, was used as a lingua franca during the main church functions, with other resources such as Cantonese sometimes being used in smaller Bible study groups. English was used by some of the younger parishioners with friends for more personal conversations about things like relationships and make-up. While not all parishioners were highly competent in Putonghua, and some even had limited competence in written Chinese, Putonghua served not just as a common resource for communication but also as an emblem of belonging to the congregation. Other resources were used in situations where more local identities (such as Hong Konger) were relevant or as tools to help people navigate their truncated competence in Mandarin or written Chinese. One participant, for example, reported using pinyin transliterations for hymns because of her limited competence with written Chinese.

The investigation of the Lhotshampa community focused on two main sites: an informal ESL class organised by residents and the common garden where residents in the complex grew vegetables. The informal English language class was organised partly as the result of the monolingual pedagogies used by the teacher in the formal class offered by the adult basic education centre, where students were prohibited from using languages other than English to aid their learning (see Chapter 5). In these informal classes, Nepali arose as the lingua franca among the different participants who brought to these interactions a range of different resources and competencies. Participants who were less proficient in Nepali were helped by others who translated Nepali and English words and phrases they had difficulty with into other languages, and sometimes Devanagari script was used not just to write Nepali but also to represent sounds in other languages like Magar.

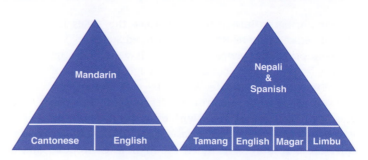

FIGURE 9.2
'(Re)scaled' language
hierarchies
(adapted from Altherr
Flores et al. 2020: 129)

The situation was different, however, in the common garden where participants interacted with other residents of the complex. Here, Spanish (not English) arose as the lingua franca. Participants made use of their sometimes-limited command of Spanish as a way of integrating with the community and creating a feeling of solidarity with the other residents.

Altherr Flores and her colleagues illustrate the hierarchical relationship among these different resources in the two communities with the charts shown in Figure 9.2.

What is interesting about these findings is that, although English was an important resource for both communities in the larger context of the United States, they chose to use other languages as lingua francas in their everyday lives. Altherr Flores and her colleagues describe these situations as examples of strategic '(re)scaling' where people relocated local and translocal resources within existing hierarchies to manage their ethnic and migrant identities and to cope with day-to-day practical communication challenges.

Often, we think of globalisation as involving higher scales and the institutions associated with them exerting downward pressure on citizens when it comes to which communicative resources are valued and deemed appropriate in different situations. This article provides examples of how globalised immigrants can also engage in what Altherr Flores and her colleagues call 'globalisation processes from below' (p. 130), resisting the downward pressure to use English in the United States and instead using lingua francas that were neither English nor their first language with people with different communicative repertoires, thus strategically (re)scaling language hierarchies in order to help them manage their participation and membership in their particular communities.

Bailey, A. J., Canagarajah, S., Lan, S., and Powers, D. G. (2016) Scalar politics, language ideologies, and the sociolinguistics of globalization among transnational Korean professionals in Hong Kong. *Journal of Sociolinguistics*, 20(3), 312–34 In this article Adrian Bailey and his colleagues explore the language experiences of Korean migrants in Hong Kong using the concept of scales, focusing on how they negotiate the uneven values assigned to different resources in the linguistic marketplace of globalisation.

In their study they interviewed ten Korean migrants living in Hong Kong, all of them middle-class professionals working in fields like higher education, banking, advertising, and medicine. Most of them had transnational life trajectories, involving not just having lived in South Korea, but also having worked or gone to school in other countries such as the United States.

The context for this study, Hong Kong, is a good example of the kind of superdiverse society we talked about above. A former British colony, it is a major world port and financial centre with residents from all over the world from different economic, social, cultural, and linguistic backgrounds. Because of this, it has what Bailey and his colleagues (p. 316) call 'a diverse linguascape in which the daily experience of language goes beyond a simple native/non-native or fluent/non-fluent binary'. At the same time, it is also subject to the scalar values of globalisation, with English occupying the top of the hierarchy, despite the fact that most local residents speak Cantonese and the national language of the country (the People's Republic of China) is Putonghua.

Bailey and his colleagues are particularly interested in how the Korean migrants they interviewed navigated these scales, particularly with regard to English, and how they strategically referenced different scales in different contexts to manage their social identities and social relationships. One of the main ways they did this was by articulating different language ideologies when discussing their experiences of using different languages in Hong Kong and their feelings about their proficiencies in these languages.

We have been talking about language ideologies throughout this book, mostly as dominant sets of ideas and values related to what sorts of language practices are considered 'prestigious', 'correct', and 'appropriate' in a given society. Bailey and his colleagues, however, take a more local perspective on language ideologies, pointing out how individuals deploy various ideas about language as a way of justifying their language practices and performing their social identities. Here they quote linguistic anthropologist Michael Silverstein in defining language ideologies as 'sets of beliefs about language *articulated* by users as a *rationalization or justification* of perceived language structure and use' (1979: 193, emphasis ours).

In their interviews they noted three sets of contrasting language ideologies their participants articulated as they discussed their experiences with different languages (and especially different kinds of Englishes) and their perception of their values in different contexts. They were: (1) Pragmatic English/Perfect English, (2) Multilingualism/English Only, and (3) Global Language/Local Language.

First, they noted that their participants made the distinction between 'Pragmatic English', the kind of English which they felt was highly valued in their workplaces, especially in interactions with colleagues from diverse ethnic and linguistic backgrounds, and 'Perfect English', typically associated with American or British 'standard' varieties, which was valued on the scale of global business and professional life. It was this latter kind of English that they felt facilitated mobility and career advancement, but most felt they had limited competence in it. One participant explicitly described the values she ascribed to different kinds of

English in Hong Kong in terms of a hierarchy, with American English on the top, Hong Kong English second, and Korean English on the bottom of the hierarchy.

The second set of ideologies they talked about involved the tension between 'Multilingualism' and 'English Only', and like the 'languages' they described in the first set of ideologies, these linguistic practices were valued differently on different scales, with multilingual practices valued in interactions with friends and family members, and English-only practices valued in more formal professional contexts and in the context of their longer career trajectories. In fact, some of them considered their multilingual practices to be a detriment to their acquiring 'pure' English.

Finally, the participants made distinctions between what they considered to be 'Global Languages' and 'Local Languages', with English being considered a global language, and other languages, including Korean, being considered local. In the context of Hong Kong, they made a distinction between Cantonese, which they viewed as a local language, and Putonghua, which they considered a more global variety of Chinese. Consequently, while mastery of Cantonese was valued for its ability to help them communicate better with the local population, Putonghua was valued for its potential to help them advance their careers.

An important point that Bailey and his colleagues make is that the hierarchical scales and values reflected in these ideologies were not entirely determinative of their experiences and opportunities, but that their participants were able to strategically rework or reconfigure these scales through their linguistic practices in different kinds of situations for different kinds of purposes. One strategy they used was to realign these scales and values in relation to their transnational life courses, referencing different scales and articulating different ideologies as they moved from place to place, seeking 'to combine locations and live across borders, rather than maintain binaries between here and there, or between the global and the local' (p. 324). Another strategy they used was what Bailey and his colleagues refer to as 'hybridizing identities', defining themselves in ways that combined identities and scales, using labels, for example, like 'overseas-Korean' and 'Korean American'. Finally, they sometimes incorporated their experiences of racial discrimination and acknowledged the racial undertones of different scalar values, describing, for instance, how their way of speaking English was stigmatised when they lived in the US but not in Hong Kong where more people were also 'Asian' and spoke English with a variety of accents.

Bailey and his colleagues say that their study shows how paying attention to what they call 'scalar politics', the ability of people to navigate and reconfigure scalar relations and the values associated with them in their everyday linguistic practices, provides a way of understanding both how migrants are constrained by sociolinguistic scales and how they can exercise agency in relation to them.

Project Ideas

1. Explore how migration has changed the city, town, village where you live. Observe any new 'languages' that newcomers have brought with them. Some good ways to find out are to identify which codes are visible on public signs in the linguistic landscape, or obtain some census data from local municipalities, or look at what schools or religious establishments exist in the area. Once you complete your initial observations, design a questionnaire that investigates local people's awareness and reactions to changes due to migration, and also their reactions towards new codes and their speakers. Distribute your questionnaire to at least thirty informants either online or in person.

2. Conduct a focus group interview with five people to investigate their communicative practices in relation to the trajectory of their mobilities. Start by eliciting information about each person's reasons behind their mobilities (e.g., trade/business, education, tourism, conflict, pursuit of better life, religion, colonisation). Then ask them what communicative resources they used with different people, in different contexts, at different times and whether they have had to adjust them along the way.

3. For this project you will explore the family language policy of a migrant multilingual family. Ask the members of the family to keep a 'language diary' for a week, indicating which codes they use throughout their everyday activities. If they have very young children, ask the parents to note down their children's linguistic practices. Then conduct a short interview with the family to discuss what kind of changes they made in preparation for their migration, the parents' expected and actual language practices at home, the children's language practices and preferences, and any language barriers they have experienced in their new country.

4. Investigate a creole language like Tok Pisin, Famagalo, Haitian Creole, or a different one. Identify the historical reasons behind the emergence of this 'language'. Then focus on linguistic aspects like its lexifier language and typical linguistic features in terms of grammar, vocabulary, and so on. Then explore its functions in the community and how it is used on a daily basis.

Appendix: A Sociolinguist's Toolkit

A.1 Introduction

At the end of each chapter, we presented some project ideas to inspire you to conduct your own sociolinguistic projects. Embarking on a project, however, is not an easy task. A lot of preparation is required before collecting data, like designing research tools, finding participants, considering the ethics of your project, and planning how you are going to analyse your data once you have it and how you are going to present it to others. Here we present some methodological tools that have been widely used by sociolinguists over the past sixty years. The approaches we will talk about range from classic methods like the sociolinguistic interview and the matched guise technique, to novel ones used for linguistic landscape and computer-mediated communication research. As we go through each approach, we will offer suggestions and tips that will help you to plan and carry out your research project and recommend some books and articles you can read to find out more about the method.

A.2 Methods

i. Sociolinguistic Interviews

a. **What are they?** This classic method is used chiefly to study language variation. It was developed by William Labov and has been widely used by other scholars like Peter Trudgill (see Chapter 3). This interview method works best for studying the frequency with which different kinds of people produce phonological, grammatical, and lexical variants. The researcher explores how linguistic variables are related to social factors such as gender, age, social class, and education, as well as the effect of different 'styles' of speaking, from casual to formal, on the production of linguistic variants.

b. **How do they work?** Participants are recruited based on the social variables the researcher is interested in (such as class or gender). The sample is usually 'stratified', with the same or a similar number of participants from each category. They engage in a variety of tasks during the interview, from reading aloud lists of words to having a casual conversation. The researcher designs these tasks in order to elicit the production of the linguistic variables that they wish to test. Each of the tasks is designed to create in participants a different level of awareness about their language use. The idea is that, when they are paying more attention to how they speak, they are more likely to talk the way they think they *should* talk, and when they are paying less attention, they are more likely to talk the way they 'normally' talk. Sociolinguistic interviews are usually recorded to enable the researcher to perform close analysis after the completion of all the interviews. The biggest challenge in such interviews is known as the 'observer's paradox' (Labov 1972), the fact that people inevitably change the way they speak when they know they are being observed. There are various strategies to mitigate the effects of observation in order to elicit 'casual' speech, for example asking informants to tell a funny story about themselves or asking them a disarming question like: 'Have you been in a situation where you were in serious danger of being killed?'

c. **How can I analyse my data?** Data from sociolinguistic interviews is usually analysed quantitatively. The researcher counts how many times a given linguistic variable occurred in the groups of participants under the conditions of the different tasks. Frequencies are then often analysed using statistical methods. Findings are usually presented as percentages in the form of graphs or tables.

d. **Useful readings**
   o Becker, K. (2017). The sociolinguistic interview. In C. Mallinson, B. Childs, and G. van Herk (Eds.), *Data collection in sociolinguistics* (pp. 91–100). London: Routledge.
   o Hoffman, M. (2014). Sociolinguistic interviews. In J. Holmes and K. Hazen (Eds.), *Research methods in sociolinguistics: A practical guide* (pp. 25–41). Malden: Wiley-Blackwell.
   o Labov, W. (1972). *Sociolinguistic patterns*. Philadelphia: University of Pennsylvania Press.
   o Labov, W. (1984). Field methods of the project on linguistic change and variation. In J. Baugh and J. Sherzer (Eds.), *Language in use: Readings in sociolinguistics* (pp. 28–53). Englewood Cliffs: Prentice Hall.
   o Meyerhoff, M., Schleef, E., and MacKenzie, L. (2015). *Doing sociolinguistics: A practical guide to data collection and analysis*. London: Routledge.

ii. Surveys and Questionnaires
a. **What are they?** A questionnaire is a list of questions that is usually presented in writing to informants. We can use

questionnaires to explore different sociolinguistic problems relating to behaviour, knowledge, beliefs, attitudes, and attributes. For example, questionnaires can help us reveal language attitudes, perceptions, and experiences, elicit information about language practices, investigate which languages are used in a given area, school, or family, understand people's motivations for learning other languages, and so on. The benefit of questionnaires is that they enable researchers to collect data from a large number of people. However, one limitation is that they are not particularly suited to exploring in depth the reasons or motivations for people's responses.

b. **How do they work?** Designing a good questionnaire is not an easy task. This process should be well thought out to ensure that questions are designed to elicit the kind of information that the researcher needs. Different kinds of questions can be included to generate different kinds of data, either quantitative or qualitative. Most common are closed questions in which respondents are asked to choose from a limited number of options when they answer (e.g., multiple-choice questions, true–false questions, rating scales). These questions generate quantitative data that can be easily compared across respondents. To obtain qualitative data, open-ended questions can be used. These enable the informants to expand on their own ideas, experiences, opinions, and attitudes and to provide more personal responses. It is always a good idea to *pilot* the questionnaire with a few people before distributing it to a large number of informants in order to identify aspects in the questionnaire that may not be clear or that do not elicit the kind of data that is needed.

c. **How can I analyse my data?** Answers obtained from closed questions can be quantified and expressed as frequencies and averages. Researchers also often use inferential statistics to further explore different aspects of the data, such as the relationships between responses to different questions. Data obtained from open questions can be analysed qualitatively by identifying themes. Quotes from qualitative responses can be included in your report to provide support for your findings.

d. **Useful readings**
   o Boberg, C. (2017). Surveys: The use of written questionnaires in sociolinguistics. In C. Mallinson, B. Childs, and G. van Herk (Eds.), *Data collection in sociolinguistics* (pp. 131–41). London: Routledge.
   o Iwaniec, J. (2019). Questionnaires: Implications for effective implementation. In J. McKinley and H. Rose (Eds.), *The Routledge handbook of research methods in applied linguistics* (pp. 324–35). London: Routledge.
   o Meyerhoff, M., Schleef, E., and MacKenzie, L. (2015). *Doing sociolinguistics: A practical guide to data collection and analysis*. London: Routledge.

o Schleef, E. (2014). Written surveys and questionnaires in sociolinguistics. In J. Holmes and K. Hazen (Eds.), *Research methods in sociolinguistics: A practical guide* (pp. 42–57). Malden: Wiley-Blackwell.

iii. Controlled Experiments

a. **What are they?** Experiments have been widely used in sociolinguistic research. They involve participants being asked to perform tasks (such as listening to speech samples) under controlled conditions. Through the years various experimental designs have been developed, such as the matched guise technique (see Chapter 7). The way experiments are designed depends on the aims of the study and the research questions. While data obtained from controlled experiments is sometimes considered 'artificial', a well-planned experiment enables the researcher to obtain large amounts of comparable data that can provide clear findings. Experiments can be used alone or in combination with other data collection methods (such as interviews), enabling us to investigate a given sociolinguistic phenomenon from different perspectives.

b. **How do they work?** The matched guise technique (Lambert et al. 1960) is a good example of an experimental design. Different versions of this method have emerged over the years, but the main idea is that informants listen to carefully prepared recordings and then evaluate them using scales. In identification tasks, listeners might listen to words that are relatively similar (e.g., *bad* vs. *bed*) and then indicate on a response sheet which word they heard. This design is often used to explore things like phonological perception. Informants can also be asked to complete tasks where they produce different kinds of output under controlled conditions.

c. **How can I analyse my data?** Data obtained using controlled experiments are usually quantitative. Frequencies of different kinds of responses under different conditions are calculated, and inferential statistics are usually performed. Findings are presented in tables and graphs.

d. **Useful readings**

o Drager, K. (2014). Experimental methods in sociolinguistics. In J. Holmes and K. Hazen (Eds.), *Research methods in sociolinguistics: A practical guide* (pp. 58–71). Malden: Wiley-Blackwell.

o Drager, K. (2018). *Experimental research methods in sociolinguistics*. London: Bloomsbury Academic.

o Clopper, G. (2017). Experiments. In C. Mallinson, B. Childs, and G. Van Herk (Eds.), *Data collection in sociolinguistics: Methods and applications* (pp. 154–62). London: Routledge.

iv. Observation/Collection of 'Naturally Occurring' Data

a. **What is it?** The observation and collection of 'naturally occurring' data are ways for researchers to obtain data about how people communicate in 'natural' situations. These might include situations such as service encounters, classrooms, or interactions with friends or family members. Sometimes researchers take notes about what they observe using protocols designed to help them focus on the kind of behaviour they are interested in, but usually interactions in these situations are audio or video recorded.

b. **How does it work?** The most important thing about collecting 'naturally occurring' data is that all of the people involved know they are being observed or recorded and have given their consent (see below). Choices about whether to simply observe or to audio/video record participants' behaviour and how depends on the kind of data the researcher wishes to obtain and how it will be analysed. Observation protocols can be used when the researcher has a good idea of the specific kind of behaviour they are interested in. Recording results in much richer data that the researcher can analyse for a greater range of features. When situations are recorded, recording devices are either placed in the situation or participants are equipped with small recorders or radio microphones to carry around with them. Participants are typically given a choice about what aspects of their behaviour they wish to be recorded and when to pause or stop the recording. One challenge with this method is the 'observer's paradox', the fact that people might behave differently when they know they are being recorded or observed. This is why quotation marks are used for the phrase 'naturally occurring'; situations that are being observed or recorded are never entirely 'natural'. Researchers often deal with this challenge by observing or recording over longer periods of time to give participants the opportunity to become more comfortable with the process.

c. **How can I analyse my data?** Data obtained from observations and recordings can be analysed quantitatively or qualitatively. Recordings are usually transcribed using particular transcription conventions designed to represent the kinds of features the researcher is interested in. In the case of quantitative analysis, a researcher might calculate the frequency with which participants produce a particular feature as a percentage of all of the instances where that feature could be produced. The aim of qualitative analysis is to identify patterns in the data using various forms of discourse analysis, such as conversation analysis (see Chapter 5) or interactional sociolinguistics.

d. **Useful readings**
   o D'Arcy, A. (2017). Advances in sociolinguistic transcription methods. In C. Mallinson, B. Childs, and G. Van Herk (Eds.),

Data collection in sociolinguistics: Methods and applications (pp. 187–90). London: Routledge.

o Golato, A. (2017). Naturally occurring data. In A. Barron, Y. Gu, and G. Steen (Eds.), *The Routledge handbook of pragmatics* (pp. 21–6). London: Routledge.

o Hyland, K., and Paltridge, B. (Eds.) (2021). *The Bloomsbury companion to discourse analysis*. London: Bloomsbury Academic.

v. Ethnographic Fieldwork

a. **What is it?** Ethnography originates from the field of cultural anthropology and aims to answer the question: 'Why do people in this particular community behave and use language as they do?' Ethnographic fieldwork is not easy to conduct. It is a time-consuming method which is also personally and intellectually challenging. However, scholars who use this approach report that it is one of the most rewarding methods of sociolinguistic research. Ethnographers usually engage in *participant observation*, taking part in the daily activities, interactions, and rituals of a group of people to collect authentic, non-elicited data from them. Interviews are also often used in ethnography, but they tend to be less structured than traditional sociolinguistic interviews. Ethnography can provide a holistic view of how language is used in a given context, but one limitation is that it is difficult to predict what sort of data we'll get. Also, unlike experimental and survey studies, ethnographic studies are difficult to replicate.

b. **How does it work?** Ethnography is not a single method. It actually consists of different data collection methods, like observations and field notes, audio or video recording of interactions, interviews with participants, and the collection of documents and artefacts like maps and drawings. During the fieldwork, researchers usually take field notes, carefully noting down their observations. Before embarking on ethnography, it is important that we develop adequate knowledge about the community we plan to investigate. Gaining access to a given community can be challenging, especially if the researcher is not an 'insider'. It is important therefore to establish relationships with 'insiders' that can help us gain access and guide us through the field. These are sometimes called 'key informants'. It is also essential that the ethnographer clearly identifies themself as a researcher and that all of the participants understand that they are being observed. Ethnographers normally spend a considerable amount of time with their participants, and they often immerse themselves in their everyday social interactions and activities.

c. **How can I analyse my data?** Unlike other approaches in which analysis takes place once data collection is complete, in ethnographic studies researchers usually analyse the data along the way. In this way they can obtain preliminary findings which might affect the future focus or direction of the study. For example, based on preliminary findings, we may choose to explore in more detail specific language practices or linguistic features. Data is usually analysed qualitatively using methods such as thematic analysis or discourse analysis.

d. **Useful readings**
- o De Fina, A. (2019). The ethnographic interview. In K. Tusting (Ed.), *The Routledge handbook of linguistic ethnography* (pp. 154–67). Milton: Routledge.
- o Levon, E. (2017). Ethnographic fieldwork. In C. Mallinson, B. Childs, and G. Van Herk (Eds.), *Data collection in sociolinguistics: Methods and applications* (pp. 71–9). London: Routledge.
- o Li Wei, (2019). Ethnography: Origins, features, accountability, and criticality. In J. McKinley and H. Rose (Eds.), *The Routledge handbook of research methods in applied linguistics* (pp. 154–64). London: Routledge.
- o Papen, U. (2019). Participant observation and field notes. In K. Tusting (Ed.), *The Routledge handbook of linguistic ethnography* (pp. 141–53). Milton: Routledge.
- o Tusting, K. (2019). *The Routledge handbook of linguistic ethnography*. Milton: Routledge.

vi. Collecting Texts and Other Artefacts

a. **What is it?** While some researchers obtain their data from participants using interviews, questionnaires, and observations, others might opt to examine written texts, media texts such as radio or television interviews, or other artefacts. Such texts are often treated as records of people's communicative behaviour, and so they are sometimes used if we are interested in the way people wrote or talked in the past. Texts like songs or television programmes are a good source of data about how people 'perform' language. Researchers might also pose questions like: 'How does the way communicative resources are used in this particular text compare to other similar texts?' or 'How might this text or artefact influence, reflect, or challenge norms, attitudes, or ideologies in a given society or community?'

b. **How does it work?** Texts and artefacts can consist of, but are not limited to, books, newspapers, magazines, manifestos, pamphlets, policy documents, advertisements, images, and media products like television programmes, news broadcasts, and films. Usually, researchers devise some kind of system for collecting data to make sure they are not just 'cherry picking' data to confirm their preconceived ideas. This might involve, for instance, choosing random or purposive samples of texts from particular contexts that were produced during a fixed time period.

c. **How can I analyse my data?** Data analysis is usually qualitative, but quantitative methods can also be used. Researchers usually use various kinds of content analysis or discourse analysis to examine their data. They might count the frequency with which different features or variants appear in texts. Sometimes they use computer programs (corpus tools) to analyse the frequency of different features or to find patterns in large collections of texts.

d. **Useful readings**

o Baker, P. (2010). *Sociolinguistics and corpus linguistics.* Edinburgh: Edinburgh University Press.

o Jones, R. H. (2019). *Discourse analysis: A resource book for students* (2nd edition). Abingdon: Routledge.

o Queen, R. (2017). Working with performed language: Movies, television and music. In C. Mallinson, B. Childs, and G. Van Herk (Eds.), *Data collection in sociolinguistics: Methods and applications* (pp. 217–27). London: Routledge.

o Schneider, E. (2017). Written data sources. In C. Mallinson, B. Childs, and G. Van Herk (Eds.), *Data collection in sociolinguistics: Methods and applications* (pp. 169–78). London: Routledge.

vii. Linguistic Landscape Research

a. **What is it?** Linguistic landscape research focuses on language and other semiotic resources that are visible in the physical environment. It usually involves studying public signs and other aspects of the built environment. It can also involve studying the ways people interact with and in the environment.

b. **How does it work?** To collect data, researchers usually visit a given public space (e.g., a street, neighbourhood, commercial area, mall, school) and systematically photograph the public signs that are visible to passers-by. These can include street name signs, traffic signs, billboards, shop names, posters, advertisements, warning signs, graffiti, and stickers. Researchers might also collect data about other aspects of the environment such as sounds, smells, the clothes people are wearing, or aspects of the architecture. Sometimes researchers rely on data created by other people, like images posted on social media. Interviews can be conducted with various people, such as the people who live in, work in, or visit the area or the people who have created the signs or placed them in the environment. Sometimes researchers use ethnographic methods, spending a great deal of time in a particular area and getting to know the people in it.

c. **How can I analyse my data?** There are different ways to analyse data collected using the linguistic landscape approach. Some scholars use quantitative methods, counting the different languages visible on signs and presenting their findings in tables and graphs. Others analyse signs qualitatively, by paying attention not only to which languages are used but also to other visual aspects, the locations at which the signs are placed, who created them, and who uses them. Interviews obtained from creators and audiences can be analysed thematically, by identifying and categorising the people's opinions, evaluations, and attitudes.

d. **Useful readings**
  - o Androutsopoulos, J. (2014). Computer-mediated communication and linguistic landscapes. In J. Holmes and K. Hazen (Eds.), *Research methods in sociolinguistics: A practical guide* (pp. 74–90). Malden: Wiley-Blackwell.
  - o Blommaert, J. (2013). *Ethnography, superdiversity and linguistic landscapes: Chronicles of complexity*. Bristol: Multilingual Matters.
  - o Landry, R., and Bourhis, R. (1997). Linguistic landscape and ethnolinguistic vitality: An empirical study. *Journal of Language and Social Psychology*, 16(1), 23–49.
  - o Lou, J. J. (2017). Linguistic landscape and ethnographic fieldwork. In C. Mallinson, B. Childs, and G. Van Herk (Eds.), *Data collection in sociolinguistics: Methods and applications* (pp. 94–8). London: Routledge.
  - o Scollon, R., and Wong Scollon, S. (2003). *Discourse in place: Language in the material world*. London: Routledge.
  - o Shohamy, E., Ben-Rafael, E., and Barni, M. (2010). *Linguistic landscape in the city*. Bristol: Multilingual Matters.
  - o Shohamy, E., and Gorter, D. (2009). *Linguistic landscape: Expanding the scenery*. New York: Routledge.

viii. Computer-Mediated Communication Research

a. **What is it?** Computer-mediated communication research involves collecting data from private or public communication via digital media such as emails, texts, blog posts, social media posts, and comments on discussion forums. The kinds of data that researchers obtain can change as new technologies and platforms are developed. Computer-mediated communication research can be used to explore language variation and change online, digital language practices such as code switching and how these are influenced by technological affordances and constraints, language style, identity, and relationships online, as well as broader issues that have to do with multilingualism, globalisation, and mobility.

b. **How does it work?** We can collect different kinds of data from online sources. We might collect texts and artefacts from the Internet such as tweets or TikTok videos. Or we might conduct participant observation, visiting a particular online 'space' (such as a massively multiplayer online gaming site), interacting with other users and observing how they communicate. We might also contact particular kinds of users (such as social media influencers) and interview them or distribute questionnaires to people who use a particular platform.

c. **How can I analyse my data?** This will depend on the research questions and the kind of data we have. Data can be analysed quantitatively, especially if we are interested in aspects such as language variation online. It can also be analysed qualitatively using a variety of methods, including multimodal discourse analysis. Some researchers, such as Herring, have developed frameworks for discourse analysis specially designed for data that was collected online.

d. **Useful readings**

o Androutsopoulos, J. (2017). Online data collection. In C. Mallinson, B. Childs, and G. Van Herk (Eds.), *Data collection in sociolinguistics: Methods and applications* (pp. 233–44). London: Routledge.

o Bolander, B., and Locher, M. A. (2014). Doing sociolinguistic research on computer-mediated data: A review of four methodological issues. *Discourse, Context & Media*, 3, 14–26.

o Herring, S. C. (2004). *Computer-mediated discourse analysis: An approach to researching online behaviour*. In S. A. Barab, R. Kling, and J. H. Gray (Eds.), *Learning in doing. Designing for virtual communities in the service of learning* (pp. 338–76). Cambridge: Cambridge University Press.

o Jones, R. H. and Hafner, C. A. (2021). *Understanding digital literacies: A practical introduction* (2nd edition). London: Routledge.

o Page, R., Barton, D., Unger, J. W., and Zappavigna, M. (2014). *Researching language and social media: A student guide*. London: Routledge.

ix. Citizen Sociolinguistics

a. **What is it?** Citizen sociolinguistics is a kind of 'citizen science' in which ordinary people gather and analyse data. In some cases, researchers collect the views of 'ordinary people' about particular linguistic phenomena through online searches and informal conversations. Sometimes, however, citizens are engaged as co-researchers. Citizen researchers might be involved in interviewing their friends or acquaintances or gathering texts or artefacts either from the physical world or from the Internet, or in observing their own or other people's behaviours and keeping records or diaries. Citizen sociolinguistics can be used to study a range of issues such as language variation, language attitudes, and the way different linguistic and semiotic resources are used in different settings.

b. **How does it work?** Typically, a researcher will decide on the particular linguistic phenomenon they are interested in and gather as many examples as they can of people talking about, reflecting on, or responding to this phenomenon. In cases where citizen sociolinguistics involves informants as co-researchers, the main job of the researcher is to create situations and support for citizen-sociolinguists to collect and reflect upon data. They might, for example, set up a website or a page or channel on a social media site for people to post the data they have collected and talk about it. Sometimes citizen-sociolinguists are asked to work together to produce things like video documentaries or podcasts about what they have learned.

c. **How can I analyse my data?** How data is analysed depends on the form in which the researcher receives it. Qualitative analysis can be used for written texts, observations, diary entries, etc. Quantitative analysis can be used when things like the frequency of different kinds of responses from informants are important. Often the informants who have gathered the data are also involved in helping to analyse it.

d. **Useful readings**

  o Rymes, B. (2020). *How we talk about language: Exploring citizen sociolinguistics*. Cambridge: Cambridge University Press.

  o SturtzSreetharan, C. (2020). Citizen sociolinguistics: A data collection approach for hard-to-capture naturally occurring language data. *Field Methods*, 32(3), 327–34.

  o Svendsen, B. A. (2018). The dynamics of citizen sociolinguistics. *Journal of Sociolinguistics*, 22(2), 137–60.

A.3 Ethical Considerations

Given our field's commitment to helping people to address 'real-world' problems, it is important that we take into careful consideration the well-being of the people whom we study. Aspects of ethics are discussed in nearly all of the books on research methods we have mentioned here. Also, organisations like the British Association for Applied Linguistics (BAAL 2021) and the American Association for Applied Linguistics (AAAL Ethics Guidelines Task Force 2017) have published guidelines on how to conduct ethical research in language studies.

'The general principles of ethics are: (1) respect for persons, (2) yielding optimal benefits while minimising harm, and (3) justice' (De Costa 2014, 2015). In order to ensure all these during our research, a number of important procedures should be followed.

Informed consent *must* be obtained from the participants before data collection commences. Researchers should prepare an **information sheet**, a document which gives participants information about the nature of the study, the research aims, the contact details of the researcher, and a list of activities that the participants agree to take part in (e.g., being interviewed, answering a questionnaire, being recorded). The explanation of the project must be written in a form that the participants can understand. Participants are then asked to sign and date a **consent form**, stating in writing that they give informed consent for their data to be used for the purposes of the study. Participants' **autonomy** is very important and must be ensured. A core principle of autonomy is that participants have the right to withdraw from a research project at any stage, even when they have initially agreed to take part.

You might have noticed that some studies back in the 1970s collected data without obtaining informed consent from participants. One famous example is Labov's (1966/2006) department store study in New York City, in which he conducted rapid interviews with shop assistants to elicit their pronunciation of the variable /r/. In this case, the participants were not aware that they were taking part in a study and had not given their informed consent. The benefit of doing this was that Labov was able to avoid the 'observer's paradox'. The problem is that he did not respect his participants' autonomy and right to decide for themselves whether they wanted to be part of a research study.

Covert research, namely when researchers pretend to do one thing but do another, or where researchers go 'undercover' and pretend to be a member of a group they are researching, is usually not considered ethical. There is a distinction, however, between deception and distraction. Some forms of distraction might be considered ethical. In some studies, for example, researchers might inform participants about the general aim of the research but not tell them the precise aspects of their behaviour that the researcher will focus on.

Two core principles of ethics that researchers need to ensure are anonymity and confidentiality. **Anonymity** is when participants' identities are kept secret, sometimes even from the researcher. Questionnaires usually offer anonymous data, because participants can complete them without giving their names. If a different data collection method is used, for example interviews, where the researcher spends more time with participants to collect data, then every effort should be made to protect their identities when reporting the findings. This can be achieved by using pseudonyms instead of the participants' real names, or by referring to people and places in more general terms, such as 'a school in Seville' rather than 'I.E.S. Murillo in Seville'. If data involves videos or photos, then pixilation can be used to obscure participants' faces in the data. Although some participants may state that they would like their real names to be used in the research, it is generally advisable not to agree to this.

Confidentiality is also very important. In this case, the researcher must keep participants' personal details secure where others cannot access them. These days, researchers can store their data in secure virtual storage spaces. If access to online environments is not possible, then data must be protected in other ways, for example by locking it in a drawer or cabinet.

Special attention needs to be paid to data obtained from online sources. Blogs, tweets, Facebook and Instagram posts, TikTok videos, WhatsApp chats, Wikis and LinkedIn posts provide freely available, non-elicited data. However, the ethical principles discussed above are often challenged when we deal with this kind of online data. For example, it might be difficult to contact and obtain consent from all the creators of online material, or to grant them anonymity. Or it might be challenging to distinguish between what is considered to be a public or private domain. To overcome these challenges, BAAL (2021) recommends that we adopt a flexible case-by-case 'process approach' that is responsive to emergent and developing forms of social interaction online.

Researchers should always check the terms and conditions of the digital platform they wish to investigate and make sure they understand their legal responsibilities and obligations. In research on publicly accessible data (e.g., unrestricted web forums or blogs), the identities of the participants should always be protected even if the data is publicly available. We protect the anonymity of our informants by not directly disclosing their offline identities and avoiding any clues that may lead to their identification. If private (e.g., emails, text messages) or semi-public (social networking sites) data is used, then the researcher should obtain permission to use this data.

Useful readings

o AAAL Ethics Guidelines Task Force. (2017). *AAAL ethics guidelines*. Retrieved 15 May 2021 from www.aaal.org/ethics-guidelines##.

o British Association for Applied Linguistics (BAAL). (2021). *Recommendations on good practice in applied linguistics*. Retrieved 15 May 2021 from www.baal.org.uk/wp-content/uploads/2021/03/BAAL-Good-Practice-Guidelines-2021.pdf.

o De Costa, P. I. (2014). Making ethical decisions in an ethnographic study. *TESOL Quarterly*, 48, 413–22.

o De Costa, P. I. (2015). Ethics and applied linguistics research. In B. Paltridge and A. Phakiti (Eds.), *Research methods in applied linguistics: A practical resource* (pp. 245–57). London: Bloomsbury.

o De Costa, P. I., Jongbong, L., Rawal, H., and Li Wei (2019). Ethics in applied linguistics research. In J. McKinley and H. Rose (Eds.), *The Routledge handbook of research methods in applied linguistics* (pp. 122–30). London: Routledge.

o Dörnyei, Z. (2007). *Research methods in applied linguistics: Quantitative, qualitative, and mixed methodologies*. Oxford: Oxford University Press.

o Mallinson, C. (2018). Ethics in linguistic research. In L. Litosseliti (Ed.), *Research methods in linguistics* (pp. 57–84). London: Bloomsbury.

Glossary

accent: A particular way of pronouncing a language or variety, usually associated with some geographical area or region. (CH1)

African American Vernacular English (AAVE): A variety of English used by many African Americans, especially in urban centres; sometimes referred to as African American English (AAE), Black English (BE), or Ebonics. (Introduction)

algorithm: Computer code which helps to determine how content is circulated on the Internet and appears on some websites. (CH4)

appropriation: Imitating the way other people speak not for the purpose of mockery, but for the purpose of personal gain or profit. (CH7)

audience design: The theory that people 'design' their speech in relation to their audiences. (CH6)

auditor effect: The effect that listeners *other* than the addressee (i.e., auditors, overhearers) have on a speaker's speech. (CH6)

authenticity: The degree to which a style we adopt is regarded as a sincere reflection of our 'true' identity. (CH6)

borrowing: When lexical items from one code are incorporated into another, for example English borrowed the word 'croissant' from French and the word 'ketchup' from Chinese. (CH9)

bottom-up signs: Public signs that are created by commercial and other private organisations. (CH8)

bricolage: The act of drawing on and combining diverse linguistic resources from our communicative repertoires in order to construct new meanings or perform different kinds of identities. (CH6)

citizen sociolinguistics: An approach in sociolinguistics which is concerned with the everyday ways people talk about language and elicits the assistance of ordinary citizens to collect data. (CH7)

code: A term for any variety of language; often used as an alternative for 'language' or 'dialect' to avoid the connotations of these terms. (CH2)

code mixing: Mixing linguistic units from different 'languages' within a sentence (also known as 'intrasentential' code mixing). (CH5)

code preference system: The order in which different codes appear on multilingual public signs. (CH8)

code switching: Mixing linguistic units from different 'languages' across sentence boundaries (also known as 'intersentential' code mixing). (CH5)

codification: The process of arranging rules according to a system or plan. In linguistics, this term is used to refer to the promulgation of 'standard' forms of grammar, spelling, pronunciation, and vocabulary, often through formal schooling and the writing of dictionaries and grammar books. (CH1)

Communication Accommodation Theory: A theory which predicts that people alter their language in order to manage their relationships with the people they are speaking to. (CH6)

communicative competence: A concept invented by Dell Hymes to describe the kind of competence people need to communicate successfully in real social situations. (Introduction)

community of practice: A group of people who come together because they share a common cause, interest, or mission. They usually have mutual engagement through regular interaction and develop common practices or ways of doing things. (CH3)

competency: Knowledge or understanding of something or the ability to do something successfully or efficiently. When it comes to the communicative resources in their repertoires, people have different kinds of unequal competencies. (CH2)

contact linguistics: The study of how 'languages' influence one another when they come into contact. (CH9)

context: The set of circumstances associated with a communicative situation (e.g., physical surroundings, people, relationships, people's past experiences, conversational goals, broad cultural values and expectations) that may affect the way people communicate. (CH4)

contextualisation: The creation of context through the use of communicative resources. (CH6)

convergence: When speakers change the way they talk to make it more similar to the way their addressees talk. (CH6)

conversation analysis: An approach to the study of social interaction that explores how interactions develop sequentially, paying attention to things like turn-taking and 'adjacency pairs'. (CH5)

corporeal sociolinguistics: Sociolinguistic studies which focus on the body. (CH8)

covert language attitudes: Evaluations about language not openly expressed by people, either because they think it would be somehow wrong to express them or because they are not completely aware of them themselves. (CH 7)

covert prestige: The value implicitly attached by a group of people to forms or variants which they frequently use but claim to avoid. It usually relates to local or 'non-standard' forms whose use is often frowned upon, but that at the same time also index solidarity. (CH3)

creole: A stable language variety arising from contact situations. (CH9)

crossing: Code alternation by people who are not members of the group associated with the code they employ. (CH5)

decreolisation: The process whereby a creole language reconverges with one of the 'standard' languages from which it originally derived. (CH9)

deterritorialisation: The idea that 'languages' and other resources are not fixed to a given country or region or defined by particular localities. (CH9)

dialect: A distinct variety of a language, especially one spoken in a specific part of a country or other geographical area. (CH1)

dialect levelling: The process whereby features associated with different 'dialects' reduce over time and people from different places start to speak more similarly. (CH9)

dialectology: The branch of linguistics concerned with the study of 'dialects'. (CH3)

diglossia: A term used by Charles Ferguson to describe situations in which two distinct varieties have clear functional distinctions. (CH9)

divergence: When people alter their speech to make it more unlike the speech of their addressees. (CH6)

double-voicing: A term introduced by the Russian literary critic Mikhail Bakhtin to describe when people adopt codes that are not typically associated with them, sometimes in an ironic way. (CH5)

embodiment: The ways that people use their bodies (i.e., bodily movements, clothing, tattoos, etc.) to generate meaning. (CH8)

emplacement system: Where in the physical world a given public sign is located. (CH8)

enregisterment: A semiotic process by which linguistic forms (variables, varieties, styles, or other resources) become linked to social identities, social groups, and/or specific places or activities. (CH3)

ephemeral signs: Signs that are not permanent and which are usually created by ordinary people. (CH8)

ethnography: A method that originates from anthropology which is used to investigate the social relationships people have in communities and how they affect the way they speak or write. It often involves long-term participant observation, interacting with people and getting to know their everyday lives. (CH3)

ethnolinguistic vitality: A group's ability to maintain and protect its existence as a collective entity with a distinctive identity and language. (CH8)

flows: A term used by globalisation scholar Arjun Appadurai in the 1990s to refer to the fluid and dynamic ways that resources move around the world and affect one another. (CH9)

folk linguistics: An approach developed by Dennis Preston which aims to discover language attitudes by examining overt comments about language made by non-linguists. (CH7)

genres: Types of communicative activities or texts that are structured in predictable ways (e.g., stories, arguments, Instagram posts, political slogans, and graffiti tags). (CH2)

geosemiotics: A qualitative analytical framework developed by Ron Scollon and Suzie Wong Scollon which is used to analyse code choices, visual elements, and the emplacement of public signs in the physical world. (CH8)

globalisation: The global interconnectedness of people, goods, and cultural artefacts and their ability to move across the globe as a result of travel and communication technologies. (CH9)

heteroglossia: The diversity of voices, styles of discourse, resources, or points of view in a text or interaction, each one 'pointing to' a particular social group or world view. (CH2)

icons, symbols, and indexes: Terms introduced by semiotician Charles Peirce to refer to types of relationships between a sign and what it means. (CH2)

identification: The way in which people 'identify with' or distance themselves from particular social groups and particular identities. (CH6)

indexical meaning: Instances when the meaning of a sign/resource is created by 'pointing to' aspects of the context in which it is used. (CH2)

inscription system: The multimodal aspects of public signs, including use of fonts, colours, images, and the kind of material that was used to produce the sign (e.g., paper, metal, laminate). (CH8)

koineisation: A process whereby different 'dialects' merge to form a new 'dialect'. (CH9)

language: A term that can be used to refer to language in general or to particular 'codes' (e.g. French, Urdu), or particular ways of speaking or writing. (CH1)

language ideologies: Conceptualisations and beliefs about languages, speakers, and communicative practices. (CH1)

language mocking: The intentional use of a language variety that is not native to a speaker for the purposes of teasing, joking, or insulting those who use this variety. (CH7)

language shift: A process whereby people shift to regularly using a different language variety as a result of language contact. (CH9)

language variation: Regional, social, or contextual differences in the ways that a particular 'language' is used. (CH3)

light communities: Online groups that have short lifespans, and which people move easily in and out of, often anonymously. (CH4)

linguistic landscape: An approach in sociolinguistics which investigates the display of language on public signs and other semiotic aspects of the physical environment. (CH8)

linguistic purism: The notion that 'languages' should only be used in their 'pure form'. (CH5)

linguistic resistance: An attempt by people to use certain variants in order to avoid being associated with a given social group. (CH3)

linguistic variable: A linguistic element such as a word or a sound that can be produced in different ways. (CH3)

markedness model: An approach to the study of language use that explores code switching in relation to social norms. (CH5)

matched guise technique: A approach used to investigate language attitudes in which listeners hear recordings of the same speaker speaking different 'languages' or language varieties and evaluate them using a scale. (CH7)

meaning potential: The range of meanings a particular resource can express. (CH4)

media: The material carriers of modes. These can include newspapers, telephones, magazines, radio, television, the Internet, clothing, and the human body. (CH4)

meme: A multimodal media text that goes viral, often consisting of an image with text superimposed on it which is altered and remixed as it circulates. (CH4)

metadiscourse: Talk or writing about language/communication and linguistic/communicative practices. (CH3)

metaphorical code switching: When people switch to a different code in order to express some kind of social meaning. (CH5)

mobility: When people and resources, meanings and values travel across different kinds of borders (physical, political, social) and through different communities and social contexts. (CH9)

modes: A regularised set of resources for making meaning, such as speech, writing, images, graphs, gestures, gaze, music, fonts, and tone of voice. (CH4)

monolingual ideology: The belief that monolingualism is better than multilingualism. (CH1)

monomodal ideology: The idea that one mode, usually written language, is superior to other modes of communication. (CH4)

multilingual ideology: The belief that multilingualism is normal and beneficial. (CH1)

multiliteracies: The ability to communicate effectively through multiple modes conveyed through multiple media. (CH4)

multimodality: A term associated with the work of Gunther Kress and Theo Van Leeuwen, who said that all communication is multimodal, i.e., makes use of different kinds of modes. (CH4)

networked multilingualism: Multilingual practices that are shaped by two interrelated processes: being networked, i.e., digitally connected to other individuals and groups, and being in the network, i.e., embedded in the global mediascape of the web. (CH4)

overt language attitudes: Evaluations about language which are consciously felt/thought and explicitly expressed. (CH7)

overt prestige: The value explicitly attached by a group of people to forms or variants which they consider 'correct'; it is usually associated with 'standard' forms of language. (CH3)

performativity: The way the performance of identities brings those identities into existence. (CH6)

pidgin: A language variety that arises from situations of contact where people do not share the same language. It usually has a simplified structure, and it is used in fairly restricted domains. It is sometimes a stage in the evolution of a creole. (CH9)

prestige variants: Forms or variants that are socially acknowledged as 'correct' and therefore highly valued among speakers. (CH3)

public signs: Signs displayed in the linguistic landscape either by official institutions, by commercial entities, or by the general public. (CH8)

rapid and anonymous interview: A method used by Labov in his New York department store study in the 1970s. Labov asked his participants a quick question to elicit responses which contained the variable /r/. (CH3)

recombination: How people make meanings by combining and recombining different modes and other resources when they communicate. (CH4)

recontextualisation: When the meaning of a particular text or resource changes depending on the context into which it is deployed. (CH4)

referee: A person or group that people 'refer to' in their heads when they are speaking. (CH6)

registers: Different ways of speaking or writing associated with particular people, activities, attitudes, and social identities. (CH2)

repertoires: Collections of resources that people have available to them and the ways they deploy these resources in different situations. (CH2)

resemiotisation: The process whereby meanings are translated from one mode to another. (CH4)

resources: Codes, registers, genres, and other things like pictures, gestures, and clothing which enable people to communicate not just what they mean but also who they are. (CH2)

scales: Hierarchically layered contexts in which communication takes place. (CH9)

semantic meaning: The denotative meaning of words and phrases. (CH2)

semiotic landscapes: An approach in sociolinguistics which explores the use of different semiotic resources in public spaces. (CH8)

situational code switching: When switching codes relates to changes in the situation (e.g., participants, topic of discussion, activities people are doing). (CH5)

social network: A social structure that consists of people with different kinds of relationships and ties. (CH3)

social variable: A social factor which might influence or correlate with language variation. (CH3)

sociolinguistic interview: A data collection method used in sociolinguistics to elicit different kinds of speech from different kinds of people. (CH3)

sociolinguistics: The study of the relationship between language and social life. (Introduction)

speech community: A group of people who share a set of linguistic norms and expectations regarding the use of language. (Introduction)

standard language ideology: The belief that there is only one 'standard' and 'correct' way of speaking or writing a particular 'language'. (CH1)

stereotype: A generalised belief about the characteristics of a particular group of people. (CH7)

style: The different ways individuals talk in different situations to enact different identities or respond to different audiences. (CH6)

styling: The act of picking and choosing resources from our communicative repertoires in order to enact different identities. (CH6)

stylisation: Imitating the ways other people or other groups speak by adopting certain stereotypical features. (CH6)

superdiversity: A term coined by the anthropologist Steven Vertovec to describe the unprecedented diversity of people from different backgrounds that find themselves living in proximity to one another as a result of increased mobility. (CH9)

top-down signs: Public signs that are produced by governments, official institutions, and municipalities. (CH8)

transient signs: Mobile signs, in other words, signs that are not permanently fixed in one particular location. (CH8)

translanguaging: When multilingual people select features from their entire linguistic and semiotic repertoires and create new, original, and complex constructions that cannot be assigned to one or another 'language'. (CH5)

variant: A particular way of producing a variable. (CH3)

verbal hygiene: Practices by which people attempt to regulate, improve, or 'clean up' language. (CH1)

walking-tour interviews: A method of data collection which involves researchers walking with participants through the linguistic landscape discussing the different public signs and other features they notice around them. (CH8)

we-code/they-code: An approach to studying code switching proposed by Gumperz. A we-code is a code associated with one's 'in-group'; a they-code is associated with an 'out-group'. (CH5)

wicked problems: A term used to describe problems that are made up of many different interdependent components, which are often themselves symptoms of yet other problems. Because of this, often when we try to solve one aspect of a wicked problem, we can actually make other aspects of it worse.

References

Abdelhamid, F. (2020). *Communicative digital practices of Algerians on Facebook*. Unpublished PhD thesis, University of Reading.

Adami, E. (2017). *Multimodality and superdiversity: Evidence for a research agenda*. Tilburg Papers in Culture Studies, 177.

Agha, A. (2003). The social life of a cultural value. *Language and Communication*, 23, 231–73.

Agha, A. (2007). *Language and social relations*. New York: Cambridge University Press.

Alim, H. S. (2006). *Roc the mic right: The language of Hip Hop Culture*. London: Routledge.

Alim, H. S. (2009). Translocal style communities: Hip Hop youth as cultural theorists of style, language, and globalization. Pragmatics. *Quarterly Publication of the International Pragmatics Association (IPrA)*, 19(1), 103–27.

Alim, H. S., & Pennycook, A. (2007). Glocal linguistic flows: Hip-Hop culture(s), identities, and the politics of language education. *Journal of Language, Identity & Education*, 6(2), 89–100.

Altherr Flores, J. A., Hou, D., & Diao, W. (2020). Lingua francas beyond English: Multilingual repertoires among immigrants in a southwestern US border town. *International Journal of Multilingualism*, 17(2), 107–33.

Althusser, L. (1971). Ideology and ideological state apparatuses. In L. Althusser (Ed.), *Lenin and philosophy and other essays*. New York: Monthly Review Press.

Anderson, B. (1991). *Imagined communities: Reflections on the origin and spread of nationalism*. London: Verso.

Androutsopoulos, J. (2011). From variation to heteroglossia in the study of computer-mediated discourse. In C. Thurlow & K. Mroczek (Eds.), *Digital discourse: Language in the New Media* (pp. 277–98). Oxford: Oxford University Press.

Androutsopoulos, J. (2013). Networked multilingualism: Some language practices on Facebook and their implications. *International Journal of Bilingualism*, 19(2), 185–205.

Androutsopoulos, J. (2014). Languaging when contexts collapse: Audience design in social networking. *Discourse, Context & Media*, 4–5, 62–73.

Appadurai, A. (1990). Disjuncture and difference in the global cultural economy. *Theory, Culture & Society*, 7(2–3), 295–310.

Aslan, E., & Vásquez, C. (2018). 'Cash me ousside': A citizen sociolinguistic analysis of online metalinguistic commentary. *Journal of Sociolinguistics*, 22(4), 406–31.

Ateek, M., & Rasinger, S. M. (2018). Syrian or non-Syrian? Reflections on the use of LADO in the UK. In I. M. Nick (Ed.), *Forensic linguistics: Asylum-seekers, refugees and immigrants* (pp. 75–93). Wilmington, DE: Vernon Press.

Auer, P. (1984). *Bilingual conversation*. Amsterdam: John Benjamins.

Auer, P. (1998). *Code-switching in conversation: Language, interaction and identity*. London: Routledge.

Backhaus, P. (2007). *Linguistic Landscapes: A comparative study of urban multilingualism in Tokyo*. Clevedon: Multilingual Matters.

Bailey A. J., Canagarajah S., Lan S., & Powers, D. G. (2016). Scalar politics, language ideologies, and the sociolinguistics of globalization among transnational Korean professionals in Hong Kong. *Journal of Sociolinguistics*, 20(3), 312–34.

Bakhtin, M. (1981). *The dialogic imagination: Four essays*. C. Emerson & M. Holquist (Trans.), M. Holquist (Ed.). Austin: University of Texas Press.

Barrett, R. (2006). Language ideology and racial inequality: Competing functions of Spanish in an Anglo-owned Mexican restaurant. *Language in Society*, 35(2), 163–204.

Bauman, R. (1977). *Verbal art as performance*. Prospect Heights, IL: Waveland Press.

Bauman, R., & Briggs, C. L. (1990). Poetics and performance as critical perspectives on language and social life. *Annual Review of Anthropology*, 19, 59–88.

BBC. (2018). Rugby World Cup: Cover up your tattoos in Japan, players told. *BBC News*, 20 September. Retrieved 7 May 2021 from www.bbc.com/news/world-asia-45586210.

Beal, J. C. (2000). From Geordie Ridley to Viz: Popular literature in Tyneside English. *Language and Literature*, 9(4), 343–59.

Beal, J. C. (2009). 'You're not from New York City, you're from Rotherham': Dialect and identity in British Indie music. *Journal of English Linguistics,* 37(3), 223–40.

Bell, A. (1977). *The language of radio news in Auckland: A sociolinguistic study of style, audience and subediting variation.* PhD dissertation, University of Auckland, New Zealand.

Bell, A. (1984). Language style as audience design. *Language in Society*, 13, 145–204.

Bell, A. (2001). Back in style: Re-working audience design. In J. R. Rickford & P. Eckert (Eds.), *Style and variation* (pp. 139–69). Cambridge: Cambridge University Press.

Bell, A. (2014). *The guidebook to sociolinguistics.* Chichester: Wiley-Blackwell.

Ben-Rafael, E., Shohamy, E., Muhammad Hasan, A., & Trumper-Hecht, N. (2006). Linguistic landscape as symbolic construction of the public space: The case of Israel. *International Journal of Multilingualism*, 3(1), 7–30.

Blackledge, A. (2009). 'As a country we do expect': The further extension of language testing regimes in the United Kingdom. *Language Assessment Quarterly*, 6(1), 6–16.

Blackledge, A., & Creese, A. (2017). Translanguaging in mobility. In S. Canagarajah (Ed.), *The Routledge handbook of migration and language* (pp. 31–46). Abingdon: Routledge.

Blom, J. P., & Gumperz, J. J. (1972). Social meaning in linguistic structure: Code-switching in Norway. In J. J. Gumperz & D. Hymes (Eds.), *Directions in sociolinguistics* (pp. 407–34). New York: Holt, Rinehart & Winston.

Blommaert, J. (2001). Investigating narrative inequality: African asylum stories in Belgium. *Discourse & Society,* 12(4), 413–49.

Blommaert, J. (2005). *Discourse: A critical introduction.* Cambridge: Cambridge University Press.

Blommaert, J. (2007). Sociolinguistic scales. *Intercultural Pragmatics*, 4, 1–19.

Blommaert, J. (2009). Ethnography and democracy: Hymes's political theory of language. *Text & Talk*, 29 (3), 257–76.

Blommaert, J. (2010). *The sociolinguistics of globalization.* Cambridge: Cambridge University Press.

Blommaert, J. (2013a). Citizenship, language, and superdiversity: Towards complexity. *Journal of Language, Identity & Education*, 12(3), 193–6.

Blommaert, J. (2013b). *Ethnography, superdiversity and linguistic landscapes: Chronicles of complexity.* Bristol: Multilingual Matters.

Blommaert, J. (2017). Online-offline modes of identity and community: Elliot Rodger's twisted world of masculine victimhood. *Tilburg Papers in Culture Studies*, 200.

Blommaert, J. (2018). *Durkheim and the internet: Sociolinguistics and the sociological imagination.* London: Bloomsbury Academic.

Blommaert, J., & Backus, A. (2011). Repertoires revisited: 'Knowing language' in superdiversity. *Working Papers in Urban Language and Literacies,* paper 67, Tilburg University.

Blommaert, J., & Backus, A. (2013). Superdiverse repertoires and the individual. In I. de Saint-Georges & J. J. Weber (Eds.), *Multilingualism and multimodality: Current challenges for educational studies* (pp. 11–32). Rotterdam: Sense Publishers.

Blommaert, J., Collins, J., & Slembrouck, S. (2005). Spaces of multilingualism. *Language and Communication*, 25(3), 197–216.

Bloomfield, L. (1933). *Language.* New York: Holt, Rinehart & Winston.

Bourdieu, P. (1977). *Outline of a theory of practice* (R. Nice, Trans.). Cambridge: Cambridge University Press.

Bourdieu, P. (1984). *Distinction: A social critique of the judgement of taste* (R. Nice, Trans.). Cambridge, MA: Harvard University Press.

Bourhis, R. Y., & Giles, H. (1977). The language of intergroup distinctiveness. In H. Giles (Ed.), *Language, ethnicity, and intergroup relations* (pp. 119–35). London: Academic Press.

boyd, d. (2012). Networked privacy: How teenagers negotiate context in social media. *Surveillance & Society*, 10(3/4), 348–50.

Briggs, C. L. (1996). Introduction. In C. L. Briggs (Ed.), *Disorderly discourse: Narrative, conflict, & inequality* (pp. 1–30). New York: Oxford University Press.

Brumberg, S. (1986). *Going to America, going to school: The Jewish immigrant public school encounter in turn-of-the-century New York City.* New York: Praeger.

Bucholtz, M. (1999). 'Why be normal?': Language and identity practices in a community of nerd girls. *Language in Society*, 28(2), 203–23.

Bucholtz, M., & Lopez, Q. (2011). Performing blackness, forming whiteness: Linguistic minstrelsy in Hollywood film. *Journal of Sociolinguistics*, 15(5), 680–706.

Butler, J. (1988). Performative acts and gender constitution: An essay in phenomenology and feminist theory. *Theatre Journal*, 40(4), 519–31.

Cameron, D. (1992). 'Respect, please!': Investigating race, power and language. In D. Cameron, E. Frazer, P. Harvey, B. Rampton, & K. Richardson (Eds.), *Researching language: Issues of power and method* (pp. 113–30). London: Routledge.

Cameron, D. (1995). *Verbal hygiene*. London: Routledge.

Canagarajah, S. (2011). Writing to learn and learning to write by shuttling between languages. In R. M. Manchón (Ed.), *Learning-to-write and writing-to-learn in an additional language* (pp. 111–32). Amsterdam: John Benjamins.

Canagarajah, S., & De Costa, P. I. (2016). Introduction: Scales analysis, and its uses and prospects in educational linguistics. *Linguistics and Education*, 34, 1–10.

Castells, M. (2000). *The rise of the network society.* Oxford: Blackwell.

Chau, D. (2021). Spreading language ideologies through social media: Enregistering the 'fake ABC' variety in Hong Kong. *Journal of Sociolinguistics*, online prepublication https://doi.org/10.1111/josl.12486.

Cheshire, J. (1982). Linguistic variation and social function. In S. Romaine (Ed.), *Sociolinguistic variation in speech communities* (pp. 153–66). London: Edward Arnold.

Cheshire, J., Kerswill, P., Fox, S., & Torgersen, E. (2011). Contact, the feature pool and the speech community: The emergence of Multicultural London English. *Journal of Sociolinguistics*, 15(2), 151–96.

Chomsky, N. (1986). *Knowledge of language: Its nature, origin, and use.* New York: Praeger.

Christodoulidou, M. (2013). Style shifting from Cypriot towards Greek phonology. *Journal of Greek Linguistics*, 13(1), 54–70.

Chun, E. W. (2001). The construction of white, black, and Korean American identities through African American Vernacular English. *Journal of Linguistic Anthropology*, 11, 52–64.

Chun, E. W. (2010). Ideologies of legitimate mockery: Margaret Cho's revoicings of Mock Asian. *Pragmatics*, 14(2), 263–89.

Cooper, T. (1826). *Lecture on the elements of political economy.* Columbia, S.C.: Doyle E. Sweeny.

Coupland, N. (2001). Dialect stylization in radio talk. *Language in Society*, 30, 345–76.

Coupland, N. (2007). *Style: Language variation and identity*. Cambridge: Cambridge University Press.

Coupland, N., & Bishop, H. (2007). Ideologised values for British accents. *Journal of Sociolinguistics*, 11(1), 74–93.

Crystal, D. (2006). *Language and the Internet.* Cambridge: Cambridge University Press.

Cutler, C. A. (1999). Yorkville crossing: White teens, hip hop and African American English. *Journal of Sociolinguistics*, 3(4), 428–42.

Cutler, C. A. (2003). 'Keepin' it real': White hip hoppers' discourses of language, race, and authenticity. *Journal of Linguistic Anthropology*, 13, 1–23.

D'Addario, D. (2013). Pop music's race problem: How white artists profit from mocking hip-hop. Accessed 9 June 2015 from www.salon.com/2013/11/21/pop_musics_race_problem_how_white_artists_profit_from_mocking_hip_hop/.

Dirim, I., & Hieronymus, A. (2003). Cultural orientation and language use among multilingual youth groups: 'For me it is like we all speak one language'. In J. N. Jørgensen (Ed.), *Bilingualism and social relations: Turkish speakers in North Western Europe* (pp. 42–55). Clevedon: Multilingual Matters.

Dixon, J., Tredoux, C., Durrheim, K., & Foster, D. (1994). The role of speech accommodation and crime type in attribution of guilt. *The Journal of Social Psychology*, 134, 465–73.

Drummond, R. (2018a). Maybe it's a grime [t]ing: TH-stopping among urban British youth. *Language in Society*, 47, 171–96.

Drummond, R. (2018b). *Researching urban youth language and identity*. Switzerland: Palgrave Macmillan.

Du Bois, W. E. B. (1994). *The souls of black folks*. New York: Dover.

Dufva, H., Suni, M., Aro, M., & Salo, O. (2011). Languages as objects of learning: Language learning as a case of multilingualism. *Apples – Journal of Applied Language Studies*, 5(1), 109–24.

Eberhardt, M., & Freeman, K. (2015). 'First things first, I'm the realest': Linguistic appropriation, white privilege, and the hip-hop persona of Iggy Azalea. *Journal of Sociolinguistics*, 19(3), 303–27.

Eckert, P. (1989). *Jocks and Burnouts: Social categories and identity in the high school*. New York: Teachers College Press.

Eckert, P. (1997). Age as a sociolinguistic variable. In F. Coulmas (Ed.), *The handbook of sociolinguistics* (pp. 151–67). Oxford: Blackwell.

Eckert, P. (2000). *Linguistic variation and social practice: The linguistic construction of identity in Belten High*. Malden: Blackwell.

Eckert, P. (2004). The meaning of style. Research paper, Stanford University. Retrieved 15 May 2021 from https://web.stanford.edu/~eckert/PDF/salsa2003.pdf.

Eckert, P., & McConnell-Ginet, S. (2003). *Language and gender*. Cambridge: Cambridge University Press.

The Economist. (2021). Grime and UK drill are exporting multicultural London English, 30 January. Retrieved 21 April 2021 from www.economist.com/britain/2021/01/30/grime-and-uk-drill-are-exporting-multicultural-london-english.

Evans, B. (2002). Seattle to Spokane: Mapping perceptions of English in Washington State. *Journal of English Linguistics*, 41(3), 268–91.

Ferguson, C. (1959). Diglossia. *Word*, 15(2), 325–40.

Fichte, J. G. (1968 [1808]). *Addresses to the German nation* (R. F. Jones & G. H. Turnbull, Trans.) (G. A. Kelly, Ed.) New York: Harper & Row.

Gal, S. (1978). Peasant men can't get wives: Language change and sex roles in a bilingual community. *Language in Society*, 7(1), 1–16.

García, O., & Li Wei (2014). *Translanguaging: Language, bilingualism and education*. Basingstoke: Palgrave Macmillan.

García, O., Flores, N., & Spotti, M. (Eds.). (2016). *The Oxford handbook of language and society*. Oxford: Oxford University Press.

Garrett, P. (2010). *Attitudes to language*. Cambridge: Cambridge University Press.

Gee, J. P. (2004). *Situated language and learning: A critique of traditional schooling*. New York: Routledge.

Gibson, J. J. (1979). *The ecological approach to visual perception*. Boston: Houghton Mifflin.

Giles, H., & Powesland, P. F. (1975). *Speech style and social evaluation*. London: Academic Press.

Giles, H., & Smith, P. M. (1979). Accommodation theory: Optimal levels of convergence. In H. Giles & R. N. St. Clair (Eds.), *Language and social psychology* (pp. 45–65). Oxford: Blackwell.

Giles, H., Wilson, P., & Conway, A. (1981). Accent and lexical diversity as determinants of impression formation and perceived employment suitability. *Language Sciences*, 3, 91–103.

Goffman, E. (1959). *The presentation of self in everyday life*. New York: Doubleday.

Goodwin, M., & Alim, H. S. (2010). 'Whatever (neck roll, eye roll, teeth suck)': The situated coproduction of social categories and identities through stancetaking and transmodal stylization. *Linguistic Anthropology*, 20(1), 179–94.

Grierson, G. A. (1903). *Linguistic survey of India*. Calcutta: Office of the Superintendent of Government Printing, India.

Gumperz, J. J. (1964). Linguistic and social interaction in two communities. *American Anthropologist*, 66(6/2), 137–53.

Gumperz, J. J. (1982). *Discourse strategies*. Cambridge: Cambridge University Press.

Gumperz, J. J., & Hymes, D. H. (1972). *Directions in sociolinguistics: The ethnography of communication*. New York: Holt, Rinehart & Winston.

Hall, K., Goldstein, D., & Ingram, M. (2016). The hands of Donald Trump: Entertainment, gesture, spectacle. *Journal of Ethnographic Theory*, 6(2), 71–100.

Halliday, M. A. K. (1978). *Language as social semiotic: The social interpretation of language and meaning*. London: Arnold.

Haugen, E. (1966). Dialect, language, nation. *American Anthropologist*, 68(4), 922–35.

Hill, J. H. (1998). Language, race, and white public space. *American Anthropologist*, 100(3), 680–9.

Hill, J. H. (2008). *The everyday language of white racism*. Malden, MA: Wiley-Blackwell.

Hinnenkamp, V. (2003). Mixed language varieties of migrant adolescents and the discourse of hybridity. *Journal of Multilingual and Multicultural Development*, 24 (1–2), 12–41.

Hobsbawm, E. J. (2012). *Nations and nationalism since 1780: Programme, myth, reality*. Cambridge: Cambridge University Press.

Hurley, L. (2018, 21 July). An image of Putin and Trump kissing isn't funny. It's homophobic. *The Guardian*. Retrieved 15 May 2021 from www .theguardian.com/commentisfree/2018/jul/21/trump-putin-kissing-homophobic-queer-joke.

Hymes, D. (1966). Two types of linguistic relativity. In W. Bright (Ed.), *Sociolinguistics* (pp. 114–58). The Hague: Mouton.

Hymes, D. (1974). *Foundations in sociolinguistics: An ethnographic approach*. London: Tavistock.

Hymes, D., & Cazden, C. (1980). Narrative thinking and story-telling rights: A folklorist's clue to a critique of education. In D. Hymes (Ed.), *Language in education: Ethno-linguistic essays* (pp. 126–38). Washington, DC: Center for Applied Linguistics.

Irvine, J. (1989). When talk isn't cheap: Language and political economy. *American Ethnologist*, 16(2), 248–67.

Jansen, L., & Westphal, M. (2017). Rihanna works her multivocal pop persona: A morpho-syntactic and accent analysis of Rihanna's singing style. *English Today*, 33(2), 46–55.

Jaworska, S., & Themistocleous, C. (2018). Public discourses on multilingualism in the UK: Triangulating a corpus study with a sociolinguistic attitude survey. *Language in Society*, 47(1), 57–88.

Jaworski, A., & Thurlow, C. (2010). *Semiotic landscapes: Language, image, space*. London: Continuum.

Jewitt, C., & Kress, G. (2003). *Multimodal literacy*. New York: Peter Lang.

Johnstone, B. (2009). Pittsburghese shirts: Commodification and the enregisterment of an urban dialect. *American Speech*, 84(2), 157–75.

Johnstone, B. (2011). Dialect enregisterment in performance. *Journal of Sociolinguistics*, 15(5), 657–79.

Johnstone, B. (2013). *Speaking Pittsburghese: The story of a dialect*. Oxford: Oxford University Press.

Johnstone, B. (2016). Enregisterment: How linguistic items become linked with ways of speaking. *Language and Linguistics Compass*, 10, 632–43.

Johnstone, B., Andrus, J., & Danielson, A. (2006). Mobility, indexicality and the enregisterment of 'Pittsburghese'. *Journal of English Linguistics*, 34(2), 77–104.

Jones, R. H. (2001). Beyond the screen: A participatory study of computer-mediated communication among Hong Kong youth. Paper presented at the Annual Meeting of the American Anthropological Association, Washington DC, 28 November– 2 December.

Jones, R. H. (Ed.). (2021a). *Viral discourse*. Cambridge: Cambridge University Press.

Jones, R. H. (2021b). *Digital literacies and synthetic embodiment: The ethics of mimicry on TikTok*. A talk delivered at the Berkeley Language Center, University of Berkeley, CA, 12 March. Available at https://youtu .be/nAIi0engvng.

Jones, R. H., & Chau, D. (2021). Metalinguistic tactics in the Hong Kong protest movement. *Journal of Language and Politics*. Online pre-publication available at www.jbe-platform.com/content/journals/10.1075/ jlp.21017.jon.

Jørgensen, J. N. (1998). Children's acquisition of code-switching for power wielding. In P. Auer (Ed.), *Code-switching in conversation: Language, interaction and identity* (pp. 418–59). London: Routledge.

Jørgensen, J. N. (2008). Polylingual languaging around and among children and adolescents. *International Journal of Multilingualism*, 5(3), 161–76.

Joseph, J. E. (2006). *Language and politics*. Edinburgh: Edinburgh University Press.

Kalin, R., & Rayko, D. (1980). The social significance of speech in the job interview. In R. St. Clair & H. Giles (Eds.), *The social and psychological contexts of language* (pp. 39–50). Hillsdale: Erlbaum.

Kasanga, L. A. (2019). Crossing in popular music in D.R. Congo: The mixing of English in Lingala lyrics. *Journal of African Cultural Studies*, 3(1), 89–105.

Kerswill, P., & Williams, A. (2000). Creating a New Town koine: Children and language change in Milton Keynes. *Language in Society*, 29(1), 65–115.

King, B. W. (2018). Hip Hop headz in sex ed: Gender, agency, and styling in New Zealand. *Language in Society*, 47(4), 487–512.

Kirkpatrick, D. (2011). *The Facebook effect: The real inside story of Mark Zuckerberg and the world's fastest growing company*. London: Virgin Books.

Kitis, D., & Milani, T. (2015). The performativity of the body: Turbulent spaces in Greece. *Linguistic Landscape*, 1(3), 268–90.

Kress, G. (2000). Design and transformation: New theories of meaning. In B. Cope & M. Kalantzis (Eds.), *Multiliteracies: Literacy learning and the design of social futures* (pp. 153–61). New York: Routledge.

Labov, W. (1963). The social motivation of a sound change. *Word*, 18, 1–42.

Labov, W. (1966/2006). *The social stratification of English in New York City*. Cambridge: Cambridge University Press.

Labov, W. (1972). *Sociolinguistic patterns*. Philadelphia: University of Pennsylvania Press.

Labov, W. (1982). Objectivity and commitment in linguistic science: The case of the Black English trial in Ann Arbor. *Language in Society*, 11(2), 165–201.

Lakoff, R. T. (1975). *Language and woman's place*. New York: Harper & Row.

Lambert, W., Hodgson, R., Gardner, R., & Fillenbaum, S. (1960). Evaluational reactions to spoken languages. *Journal of Abnormal and Social Psychology*, 60, 44–51.

Landry, R., & Bourhis, R. (1997). Linguistic landscape and ethnolinguistic vitality: An empirical study. *Journal of Language and Social Psychology*, 16(1), 23–49.

Le Page, R. B., & Tabouret-Keller, A. (1985). *Acts of identity: Creole-based approaches to language and ethnicity*. Cambridge: Cambridge University Press.

Lee, C. (2007). Linguistic features of email and ICQ Instant messaging in Hong Kong. In B. Danet & S. Herring (Eds.), *The multilingual internet: Language, culture, and communication online* (pp. 184–208). Oxford: Oxford University Press.

Lee, J. S. (2011). Globalization of African American Vernacular English in popular culture: Blinglish in Korean Hip Hop. *English World-Wide*, 32(1), 1–23.

Li Wei (2018). Translanguaging as a practical theory of language. *Applied Linguistics*, 39(1), 9–30.

Lippi-Green, R. (2012). *English with an accent: Language, ideology and discrimination in the United States* (2nd edn.). London: Routledge.

lola. (2017, 4 June). Hey Bieber, Singing in Spanish is hard, but don't make fun of the language. Retrieved 15 May 2021, from HipLatina website: https://hiplatina.com/justin-bieber-despacito-spanish-mixup/.

Lou, J. J. (2016). *The linguistic landscape of Chinatown: A sociolinguistic ethnography*. Bristol: Multilingual Matters.

Lou, J. J. (2017). Spaces of consumption and senses of place: A geosemiotic analysis of three markets in Hong Kong. *Social Semiotics*, 27(4), 513–31.

Lundervold, L. (2013). *Harry Potter and the different accents: A sociolinguistic study of language attitudes in Harry Potter and Game of Thrones*. Unpublished MA dissertation, University of Bergen, Norway.

MacKinnon, K. (1981). Scottish opinion on Gaelic. Hatfield Polytechnic Social Science Research Publications SS14.

Makoni, S. (2003). From misinvention to disinvention of language: Multilingualism and the South African Constitution. In S. Makoni, G. Smitherman, A. F. Ball, & A. K. Spears (Eds.), *Black linguistics: Language, society, and politics in Africa and the Americas* (pp. 132–51). London: Routledge.

Makoni, S., & Pennycook, A. (Eds.). (2007). *Disinventing and reconstituting languages*. Clevedon: Multilingual Matters.

Marwick, A. E., & boyd, d. (2010). I tweet honestly, I tweet passionately: Twitter users, context collapse, and the imagined audience. *New Media & Society*, 13(1), 114–33.

Marwick, A. E., & Caplan, R. (2018). Drinking male tears: Language, the manosphere, and networked harassment. *Feminist Media Studies*, 18(4), 543–59.

Matamoros-Fernandez, A. (2020). 'El Negro de WhatsApp' meme, digital blackface, and racism on social media. *First Monday*, 25(1).

Mather, P. A. (2012). The social stratification of /r/ in New York City: Labov's department store study revisited. *Journal of English Linguistics*, 40(4), 338–56.

Matsuda, M. J. (1991). Voices of America: Accent, antidiscrimination law, and a jurisprudence for the last reconstruction. *The Yale Law Journal*, 100(5), 1329.

McCool, S. (1982). *Sam McCool's new Pittsburghese: How to speak like a Pittsburgher*. Pittsburgh: Hayford Press.

Mendoza-Denton, N. (2008). *Homegirls: Language and cultural practice among Latina youth gangs*. Malden: Blackwell.

Milroy, J. (2007). The ideology of the standard language. In C. Llamas, L. Mullany, & P. Stockwell (Eds.), *The Routledge companion to sociolinguistics* (pp. 133–9). London: Routledge.

Milroy, J., & Milroy, L. (2012). *Authority in language: Investigating Standard English*. London: Routledge.

Milroy, L. (1987). *Language and social networks*. Oxford: Blackwell.

Mirror Online. (2011). David Starkey claims 'the whites have become black' during UK riots Newsnight debate. *Mirror Online*, 13 August. Retrieved 15 May 2021 from www.mirror.co.uk/news/uk-news/david-starkey-claims-the-whites-184964.

Moreno, C. (2017, June 5). Luis Fonsi responds to Justin Bieber butchering 'Despacito' lyrics. Retrieved 15 May 2021, from HuffPost UK website: www.huffpost.com/entry/luis-fonsi-responds-to-justin-bieber-butchering-despacito-lyrics_n_5935ae1ee4b0099e7fae451a.

Myers-Scotton, C. (1993). *Social motivations for codeswitching: Evidence from Africa*. Oxford: Oxford University Press.

New London Group. (1996). A pedagogy of multiliteracies: Designing social futures. *Harvard Educational Review*, 66(1), 60–93.

Niedzielski, N., & Preston, D. (2003). *Folk linguistics*. Berlin: Mouton de Gruyter.

Niedzielski, N., & Preston, D. (2007). Folk pragmatics. In J. O. Östman, J. Verschueren, & E. Versluys (Eds.), *Handbook of Pragmatics* (pp. 1–12). Amsterdam: John Benjamins.

Nissenbaum, H. (2009). *Privacy in context: Technology, policy, and the integrity of social life*. Palo Alto: Stanford University Press.

Norris, S. (2004). *Analysing multimodal interaction: A methodological framework*. London: Routledge.

O'Hanlon, R. (2006). Australian Hip Hop: A sociolinguistic investigation. *Australian Journal of Linguistics*, 26(2), 193–209.

Omoniyi, T. (2008). 'So I choose to do am Naija Style': Hip Hop, language, and postcolonial Identities. In H. S. Alim, A. Ibrahim, & A. Pennycook (Eds.), *Global linguistic flows: Hip Hop Cultures, youth identities, and the politics of language* (pp. 113–35). London: Routledge.

Ong, W. J. (1971). The literate orality of popular culture today. In W. J. Ong (Ed.), *Rhetoric, romance, and technology* (pp. 284–303). Ithaca: Cornell University Press.

Ong, W. J. (1982/2003). *Orality and literacy*. London: Routledge.

Otheguy, R., & Zentella, A. C. (2012). *Spanish in New York: Language contact, dialectal levelling, and structural continuity*. Oxford: Oxford University Press.

Paolillo. J. (2007). How much multilingualism? Language diversity on the internet. In B. Danet & S. Herring (Eds.), *The multilingual internet: Language, culture, and communication online* (pp. 408–31). Oxford: Oxford University Press.

Parham, J. (2020). TikTok and the evolution of digital blackface. *Wired*, 4 August. Retrieved 8 November 2020 from www.wired.com/story/tiktok-evolution-digital-blackface/.

Peck, A., & Stroud, C. (2015). Skinscapes. *Linguistic Landscape*, 1(1/2), 133–51.

Peirce, C. S. (1977). *Semiotics and significs*. Charles Hardwick (Ed.). Bloomington: Indiana University Press.

Pennycook, A. (2003). Global Englishes, Rip Slyme, and performativity. *Journal of Sociolinguistics,* 7(4), 513–33.

Pennycook, A. (2007). *Global Englishes and transcultural flows.* London: Routledge.

Pennycook, A. (2010). Spatial narrations: Graffscapes and city souls. In A. Jaworski & C. Thurlow (Eds.), *Semiotic landscapes: Language, image, space* (pp. 137–50). London: Continuum.

Pennycook, A., & Otsuji, E. (2015). Making scents of the landscape. *Linguistic Landscape,* 1(3), 191–212.

Pérez-Sabater, C. (2019). Emoticons in relational writing practices on WhatsApp: Some reflections on gender. In P. Bou-Franch & P. Garcés-Conejos Blitvich (Eds.), *Analyzing digital discourse: New insights and future directions* (pp. 163–89). Switzerland: Springer/Palgrave Macmillan.

Probyn, M. (2009). 'Smuggling the vernacular into the classroom': Conflicts and tensions in classroom codeswitching in township/rural schools in South Africa. *International Journal of Bilingual Education and Bilingualism,* 12(2), 123–36.

Probyn, M. (2019). Pedagogical translanguaging and the construction of science knowledge in a multilingual South African classroom: Challenging monoglossic/post-colonial orthodoxies. *Classroom Discourse,* 10(3–4), 216–36.

Rampton, B. (1995). *Crossing: Language and ethnicity among adolescents.* London: Longman.

Rampton, B. (1998). Language crossing and the redefinition of reality. In P. Auer (Ed.), *Code-switching in conversation: Language, interaction and identity* (pp. 505–62). London: Routledge.

Reilly, K. (2016, May 14). Street mural of Donald Trump kissing Vladimir Putin goes viral. *Time.* Retrieved 25 April 2019 from https://time.com/4336396/lithuania-mural-donald-trump-vladimir-putin-kiss/.

Rey, A. (1977). Accent and employability: Language attitudes. *Language Sciences,* 47, 7–12.

Rheingold, H. (2000). *The virtual community: Homesteading on the electronic frontier.* Cambridge, MA: MIT Press.

Rittel, H. W. J., & Webber, M. M. (1973). Dilemmas in a general theory of planning. *Policy Sciences,* 4(2), 155–69.

Ronkin, M., & Karn, H. E. (2002). Mock Ebonics: Linguistic racism in parodies of Ebonics on the Internet. *Journal of Sociolinguistics,* 3(3), 360–80.

Roux, S. D. (2015). A multisemiotic analysis of 'skinscapes' of female students at three Western Cape universities. PhD thesis, University of the Western Cape.

Rubdy, R., & Ben Said, S. (2015). *Conflict, exclusion and dissent in the linguistic landscape.* Basingstoke: Palgrave Macmillan.

Rymes, B. (2014). *Communicating beyond language: Everyday encounters with diversity.* New York: Routledge.

Rymes, B. (2020). *How we talk about language: Exploring citizen sociolinguistics.* Cambridge: Cambridge University Press.

Sabaté-Dalmau, M. (2018). 'I speak small': Unequal Englishes and transnational identities among Ghanaian migrants. *International Journal of Multilingualism,* 15(4), 365–82.

Saowanee, A., & McCargo, D. (2014). Diglossia and identity in Northeast Thailand: Linguistic, social, and political hierarchy. *Journal of Sociolinguistics,* 18(1), 60–86.

Schuman, R. (2017, July 26). Is Schlager Music the most embarrassing thing Germany has ever produced? Retrieved 16 May 2021 from Medium website: https://medium.com/the-awl/is-schlager-music-the-most-embarrassing-thing-germany-has-ever-produced-ab1863ef0ce8.

Scollon, R., & LeVine, P. (2004). Multimodal discourse analysis as the confluence of discourse and technology. In R. Scollon & P. LeVine (Eds.), *Discourse and technology: Multimodal discourse analysis* (pp. 1–6). Washington DC: Georgetown University Press.

Scollon, R., & Wong Scollon, S. (2003). *Discourses in place: Language in the material world.* London: Routledge.

Seargeant, P., & Tagg, C. (2011). English on the internet and a 'post-varieties' approach to language. *World Englishes,* 30(4), 496–514.

Sebba, M. (1993). *London Jamaican: Language systems in interaction.* London: Longman.

Sebba, M. (1997). *Contact languages: Pidgins and creoles.* Basingstoke: Palgrave.

Sebba, M. (2003). Will the real impersonator please stand up? Language and identity in the Ali G websites. *AAA: Arbeiten Aus Anglistik Und Amerikanistik*, 28(2), 279–304.

Sebba, M. (2010). Discourses in transit. In A. Jaworski & C. Thurlow (Eds.), *Semiotic landscapes: Language, image, space* (pp. 59–76). London: Continuum.

Sebba, M., & Wootton, T. (1998). We, they and identity: Sequential versus identity-related explanation in code-switching. In P. Auer (Ed.), *Code-switching in conversation: Language, interaction and identity* (pp. 460–504). London: Routledge.

Shohamy, E. (2006). *Language policy: Hidden agendas and new approaches.* New York: Routledge.

Siebetcheu, R. (2016). Semiotic and linguistic analysis of banners in three European countries' football stadia: Italy, France and England. In R. Blackwood, E. Lanza, & H. Woldemariam (Eds.), *Negotiating and contesting identities in linguistic landscapes* (pp. 181–94). London: Bloomsbury.

Silverstein, M. (1985). Language and the culture of gender: At the intersection of structure, usage, and ideology. In E. Mertz & R. Parmentier (Eds.), *Semiotic mediation* (pp. 219–60). Orlando: Academic Press.

Silverstein, M. (1979). Language structure and linguistic ideology. In P. R. Clyne, W.F. Hanks, & C. L. Hofbauer (Eds.), *The elements* (pp. 193–248). Chicago: Chicago Linguistic Society.

Simpson, P. (1999). Language, culture and identity: With (another) look at accents in pop and rock singing. *Multilingua*, 18(4), 343–67.

Squires, L. (2010). Enregistering internet language. *Language in Society*, 39(4), 457–92.

Swain, M. (2006). Languaging, agency and collaboration in advanced second language learning. In H. Byrnes (Ed.), *Advanced language learning: The contribution of Halliday and Vygotsky* (pp. 95–108). London: Continuum.

Tannen, D., & Wallat, C. (1987). Interactive frames and knowledge schemas in interaction: Examples from a medical examination/interview. *Social Psychology Quarterly*, 50(2), 205–16.

TEDx Talks. (2012). *Anita Sarkeesian at TEDxWomen 2012.* The Paley Center for Media. Retrieved 15 May 2021 from www.youtube.com/watch?v=GZAxwsg9J9Q.

Thatcher, M. (1987). Interview. *Women's Own*, 1 October. Retrieved 13 May 2021 from www .margaretthatcher.org/document/106689.

Themistocleous, C. (2019). Conflict and unification in the multilingual landscape of a divided city: The case of Nicosia's border. *Journal of Multilingual and Multicultural Development*, 40(2), 94–114.

Themistocleous, C. (2020). Multilingual voices of unification in 'No man's land': Evidence from the linguistic landscape of Nicosia's UN-controlled buffer zone. *Linguistic Landscape*, 6(2), 155–82.

Themistocleous, C. (2021). From public to digital spaces: Spatial and media practices of the 2017 'Unite Cyprus Now' peace protests. *Discourse, Context & Media*, 42.

Thurlow, C. (2014). Disciplining youth: Language ideologies and new technologies. In A. Jaworski & N. Coupland (Eds.), *The discourse reader* (pp. 481–96). London: Routledge.

Times of Israel. (2016). 'Trump-Putin kiss' graffiti shows misgivings in Baltic states, 14 May. Retrieved 4 July 2021 from www.timesofisrael.com/trump-putin-kiss-graffiti-shows-misgivings-in-baltic-states/.

Timming, A. (2017). The effect of foreign accent on employability: A study of the aural dimensions of aesthetic labour in customer-facing and non-customer-facing jobs. *Work, Employment and Society*, 3 (3), 409–28.

Trudgill, P. (1974). *The social stratification of English in Norwich.* Cambridge: Cambridge University Press.

Trudgill, P. (1981). Linguistic accommodation: Sociolinguistic observations on a sociopsychological theory. In C. S. Masek, R. A. Hendrick, & M. F. Miller (Eds.), *Papers from the parasession on language and behavior* (pp. 18–37). Chicago: Chicago Linguistic Society.

Trudgill, P. (1983). Acts of conflicting identity: The sociolinguistics of British pop-song pronunciation. In P. Trudgill (Ed.), *On dialect: Social and geographical perspectives* (pp. 141–60). Oxford: Basil Blackwell.

Vaish, V. (2019). Challenges and directions in implementing translanguaging pedagogy for low achieving students. *Classroom Discourse*, 10,(3–4), 274–89.

Vertovec, S. (2007). Super-diversity and its implications. *Ethnic and Racial Studies*, 30(6), 1024–54.

Wheeler, R. S. & Swords, R. (2006). *Code-switching: Teaching Standard English in urban classrooms.* Urbana: National Council of Teachers of English.

Woolard, K. A. (2004). Codeswitching. In A. Durantic (Ed.), *A companion to linguistic anthropology* (pp. 73–94). Malden: Blackwell Publishing.

World Economic Forum. (2017). *Global shapers annual survey.* Retrieved 15 May 2021 from www.es.amnesty.org/fileadmin/noticias/ShapersSurvey2017_Full_Report_24Aug_002_01.pdf.

Young, V. S. (2009). 'Nah, we straight': An argument against code switching. *JAC*, 29(1–2), 49–71.

Zhu Hua (2021). Sense and sensibility: Urban public signs during a pandemic. In R. H. Jones (Ed.), *Viral discourse* (pp. 37–48). Cambridge: Cambridge University Press.

Zimman, L. (2017). Gender as stylistic bricolage: Transmasculine voices and the relationship between fundamental frequency and /s/. *Language in Society*, 46 (3), 339–70.

Zimman, L., & Hall, K. (2010). Language, embodiment and the 'third sex'. In C. Llamas & D. Watt (Eds.), *Language and identities* (pp. 166–78). Edinburgh: Edinburgh University Press.

Index